W. J. (William John) Deane

Pseudepigrapha

An Account of Certain Apocryphal Sacred Writings of the Jews....

W. J. (William John) Deane

Pseudepigrapha

An Account of Certain Apocryphal Sacred Writings of the Jews....

ISBN/EAN: 9783337135195

Printed in Europe, USA, Canada, Australia, Japan

Cover: Foto ©Lupo / pixelio.de

More available books at **www.hansebooks.com**

PSEUDEPIGRAPHA:

*AN ACCOUNT OF CERTAIN
APOCRYPHAL SACRED WRITINGS OF THE JEWS
AND EARLY CHRISTIANS.*

BY THE

REV. WILLIAM J. DEANE, M.A.,

RECTOR OF ASHEN, ESSEX;

AUTHOR OF "THE BOOK OF WISDOM, WITH PROLEGOMENA AND COMMENTARY
(OXFORD: CLARENDON PRESS), ETC. ETC.

IMPORTED BY
CHARLES SCRIBNER'S SONS,
NEW YORK.

PRINTED BY MORRISON AND GIBB,

FOR

T. & T. CLARK, EDINBURGH.

LONDON,	HAMILTON, ADAMS, AND CO.
DUBLIN,	GEORGE HERBERT.
NEW YORK,	CHARLES SCRIBNER'S SONS.

PREFACE.

THE present work consists chiefly of a reproduction of certain articles (with additions and corrections) contributed by me to various religious periodicals during the last few years. It treats of some curious Pseudepigraphal Jewish and Christian writings composed in the times immediately preceding or following the commencement of the Christian era, and aims at giving a succinct account of these productions for readers who are not familiar with the originals. The books comprised in our English Bibles under the name of "Apocrypha" are excluded, as they have been sufficiently examined of late years, and commentaries upon them are readily available. Some of the works treated in this volume are comparatively unknown to English readers, but those (like the Book of Enoch) which have obtained more currency among us could not be omitted from our survey, especially as they form an integral part of the literature of the period, and are often referred to and cited. The whole of the writings here examined have not hitherto been collected into one volume. The original text or versions of some of them have been printed in Fabricius' *Codex Pseudepigraphus Veteris Testamenti;* and in Fritzsche's *Libri Apocryphi Vet. Test.;* the others have been published by various editors at various times, as noted in the following accounts.

CONTENTS.

―――o―――

	PAGE
INTRODUCTION, ...	1
I. LYRICAL—	
The Psalter of Solomon, ...	25
II. APOCALYPTICAL AND PROPHETICAL—	
The Book of Enoch, ...	49
The Assumption of Moses, ...	95
The Apocalypse of Baruch, . . .	130
The Testaments of the Twelve Patriarchs, . .	162
III. LEGENDARY—	
The Book of Jubilees, . . .	193
The Ascension of Isaiah, . . .	236
IV. MIXED—	
The Sibylline Oracles, . . .	276

INTRODUCTION.

In the times immediately preceding and succeeding the commencement of the Christian era there arose among the Jews a style of writing to which the name Pseudepigraphic has been given, because most of the works so composed appeared under the assumed name of some famous person. They must not be considered in the light of literary forgeries; they are not like Macpherson with his Ossian, or Chatterton with his Rowley, fraudulent attempts at imposture; but the authors, having something to say which they deemed worthy of the attention of contemporaries, put it forth under the ægis of a great name, not to deceive, but to conciliate favour. A writer who ventured to appropriate a celebrated title would take care to satisfy the expectations raised by his pseudonym, and readers would believe that no one would dare to challenge comparison with a great original who was not qualified to sustain the character assumed. The most familiar instance is, perhaps, the book known as the Wisdom of Solomon, wherein the writer assumes the person of the great Israelite king, certainly with no idea of deceiving his readers (for the language of the treatise, the date and place of its composition, alike forbid any notion of fraud), but with the view of supporting his opinions by the highest authority, and as embodying sentiments which are such as the son of David might have enunciated. A similar impersonation is familiar to us in the Book of Ecclesiastes, where Koheleth utters his varied experiences through the mouth of Solomon, "son of David, king in Jerusalem." Such a use of fiction has been common in all ages; it is found in classical authors. Plato and Cicero introduced real characters as vehicles for supporting or opposing their views. The Apologies of Socrates, the speeches in Thucydides and Livy, are never deemed to be intentional deceptions; the *animus decipiendi* is lacking; and though they utter the words of the writers, and not those of the persons represented, no one sees in them fraud and chicanery, but every one regards them as legitimate examples of dramatic personation. The Old Testament authors do not prefix their names to their works, as they write, not for self-glorification, but to serve far higher purposes. The only exception to this rule is found in the case of the prophets, whose names and credentials were necessarily required, in order to give weight and credibility to their announcements. In accordance with this practice the uninspired apocalyptic writers publish their visions and lucubrations under the appellation of some earlier worthy, whom with transparent impersonation they introduce into their compositions. They might also claim the authority of the titles of many books in the Old Testament which are presented under the names of authors who certainly did not write them. No one supposes that Ruth or Esther composed the books which bear their names, and very little of the two books of

Samuel are the work of that great prophet. The Psalmists adopted the designations of David, or Asaph, or the sons of Korah, because they echoed the spirit or employed the forms found in their prototypes. Those who followed the footsteps of these great predecessors, without their claim to inspiration, thought themselves justified in winning attention to their utterances by adventitious means, and boldly personated the eminent characters in whose spirit they wrote.[1]

At the cessation of prophecy among the Jews, when no longer the utterances of inspired seers denounced abuses, pointed the right way, proclaimed the will of God, great attention was paid by devout men to the study and interpretation of canonical Scripture. In contrast with the heathenism of surrounding nations, the Hebrew pored over his Heaven-sent law, and, by attention thereto, confirmed his abhorrence of idolatry and his adherence to his monotheistic faith. The degradation of Israel under its pagan oppressors, and the temporary triumph of the chosen people in the Maccabean period, gave rise to the apocalyptic literature of which we are speaking. An unswerving zeal for the Law, and a glowing hope of a happy future, formed the characteristics of this period. From the storm and tumult and confusion of their own times good men looked forward to a reign of peace and happiness, and strove to impart their own hopes to their desponding countrymen. Taking their tone from, and founding their views upon, the ancient prophets, and more especially employing the imagery and developing the annunciations of Daniel,

[1] See Dr. Edersheim, *Life and Times of Jesus,* i. 37 f.

these writers, under various forms, and with very different success, gradually put forth their notions of the future, and anticipate the kingdom of Messiah. Often in their treatises they enter on the history of the past, putting their words into the mouth of an ancient prophet; but all such details are preparatory to the predictive portion, and lead up to this important element. The grand destiny which awaits Israel fills their minds; they dream of an universal judgment, followed by the supremacy of the chosen people; they are fired with an enthusiasm which is not fettered by probabilities, and they boldly announce events as certain which they have no real claim to foretell, and which nothing but an imaginative and ardent zeal could have induced them to publish.

The value of these writings is considerable, and this for many reasons; but that which chiefly concerns us is the light which they throw upon Jewish belief at the most important era. Those which are plainly antecedent to Christian times have their own special utility; while the later productions, which belong to the first Christian centuries, show the influence of new ideas even on those who retained their affection for the old religion. And both series are necessary for every study of the religious history of the Jews. It is perhaps true that this apocalyptic literature was regarded with little favour by the Rabbinic schools, and no dogmatic authority was attributed to it; but it can be used as indicating current thought, just as we refer to any contemporary document to denote popular opinion, though it be not stamped with the authority of a teaching body. The number of these writings which are still extant, and the many more of which the titles only have remained to our times, prove the wide prevalence of the feelings which are embodied in them, and the profound impression which such thoughts had made on the hearts of the people. Omitting the works which either in whole or in part have been submitted to modern criticism, we have notices of the existence of many other apocalyptic and pseudepigraphic compositions, whose titles pretty fairly explain their contents. Of course, very many of the works enumerated in the catalogues of extra-canonical writings are of Christian origin; but even these are framed on the same lines as the earlier, and very often repeat the ideas and give expression to the hopes found in the others. In the Fourth Book of Esdras, which is called the Second in our English Bibles, the sacred books are counted as ninety-four, twenty-two of which would be the received items of the Jewish Canon, and seventy-two apocryphal. These last, which in round numbers are called seventy, were directed to be reserved for the wise among the people; "for in them is the spring of understanding, the fountain of wisdom, and the stream of knowledge."[1] Hilgenfeld[2] reckons the number of those whose titles have survived at thirty-six. Many of these, however, would scarcely come under our view as Jewish productions, being of gnostic or heretical origin, and are rather to be reckoned among New Testament pseudepigrapha. The term applied to the books

[1] 2 Esdr. xiv. 44-47. Some Latin MSS., instead of "ninety-four," give "nine hundred and four;" the Vulgate has "two hundred and four;" other versions, "ninety-four," which from what follows seems to be correct.

[2] In Herzog's *Encyklop.* xii. 341 ff. (ed. 1883).

with which we are concerned is used by Jerome in allusion to the Wisdom of Solomon, and has thence come to be employed for the whole class, though not strictly true of them all. In his preface to the Books of Solomon, Jerome says, "Fertur et Panaretos Jesu filii Sirach liber, et alius pseudepigraphus, qui sapientia Salomonis inscribitur." Not that Jerome invented the word which so happily describes the leading characteristic of such productions. It is found in Greek authors long before his time. Thus Polybius (*Hist.* xxiv. 5. 5) calls the tricksy and unreliable Messenian, Deinocrates, ψευδεπίγραφος καὶ ῥωπικός. Spuriousness of authorship belongs to most of the series, and is a mark of the writings which were produced in such luxuriance towards the time of the commencement of the Christian era; and a term denoting this peculiarity may well be adopted as their designation.

The documents fall naturally into three classes. The first, of which few representatives have reached us, may be called Lyrical. There is a spurious production of this nature assigned to David in the *Apostolical Constitutions*,[1] but it is no longer extant. The only important contribution to this class is the Psalter of Solomon, a collection of eighteen psalms, written probably originally in Hebrew, about half a century before the Christian era, but known to us only in a Greek version. They are conceived in the spirit of Old Testament prophecy, and are designed to console the Jews under national calamity by confirming their faith in future retribution and Messianic hopes.

[1] *Apost. Constit.* vi. 16.

The second class may be called Prophetical, and may be divided into two sections, composed respectively of Apocalypses and Testaments. Apocalyptic writings are very numerous, the most celebrated being the Fourth Book of Esdras and the Book of Enoch. The former of these, as it forms a portion of the Apocrypha in the Authorised Version of our English Bible, has been copiously annotated of late years; the latter from its length and importance demands special study. There are many others which are most interesting, and claim notice at our hands. The Assumption of Moses is the document from which, according to Origen, St. Jude borrowed his allusion to Michael's dispute with Satan about the body of Moses. It consists of an address of the great lawgiver to his successor Joshua, enunciating the future fate of Israel, partly historical down to the author's time, and partly predictive. The Apocalypse of Baruch is a different work from the Book of Baruch and the Epistle of Jeremy in our English Apocrypha. Written originally in Greek, it has been preserved only in Syriac and Latin versions. It contains a series of *post facto* predictions supposed to be uttered by Baruch about the time of the first destruction of Jerusalem, and a revelation of the reign and judgment of Messiah. The Ascension and Vision of Isaiah describe the martyrdom of the prophet by his being sawn asunder, an allusion to which is supposed to be made in Heb. xi. 37, and contain an account of what he saw when rapt to heaven. The above are the works which have come to us in a more or less perfect shape. There are many others of which we know little more than the titles which indeed are often very similar to those of extant productions, but appertain to distinct works. There is a Prophecy and Revelation of the holy and beloved prophet Esdras, another of Baruch; then Elijah, Jeremiah, Zephaniah, Ezekiel, Habakkuk, Zechariah, have each their special Apocalypses; a spurious Daniel also is mentioned; and Adam, Lamech, Moses, and Abraham are not unrepresented, but contribute their revelations. Hermas Pastor[1] refers to a Prophecy of Eldad and Modat which was well known in the early Church; but this with many others has perished long ago; and the vague allusions to such works in the pages of the Fathers and in some ancient catalogues of Scripture do not allow us to judge of their contents and character. Among the productions which assume the testamentary form we have the titles only of some, *e.g.* the Diatheke of the Protoplast, of Jacob, Moses, Hezekiah, Adam, Noah, Solomon, Abraham; the Last Prayer and Blessing of Joseph, a work continually quoted by Origen as "a writing not to be despised," and said by him to be in circulation among the Hebrews. But the work of this character that is still extant is called the Testaments of the Twelve Patriarchs. This is an account of the lives of the sons of Jacob, containing many legendary particulars not found in Scripture, revelations of the future, and Messianic predictions.

The third class takes a historical or Haggadistic character. Its chief representative is the Book of Jubilees, or Micro-Genesis, an enlarged account of Biblical history down to the institution of the Passover, with the chronology reduced to Jubilee periods. Other works of

[1] *Vis.* ii. 3. 4.

which little is known are these: the History of Jannes and Jambres, the magicians who opposed Moses at the court of Pharaoh; the Conversion of Manasses, a different work from the Prayer of Manasses in our Apocrypha; the Life of Adam; the Revelation of Adam; the Repentance of Adam; the Daughters of Adam; the Gospel of Eve; the Story of Asenath, Joseph's wife, and that of Noria, the wife of Noah.

We have omitted mention of the Sibylline Oracles, not because they are of less importance than other works, but because they partake of the nature of all three classes, and cannot be assigned specially to any one of them. They are lyrical, being written in measured verse, and very often in a highly poetical strain; they are historical, detailing the events in the history of various peoples down to Christian times, with an admixture of truth and fiction which is hard to unravel; and they are apocalyptic, in that they foreshadow the future of Messiah's kingdom and the destiny of the elect. While a large proportion of these poems is of post-Christian origin, there are considerable fragments of earlier date which are of important utility in determining prevalent Jewish views. Schürer happily calls them "Jewish Propaganda under a heathen mask," and classes them with the so-called productions of Hystaspes, Hecatæus, Aristæus, and Phocylides.

Without anticipating details which belong to the special account of each of these works, we may here gather up some general results of the doctrine enunciated in them.[1]

[1] I have in this sketch gladly availed myself of Prof. Drummond's *The Jewish Messiah*, and Mr. Stanton's *The Jewish and Christian*

First, as to the divisions of time, we find throughout the books that two great periods are specified—the present, and the future or coming age. This is in conformity with the view taken in the Book of Daniel. The former period is one of depression and misery, when Israel is for a time prostrate under the heel of Gentile enemies; the latter is an eternity of victory and bliss, when "the saints of the Most High shall receive the kingdom, and possess the kingdom for ever, even for ever and ever."[1] The temporary and the eternal periods are strongly contrasted, though there is no general consent as to the moment when the happy age shall dawn. But it shall be preceded by a judgment which is to take place in the last days, the end of the transition state, wherein the heathen shall receive their doom. This great day is known only to God; but it shall be revealed in due time, and meanwhile men need not disquiet themselves concerning its advent; as it is said in the Book of Enoch, "Let not your spirit be grieved on account of the times, for the Holy One hath prescribed days to all. And the righteous shall arise from sleep, and walk in the way of righteousness, and God will be gracious unto them, and give them everlasting dominion."[2] In the Psalms of Solomon we read,[3] "Behold, O Lord, and raise up for them their king, the son of David, at the time which Thou, O God, knowest." In the Fourth Book of Esdras it is said, "The Most High hath made, not one

Messiah, though most of the articles on special pseudepigraphal works were originally written before I had seen those books. Since then I have had the pleasure of perusing Schürer's valuable treatise on *The Jewish People in the time of Jesus Christ.*

[1] Dan. vii. 18.   [2] Enoch xcii. 2 ff.   [3] Ps. xvii. 23.

age, but two;" and again, "He hath made this age for the sake of many, but the future for the sake of few."[1] And, "This present age is not the end . . . but the day of judgment will be the end of this time, and the beginning of the immortal age that is to come, wherein corruption hath passed away."[2] Attempts are made to define the length of the first period more accurately, but the proposed solutions do not help much to satisfy inquiry. The Book of Enoch in one place allots seventy generations to the world's history, in another divides it into ten weeks; in the Assumption of Moses the beginning of the second age is placed "two hundred and fifty times," i.e. probably 250 weeks of years ($= 4250$), after the death of Moses, A.M. 2500. This is almost the same result as is obtained in the Book of Jubilees. In the Fourth Book of the Sibylline Oracles the time is divided into eleven generations,[3] in the last of which the judgment shall take place. In the Fourth Book of Esdras and in the Apocalypse of Baruch the age consists of twelve sections, at the end of which the new era shall commence.

Failing to define accurately the duration of the first age of the world, speculation concerned itself with the signs which should herald the approach of the last times.

[1] The former passage occurs in the fragment omitted in the old Latin editions and versions founded thereon, and will be found in Fritzsche's book as vi. 25, and in Churton's as vii. 50. In both passages the word rendered "age" is "sæculum," which some, however, translate "world."
[2] vii. 42 f.
[3] So all the MSS. Alexandre reads ἰς δεκάτην, asserting that throughout the books the last generation is always the tenth, and he refers in confirmation to vers. 47 and 86. But see Drummond, p. 206.

Theorists endeavoured to answer that question which, quite in accordance with Jewish opinion, the apostles put to Christ, "Tell us, when shall these things be? and what shall be the sign of Thy coming, and of the consummation of the age?"[1] Thus the Sibyl affirms that there shall be seen swords in the heaven, and storms of dust, and an eclipse of the sun, and armed warriors contending in the sky.[2] The Book of Enoch foretells great changes in the course of nature — the alteration of seasons, the shortening of men's lives, irregularity in the course of moon and stars, and a repetition of the wicked practices which occasioned the Flood of old.[3] To the same effect the Book of Jubilees looks forward to a season of abnormal iniquity as the precursor of the judgment day; there shall be unnatural crimes among men, and strange aberrations in the order of nature, children rising up against parents, general barrenness in earth, great destruction of the lower creatures in land and sea, perversion of all right, and universal strife.[4] The Fourth of Esdras takes up the same strain. As the world grows older it becomes weaker and more evil, men degenerate, truth flies away, leasing is hard at hand. Then shall occur earthquakes, unrest and uproar among nations, and various prodigies in heaven and earth; the sun shall shine at night, the moon in day; blood shall ooze from wood; sweet water shall be changed to salt; women shall bring forth monsters; infants of tender age shall speak.[5]

---

[1] Matt. xxiv. 3.   [2] Lib. iii. 795 ff.
[3] Chaps. xci., xcix.   [4] Book of Jub. chap. xxiii.
[5] Prof. Drummond refers to 2 Esdr. v. 1-13, 54 f., vi. 7-28, viii 63-ix. 6, xiv. 15-17.

Many of these portents are such as one reads of in classical authors; some recall our Lord's predictions, or St. Paul's warning that "in the last days perilous times shall come" (2 Tim. iii. 1). In the Apocalypse of Baruch the details of the wickedness and calamities that shall intervene are more distinctly specified, being divided into twelve parts, increasing to a climax of horror; and despair and destruction shall overtake all the world with the exception of the inhabitants of the holy land.[1] But throughout these books the advent of the second age is to be ushered in by extraordinary calamities consequent on excessive moral evil, and characterised by an universal degeneracy alike in animal and vegetable life.

We have now to see what our books say about the Messiah. Many of them, indeed, seem to have no reference whatever to Him. The writer of the Assumption of Moses expects the appearance of some great saviour to prepare the way for the visible reign of Jehovah; but this deliverer is not the Messiah, and is, in fact, not regarded as superior to Moses in action or person. In the Book of Jubilees the idea of a personal Messiah is pointedly excluded; God, says the writer, has appointed no one to reign over Israel, being Himself their only Lord and Ruler, and purposing in due time to descend from heaven and dwell with His people. The writer seems purposely to have omitted the blessings which Jacob pronounced upon his sons, and especially all mention of the house of David, which would naturally have found place in the benediction on Judah. The

[1] Apoc. Bar. chaps. xxv.-xxvii., xlviii., lxx., lxxi.

Fourth Book of the Sibylline Oracles, which is marked by some eschatological passages, omits all reference to Messiah, while announcing the resurrection and the judgment. And we may remark in passing that the apocryphal works in our English Bible are singularly devoid of all Messianic references. Ecclesiasticus has no trace of the great hope; Wisdom is equally barren; the famous passage in ii. 10-20 of that Book, about the treatment of the righteous man by the wicked, having regard to a class, and certainly not alluding to any particular individual. The Books of Maccabees look forward to the re-gathering of Israel and the appearance of a true prophet, but nothing more. In Tobit we find only hope of the conversion of the Gentiles and the restoration of Jerusalem; in Baruch and Judith, though the future judgment is intimated, absolute silence is maintained concerning the Messiah's part in that transaction. It is plain that the later conception of the Messiah, with all the hopes that gathered round His person and achievements, was not generally admitted when most of our books were composed, and it was only very gradually that the ideas obtained which we have been accustomed to associate therewith. Though it is difficult to fix the date of most of these works, probably the earliest which contains definite Messianic statements is a section of the Third Book of the Sibylline Verses, written about a century and a half before the Christian era.. The passage which is, probably correctly, assumed to bear this interpretation is the following:[1] "Then from the sun God shall send a King, who shall cause all the earth to cease from wicked

[1] Orac. Sibyll. iii. 652 ff.

war, killing indeed some, and making faithful treaties with others. Not by His own counsels shall He do all these things, but in obedience to the good decrees of the great God." Then follows a description of the happy condition that is to ensue; but there is no further mention of this King, and the governing authority of the new kingdom established by God is not one great personage, but prophets, who are "judges of mortals and righteous kings." The subordinate position assigned to Messiah is very remarkable; He, indeed, prepares the way for the great consummation, but He is not said to bear any part in the administration of the future age. In another passage,[1] which critics generally assign to some half-century B.C., the advent of the Messiah is immediately expected. Thus the Sibyl writes: " But when Rome shall rule over Egypt also, uniting it into one, then indeed the mighty kingdom of the immortal King shall appear among men; and there shall come a pure King to hold the sceptres of all the earth for all ages as time hastens onward." Evidently, it is an earthly kingdom which this Monarch establishes, and this, it is further intimated, is to come to an end when the new era dawns.

The Book of Enoch adumbrates the Messiah in symbolical language. In the vision of the seventy shepherds, and the sheep and wild animals, the Messiah appears under the figure of a white Bull. The wording of the passage is ambiguous, and the correct reading is disputed; hence it remains doubtful to which age the Messiah belongs; though the analogy of other passages

[1] Orac. Sibyll. iii. 36–92.

would place Him at the entrance of the new era. Enoch says:[1] "Then those three who were clothed in white raised me up and placed me in the midst of the sheep, before the judgment took place [2] . . . and I saw that a white Bullock was born, having great horns, and all the beasts of the field and all the birds of heaven feared him, and besought him continually. And I watched till all their tribes were changed and became white bullocks; and the first among them [was the Word, and the same Word][3] was a great beast, and had great black horns upon his head; and the Lord of the sheep rejoiced over them and over all the bullocks." The personality of this "Bullock" is not very definite, and there is no allusion to descent from the house of David; but the representation evidently embraces hopes of Messiah, and looks forward, though vaguely, to the time of His appearing. This time is fixed more accurately in the Fourth of Esdras (vii. 28 ff.), where it is announced that Messiah and the saints with Him shall rejoice four hundred[4] years, and that then he and all men are to die, and silence reign for seven days, at the end of which time "the earth that yet awaketh not shall be raised up, and that which is corrupt shall die." So in other passages, both in Esdras and Baruch, the dominion of Messiah is announced as lasting till the final judgment, confined, as it would seem, to the first, the present age.

[1] Enoch xc. 31 ff.
[2] Prof. Drummond doubts the genuineness of this clause, and Dillmann does not hold it as indisputable. It is certainly inconsistent with other statements in the same passage.
[3] The words in brackets are regarded as spurious.
[4] The Syriac reads "thirty." Churton, *in loc.*

The Messiah, according to Enoch,[1] is to be born at Jerusalem; meantime He is hidden till the hour of His revelation arrives. In the Ascension of Isaiah He passes through the seven heavens unrecognised, until He executes vengeance on the evil principalities and powers, and returns in glory to the throne of God. Esdras sees Him coming up from the midst of the sea, which denotes the mysterious and secret character of the unknown region wherein He sojourned, and in due time taking His stand upon Mount Zion.[2] "Here," says Baruch,[3] "He shall judge the last leader of His enemies, and put him to death, and shall protect God's people who are found in the place which He has chosen. And His dominion shall continue until the world of corruption is brought to an end, and the predicted times are fulfilled." Of the Messiah's descent from David and His high title, the Psalter of Solomon gives the clearest indications. "Behold, O Lord," says the Psalmist, "and raise up for them their King, the Son of David, at the time which Thou knowest. . . . He is the righteous King over them, taught of God. There shall be no injustice in His days among them, for they all shall be holy, and their King shall be Christ the Lord."[4] This last expression seems certainly to have been well known before Christian times.

[1] Enoch xc. 36 f.
[2] 2 Esdr. xiii. 26, 35.   [3] Apoc. Bar. xl.
[4] Ps. Solom. xvii. 23, 35, 36. The title is given in the MSS. without variation Χριστός Κύριος. Professor Drummond would read Κυρίου. But see xviii. 6, 8, and Lam. iv. 20. At the same time, as Ewald points out, the expression in the text may possibly be a mistranslation for "the Lord's Christ," as Luke ii. 26, and must not be taken as proving the seer's belief in the Divinity of Messiah.

In Esdras [1] the name Christ is found twice at least, though in one place it has been changed by some Christian hand into "Jesus;" and "unctus," the Anointed, also occurs, corrupted in the Latin into "ventus," the "wind;" but in the other versions appearing with an addition, "the Anointed whom the Highest hath reserved to the end of the days, who shall arise out of the seed of David." The title Messiah is constantly used in Baruch; thus we read, "It shall come to pass, when that which is to be shall have been accomplished there, that Messiah shall begin to be revealed." [2] The Book of Enoch has suffered so much from glosses and interpolations that we cannot build much upon isolated expressions; but, as the text stands, the expression "Son of God," or its equivalent, is met with in the most ancient section once. The Lord is represented as saying (cv. 2), "I and my Son will unite ourselves with them [the sons of earth] for ever and ever." Nor can much reliance be placed upon the present text of the Second of Esdras; otherwise the terms Messiah and Son of God may be observed in a few passages.[3] But although we grant that the name and designation of the Messiah are found in these books, there is very far from being any general consent as to His nature and attributes. The Catholic doctrine concerning the Christ was as yet not received, and the speculations which were rife fell far short of the great truth. Whether many of these writers believed in the pre-existence of the Messiah before His

---

[1] 2 Esdr. vii. 28, 29, xii. 32.
[2] Apoc. Bar. xxix. See also xxx., xxxix., xl., lxx., lxxii.
[3] See Drummond, pp. 285 ff.

appearance on earth is doubtful. The author of the Ascension of Isaiah certainly did; but as the portion of the work containing the assertion is probably the composition of a Christian Jew, it cannot be quoted as affording an instance of purely Jewish opinion. The expression in the Third Book of the Sibyllines already cited, which represents the future King as proceeding "from the sun," might seem to imply at least a supernatural origin, denoting that, as the Creed says, "He came down from heaven;" but the words ($ἀπ'$ $ἠελίοιο$) may mean merely "from the rising sun," *i.e.* from the East, which to a dweller in Egypt would be the land of mystery and of God's revelations. In that part of the Book of Enoch which is termed the Similitudes or Parables, He who is here called "Son of man" is seen by the seer in company with the "Ancient of Days," and is expressly stated to have existed before all worlds, and to live before God for ever; in Him all wisdom and righteousness dwell; but He is not God, though of godlike character. In another and more ancient division of the work, as we have seen above, He is figured under the representation of "a white Bull," born in due time, and in no way supernaturally distinguished from the other animals who assume the same appearance, though His supremacy is recognised by them in that they fear and pray to Him. In the Psalter of Solomon the Messiah is lauded in the highest terms, as mighty in word and deed, a just and powerful Ruler, who, living in the fear of God, shall feed the Lord's people in faith and righteousness; but He is not superhuman, He is only the ideal earthly king of David's line. The Apocalypse of Baruch speaks of the "revelation of Messiah and of His kingdom,"[1] which seems to imply pre-existence; but, as Professor Drummond points out, this expression, and the analogous one "reserved" in Second Esdras (xii. 32, xiii. 36), may merely imply the belief that Messiah after His birth should be withdrawn into concealment, from whence He should emerge in due time; or such terms may be used to denote God's predestination, and the mystery which attached to this heavenly messenger. In fact, none of these works contain any clear assertion of the Divinity of the Messiah; and the writers, while they look upon Him as abnormal and marvellous and supreme, do not attribute to Him a nature different from that of man in its highest ideal character. We may note that our Lord's own disciples were very slow to realise His Divine nature, while they readily owned His Messiahship. Again and again Jesus had to reprove their dulness of apprehension and slowness of belief. Miracles often repeated failed to convey this truth fully to their minds; and it needed the Resurrection, with all its wondrous accompaniments, to enable them fully to realise that their Master was God Almighty. So difficult was it for them to rise superior to prejudice and popular opinion.

Our general view of the pseudepigraphical books would not be complete without a brief notice of their angelology and eschatology. The existence of good and evil angels is fully recognised. The former are divided into various orders and degrees; in Enoch the names of the archangels are given as Michael, Gabriel, Suriel, and Uriel; Suriel elsewhere appears as Raphael. These four have

[1] Chap. xxix. 3, xxxix. 7; Drummond, p. 293.

their special spheres and provinces; and beside them there are myriads of inferior angels who stand before the Lord of Spirits, ready to do His will. They are archangels who reveal God's will to Enoch, and conduct him on his various journeys. It is the Angel of the Presence who is charged to transcribe the revelation in the Book of Jubilees. Angels, according to Baruch, execute God's wrath in the destruction of Jerusalem, having first committed to the earth the veil, the mercy-seat, and other sacred things appertaining to the temple. It is, as we have seen, from the Assumption of Moses that the story of the dispute between Michael and Satan over the body of Moses is derived. Esdras receives his seven visions by the intervention of Uriel. The Book of Jubilees states that on the first day of creation God made the ministering spirits, the Angel of the Presence, the Angel of Praise, and the angels that preside over the elements, as we find in the Revelation of St. John mention made of angels which have power over fire and water.[1] The angels bring men's sins before God, execute His vengeance on sinners, teach mortals useful arts and acceptable worship, and communicate God's will by dreams or visions or open manifestations. In the Testaments of the Twelve Patriarchs the heavenly hierarchy is still more systematically arranged, and the duties and offices of its various members are distinguished.

The evil angels have their ranks and orders; they are a disciplined army under chieftains. At their head appears one who is variously named Satan, Sammael,

[1] Rev. xiv. 18, xvi. 5.

Mastema, Azazel. Their fall, according to Enoch, was brought about by their connection with the daughters of men, from whence sprang a race of giants whose iniquity, fostered by their superhuman fathers, occasioned the Flood. These evil angels taught men war and bloodshed and every wicked work, and were punished by being confined in the depth of the earth till the great day of judgment, a certain portion of them only being allowed a limited liberty.

Turning to the eschatological teaching of these books, we find that in the last days, on the appearance of Messiah, there will be a great mustering of enemies to oppose the establishment of the new kingdom. Here we have the curious myth of the return to life of Nero, who, under the name of Beliar, is to lead the armies of Antichrist.[1] At other times this leader is not definitely named. In Baruch (chap. xl.) he is called merely "dux ultimus," who, as we have seen above, is to be brought to Mount Zion and there put to death by the victorious Messiah. But it is not always the Messiah who conducts the war; God Himself interposes in the Sibyl's account,[2] and Enoch predicts the great destruction of Israel's enemies before the advent of Messiah, and exults in their cruel annihilation.[3] Whether by the action of Messiah, or by the immediate intervention of the Lord, it is universally agreed that the assembled foes of Israel shall meet with signal overthrow, and that, at this "consummation," the kingdom of Messiah shall be established. This kingdom is to have its centre at Jerusalem, under

[1] Orac. Sibyll. iii. 63 ff., iv. 137 ff.
[2] *Ibid.* iii. 669 ff. [3] Enoch xc., xcviii., xcix.

the personal rule of Messiah, who is the vicegerent of God,[1] and is to extend over all nations, and to be characterised by righteousness, peace, and plenty. The material blessings of this reign are picturesquely delineated in the Sibylline Verses and elsewhere;[2] the earth shall be marvellously productive, men's lives shall be prolonged to a thousand years without disease or infirmity. The duration of this kingdom is considered in most of our books to be unlimited; Esdras alone confines its length to four hundred years, and Baruch says vaguely that it shall be continued until the world of corruption be ended. Whether the Gentiles should be converted was a question not answered in a uniform manner; while the writers with Hellenistic leanings took a merciful view, the exaggerated prejudices of others led them to anticipate with satisfaction the total annihilation of the heathen. The Sibyl looks forward to a time when the sight of the happiness and prosperity of the God-fearing Israelites will move alien nations to repentance,[3] whilst the Psalmist brings the heathen under the yoke of the chosen race, and holds out to them no hope of salvation.[4] Of the resurrection and the final judgment we have varying accounts, there being also a dissidence in the opinion as to the epochs in which these events should take place; some writers allotting the judgment to the time of Messiah's appearing, others looking for it

---

[1] Orac. Sibyll. iii. 652 ff.; Psalm. Sol. xvii.; Drummond, pp. 309 ff.
[2] Orac. Sibyll. iii. 743 ff., 776 ff.; Enoch x. 17 ff., xi. 1.; Apoc. Bar. xxix.; Jubil. xxiii.
[3] Orac. Sibyll. iii. 702 ff.; comp. Enoch x. 21, xc. 30 ff.
[4] Psalm. Sol. xvii. 25 ff.; comp. Apoc. Bar. lxxii.

at the close of that period, and as ushering in eternity. The latter view is that which most generally prevailed. The Book of Enoch gives copious details concerning the future life and the judgment. The Lord sits on a throne erected in the midst of Palestine, and passes judgment respectively on the fallen angels, the apostate Israelites, and the heathen powers. The souls of the dead have a place where they wait for their sentence, and are here divided into classes according to their earthly actions, accounts of which have been daily written down in the heavenly books; and now they shall receive their reward—unalterable punishment in the case of obstinate sinners, and eternal felicity in the case of the righteous. The resurrection of the body is nowhere expressly affirmed, though it is implied by the material nature of the penalties and the bliss accorded to the raised persons. There seems to have been no definite belief in a bodily resurrection, though a resurrection of some kind was universally expected, and blind gropings after the great Christian doctrine are occasionally found; but the general impression conveyed by these apocryphal books is that the immortality enunciated therein is incorporeal; and, as regards the righteous, the idea is that they shall be changed into angelic beings with the power of assuming any form they please.[1]

The above are the chief points of interest in the Jewish Pseudepigraphic writings; more definite details and notices of incidental matters appertain more properly to the separate accounts of the various works which are classed under this designation.

[1] Apoc. Bar. li.

I.

LYRICAL.

———o———

THE PSALTER OF SOLOMON.

AMONG the apocryphal literature of the Old Testament which has been preserved to our time, the eighteen Psalms of Solomon, so called, are an interesting monument of later Judaism, giving glimpses of contemporary history and breathing Messianic hopes. Excluded from our English version of the Bible, they have been remarkably neglected in this country, and very few students have taken the trouble of mastering this important remnant of antiquity. Germany has dealt otherwise with them. For the last thirty years critics in that country have been investigating their origin, assigning their date, settling the text, examining the contents; so that we can enter upon the study of them with a critical and exegetical apparatus which a few years ago was unattainable. They were never included in the Canonical Scriptures of the Jews, though known to early authors, and occurring in several catalogues of Scripture. The Alexandrine Manuscript of the Greek Bible, indeed, inserted them at the end of the volume, a fact which probably proves that they were used in Divine worship in the Eastern Church; but where they are named, they are included among the Antilegomena, and are apparently debarred from the Canon by the Council of Laodicea.[1] In the Stichometria of Nicephorus, and in the *Synopsis Athanasii*, they are classed with the Books of Wisdom, Ecclesiasticus, Maccabees, and other Apocrypha; in other lists they come in the same category as Enoch, the Twelve Patriarchs, the Apocalypses of Moses, etc. Being thus thrust aside in early times, they seem to have met with little attention, and to have been seldom transcribed. Hence the manuscripts which exhibited them were very few, and modern investigation has not discovered many fresh sources of information about them. Most unfortunately the leaves of the Alexandrine Codex, now in the British Museum, which once contained them, have perished, so that we are forced to rely on a late and inferior document for the exposition and correction of the text. The *Editio Princeps* of De la Cerda was printed from a MS. brought from Constantinople in the year 1615, which was once in the Augsburg Library, but has now disappeared. Three other MSS. known to exist have not been used in editing the work. Indeed, the only manuscript made available is a cursive of the

---

[1] Syn. of Laodicea, Can. 59: ὅτι οὐ δεῖ ἰδιωτικοὺς ψαλμοὺς λέγεσθαι ἐν τῇ ἐκκλησίᾳ. Zonaras and Balsamon explain the term ἰδιωτ. ψαλμ. thus: ἐκτὸς τῶν ρν´ ψαλμῶν τοῦ Δαβὶδ εὑρίσκονται καί τινες ἕτεροι λεγόμενοι τοῦ Σολομῶντος εἶναι καὶ ἄλλων τινῶν, οὓς καὶ ἰδιωτικοὺς ὠνόμασαν οἱ πατέρες καὶ μὴ λέγεσθαι ἐν τῇ ἐκκλησίᾳ διετάξαντο. They are mentioned among the Apocrypha or Antilegomena in the Catalogue of "The Sixty Books" (*ap.* Westcott, *Can. of N. T.*, Append. D. xvii.).

tenth century, Codex Vindobonensis,[1] called "V" in Fritzsche's edition, and now in the Royal Library of Vienna. In this our Psalms are found between the Book of Wisdom and Ecclesiasticus. The title prefixed to the once existing Augsburg MS. was ΨΑΛΤΗΡΙΟΝ ΣΑΛΟΜΩΝΤΟΣ, and at the end occurred the colophon Ψαλμοὶ Σαλομῶντος ιή. ἔχουσιν ἔπη ‚α· Τέλος σὺν Θεῷ. But the author himself never claims to be the son of David, and the various headings, now found in the Psalter, which attribute the Psalms to Solomon, are without dispute the work of later hands. The writer speaks of himself sometimes, *e.g.* Ps. i. 3 : "I reasoned in my heart that I was filled with righteousness, because I was prosperous and had become mighty in children;" Ps. ii. 35 : "Raising me up unto glory." But even if these and such-like passages assumed more plainly than they do Solomonic authorship, they would show merely that the poet, like the writer of the Book of Wisdom, appropriated the name of Solomon for literary purposes, with no idea of deceiving his readers or causing them to give credence to so transparent a fallacy. Or, very possibly, the name of Solomon did not occur in the original title; but, as the Psalter became well known and used, because it could not be ascribed to David, or included in the canonical Psalm-Book, it was honoured with the name of Solomon in later times, and reached the early Christian writers under that designation. The fact that in 1 Kings iv. 32 Solomon is said to have

---

[1] Codex Gr. Theol. 7. It is described by Hilgenfeld (*Zeitschr.* 1868, p. 136), who considers it superior in correctness to the Augsburg MS.

composed "a thousand and five songs" (ᾠδαὶ πεντακισ-χίλιαι, Sept.), gave a colouring to the assumed authorship, and in uncritical times, when historical allusions were little investigated or weighed, the name gained an unquestioned currency.

The references to the Book in early writers are few and uncertain. In the Stichometria of Nicephorus it is named, as we have said, among the Antilegomena of the Old Testament: to the same category it is relegated in the *Synopsis Sacræ Scripturæ* appended to the works of St. Athanasius, the date of which is doubtful, and which may possibly be founded upon the Catalogue of Nicephorus.[1] Schürer thinks it was included under the category of Antilegomena simply owing to its absence from the Hebrew Canon, position in that list being the criterion which guided the formal reception of writings; while in the Christian Church it was regarded in some quarters with greater favour. Five Odes of Solomon are quoted in the curious Gnostic book of the third century A.D., *Pistis Sophia*;[2] and St. Jerome writing against Vigilantius (cap. vi.) may possibly refer to the Psalter when he says: "Nam in commentariolo tuo quasi pro te faciens de Salomone sumis testimonium, quod Salomon omnino non scripsit, ut, qui habes alterum Esdram, habeas et Salomonem alterum." The "Second Esdras" means a passage in the Fourth Book of Esdras

---

[1] In both of these lists we find the title ψαλμοὶ καὶ ᾠδὴ Σολομῶντος; the latter adding στίχοι βρ´ = 2100. The *Synopsis* is in vol. ii. p. 154 of the Bened. edition of Athanasius. The Catalogue of Nicephorus is given in App. xix. of Canon Westcott's work on *The Canon of the New Testament*.

[2] Ed. Schwartze et Peterman, Berlin 1851.

(vi. 81, *ap.* Fritz.)[1] implying the inexpediency of certain prayers for the dead; the "Second Solomon" may perhaps indicate the following words: "Therefore this is their inheritance, Hades, and darkness, and destruction; and they shall not be found in the day of the mercy of the righteous" (Ps. xiv. 6); "for their iniquities shall make the houses of sinners desolate, and sinners shall perish in the day of the Lord's judgment for ever and ever" (xv. 13). Lactantius[2] more than once quotes passages from Solomon which do not occur in the Canonical Scriptures, and are supposed to have been once comprehended among these Psalms, though no longer extant in our copies.

[1] vii. 105, p. 98, in Canon Churton's very useful work, lately published, *The Uncanonical and Apocryphal Scriptures*, London 1884. It is called the Second Book of Esdras in the Anglican Version. The Latin runs: "Tunc non poterit quis ut deprecetur pro aliquo in illo die." Another allusion to the same passage is made by Jerome, *Adv. Vigilant.* c. 10: "Tu vigilans dormis et dormiens scribis et propinas mihi librum apocryphum, qui sub nomine Esdræ a te et similibus tui legitur, ubi scriptum est, quod post mortem nullus pro aliis gaudeat deprecari; quem ego librum nunquam legi."

[2] *Divin. Instit.* lib. iv. 18: "Solomon, filius ejus qui Hierosolymam condidit, eam ipsam perituram esse in ultionem sanctæ crucis prophetavit: 'Quod si avertimini a me, dicit Dominus, et non custodieritis veritatem meam, rejiciam Israel a terra quam dedi illis; et domum hanc, quam ædificavi illis in nomine meo, projiciam illam ex omnibus; et erit Israel in perditionem et in improperium populo; et domus hæc erit deserta; et omnis qui transibit per illam admirabitur et dicet: Propter quam rem fecit Dominus terræ huic et huic domui hæc mala? Et dicent: Quia reliquerunt Dominum Deum suum, et persecuti sunt regem suum dilectissimum Deo, et cruciaverunt illum in humilitate magna, propter hoc importavit illis Deus mala hæc.'"—On the last part of this passage the commentator (*ap.* Migne, vi. p. 509) remarks: "Hæc nescio ex qua traditione adjecit, quorum nulla 1 Reg. ix. aut 2, Paralip. vii. vestigia apparent."

The Fourth Book of Esdras, which appears to have been written towards the end of the first Christian century, contains many passages which are possibly derived from the Psalter. Some of these have been collected by Hilgenfeld in his edition of our Book, and are sufficiently apposite. Ps. viii. 34: " Gather together the dispersion of Israel with mercy and kindness." *Ibid.* xi. 3: " Stand on high, Jerusalem, and see thy children gathered once from the east and west by the Lord. They come from the north in the joy of their God; from the isles afar off God gathered them together." 4 Esdr. i. 38: "See thy people coming from the east." *Ibid.* xiii. 39: "Thou hast seen Him gathering to Himself another multitude in peace."—Ps. ix. 18: "Thou, O Lord, hast put Thy name upon us." 4 Esdr. iv. 25: "What wilt Thou do to Thy name which is invoked upon us?" *Ibid.* x. 22: "Thy name which is invoked upon us hath been profaned."—Ps. xvii. 19: "They wandered in deserts to save their souls from evil." 4 Esdr. xiii. 41 f.: "They determined to leave the multitude of nations, and to go to a distant region, there to observe their own laws."—Ps. xvii. 36: "Their king shall be Christ the Lord." 4 Esdr. vii. 28: "My son Jesus shall be revealed with those who are with him."—Ps. xvii. 37: "He shall not trust in horse and rider and bow, nor shall he multiply to himself gold and silver for war, nor put his hopes in arms ($\H{o}\pi\lambda o\iota s$, Fr.) for the day of battle." 4 Esdr. xiii. 9: "Lo, when he saw the onset of the host coming against him, he raised not his hand, nor held the shield, nor any weapon of war."—Ps. xviii. 4: "Thy chastisement shall be upon us as a first-born only-begotten son." 4 Esdr. vi. 58: "We Thy people, whom Thou hast called Thy first-born only-begotten son."

There is one passage of the Psalter (xvii. 5) which is found in the *Testaments of the Twelve Patriarchs*, that curious production of early Jewish Christianity. It occurs in the Testament of Judah, § 22: "For the Lord sware with an oath unto me that my crown shall not fail from my seed, all the days, for ever." In the Psalter: "Thou swarest to him concerning his seed for ever, that his crown should not fail before thee."[1] In the New Testament no certain intimation occurs that the work was known to the inspired writers. The only passage which bears a close likeness to a verse in the gospel is in Ps. v. 4: "One cannot take spoils from a strong man," which is parallel to Mark xii. 29: "How can one enter into a strong man's house and spoil his goods?"

On the other hand, founded as it is on the model of the Old Testament, the Psalter is replete with references to and citations from the Canonical Scriptures. To rehearse these would be to transcribe a large portion of the whole work. But it is noteworthy that what we call Apocryphal Books are not unknown to our author. And this is the more remarkable in the case of a work written, as is justly supposed, in Palestine and in the Hebrew language; since it shows how widely extended was the

---

[1] Ps. xvii. 5: καὶ σὺ ὤμοσας αὐτῷ περὶ τοῦ σπέρματος αὐτοῦ εἰς τὸν αἰῶνα, τοῦ μὴ ἐκλείπειν ἀπέναντί σου βασίλειον αὐτοῦ. *Test. XII. Patr.* v. 22: ὅρκῳ γὰρ ὤμοσέ μοι κύριος μὴ ἐκλείψειν τὸ βασίλειόν μου ἐκ τοῦ σπέρματός μου πάσας τὰς ἡμέρας ἕως αἰῶνος.

influence of that literature which grew up after the close of the Canon of the Old Testament. There are reminiscences of, if not quotations from, the Book of Wisdom in the Psalter. Thus in Ps. xvi. 8 the epithet "unprofitable" (ἀνωφελοῦς) applied to sin seems to recall the word in Wisd. i. 11: "Beware of unprofitable murmuring." In Ps. viii. 11 and in Wisd. i. 16 the making a compact (συνέθεντο συνθήκας) with sin and death is common to both. "The right hand of the Lord sheltered (ἐσκέπασε) me . . . the arm of the Lord saved us," says the Psalter (xiii. 1). "With His right hand shall He shelter (σκεπάσει) them, and with His arm shall He protect them," says Wisd. v. 16. "God is a righteous judge, and will not reverence persons (θαυμάσει πρόσωπον)," Ps. ii. 19. "The Lord of all will not cower before persons (ὑποστελεῖται πρόσωπον)," Wisd. vi. 8. The use of the very uncommon word εὐστάθεια in Ps. iv. 11, vi. 7, is probably due to a reminiscence of Wisd. vi. 26. Wisd. v. 23: "Iniquity shall lay waste (ἐρημώσει . . . ἀνομία) the whole earth," may be compared with Ps. xvii. 13: "The sinner wasted (ἠρήμωσεν ὁ ἄνομος[1]) their land." The phrase, "Man and his portion are with thee by weight (ἐν σταθμῷ)," is verbally like, though differing in intention from, the famous passage in Wisd. xi. 21: "Thou orderest all things by measure, number, and weight." The touching appeal in Wisd. xv. 2: "For even if we sin, we are Thine," finds its echo in Ps. ix. 16: "Behold, and pity us, O God of Israel, for we are Thine;" and the idea, as well as the

---

[1] The MSS. give ἄνεμος; but ἄνομος is an almost certain emendation of Ewald.

wording, of Ps. xiii. 8 : "He will admonish (νουθετήσει) the righteous man as the son of His love," is closely parallel with those of Wisd. xi. 10 : "These as a father admonishing (νουθετῶν) Thou didst prove." Between Ps. xi. and the fifth chapter of Baruch there are many close parallelisms; but the latter is probably the borrower.

Whilst we can trace the language and conceptions of the Psalter in a great measure to preceding Scriptures, we can yet claim for the author an originality for the manner in which he has developed and built upon the hints therein given, and from the outline of the prophets has presented a fairly complete picture of the ideal son of David. A few words must first be said concerning the text and the date of the original work; and then some extracts will show the pseudo-Solomon's views on various matters of the highest interest to all who desire to acquaint themselves with the progress of Jewish thought.

The revived interest in this little Book arose from the importance attributed to it by Ewald in his history of the Jewish Church; and although, as we shall show, we think that his view of the date of its production is erroneous, the learned world is largely indebted to him for raising a discussion which has contributed greatly to our knowledge of the contents and bearing of the work. Among other points which have been established may be mentioned that of the unity of the Psalter. Of course German ingenuity has endeavoured to trace the hands of various authors in the work; but the identity of ideas, the similarity of language and phrases, the homogeneousness of the composition, show that the writer is one,

C

though he may have uttered his songs at different periods and under varying circumstances. He is thoroughly imbued with the Hebraic spirit, and has framed his Psalms on the Biblical model, proving how this form of poetry endured to the latest times of the Jewish polity. Stichometrically written, the Psalter affords a fair specimen of Hebrew lyrics in their declining days; and, if we may judge by the occasional introduction of the musical term "Diapsalma" (xvii. 31, xviii. 10), the words were intended to be used in Divine service. The Psalter, as we have mentioned, was first published by La Cerda in his *Adversaria Sacra* (Lugd. 1626), from an Augsburg MS., which has since been lost.[1] The same text, with the addition of a few notes of no great value, was repeated by Fabricius in his *Codex Pseudepigraphus V. Test.* (Hamb. 1713). A careful revision of the text, aided by an additional MS., was made by Hilgenfeld, and printed in *Zeitschrift für wissenschaft. Theol.* 1868, and in *Messias Judæorum libris eorum illustratus* (Lips. 1869). Another edition, with a commentary by Geiger (*Der Psalter Salomo's*), appeared in 1871; and the same year saw Fritzsche's *Libri Apocryphi Vet. Test.*, which contains a revised text with various readings. The only English editions which I have met with are a translation of the Psalms in the first volume of W. Whiston's *Authentick Records* (London 1727), and one by Pick in the *Presbyterian Review*, October 1883.

That the Greek text, which alone is extant, is not the

---

[1] This manuscript came originally from Constantinople. How it was lost cannot now be ascertained. It is not even mentioned in the existing Catalogue of the Augsburg MSS., Hilgenf. p. 135.

original work, but a translation from the Hebrew or Aramaic, seems to be tolerably certain. The diction is thoroughly Hebraic, and the idioms of that language are too closely represented for it to have been the work of one writing Greek hymns of his own composition. And wherever the translator may have lived, the author seems to have been a native of Palestine.

But if the language and locality of the original work may be regarded as ascertained, the date of the writer is a difficult question, and one that has been the subject of much controversy. Whiston boldly cuts the knot by asserting that the author is a certain Solomon who is mentioned in the Fourth Book of Esdras [1] as rebuilding Jerusalem and restoring the true worship, after the Persian captivity, about the thirtieth year of Artaxerxes Mnemon, i.e. B.C. 375. This assertion has no support external or internal, and has been maintained by no scholar of eminence. The controversy really lies between those who refer the work to the time of Antiochus Epiphanes and those who assign it to the days of Herod or of Pompey. The determination depends entirely upon internal evidence; and we all know how uncertain this is, and how prone are critics to read their own views into the words upon which they build their argument. This is very evident in the present case. Ewald and others, who adopt the Maccabæan period as the date, found their theory especially on the language of Ps. i. ii. and xvii. In these passages the poet utters his lamentation over the oppression of his people, complains urgently of the heathen who lord it over Israel, and expresses a hope

[1] 4 Esdr. x. 46.

that God would raise up from another race one to be their saviour.[1] From these same passages other critics argue for the era of Pompey; and indeed the expressions suit either period. Some other *criteria* therefore must be found in order to settle the much disputed date.

Without entering at length into the historical question, we will just note the aspect of affairs represented in the Psalter, and then compare it with the events in Jewish history to which it seems most closely to correspond.[2] The work opens with the bitter cry of the Hebrews oppressed by the sudden attack of an enemy (i. 1, 2); a generation to which no promise of David's throne had been made had seized the royal crown (xvii.), and triumphed in the subjection of the nation. But Israel had been guilty of grievous sin; king, judge, and people alike were involved in the offence; and they were justly punished by intestine war and other calamities. These troubles were repressed by inviting foreign aid; a man of another stock rose up against them (xvii.); and the infatuated people met the foreigner with joy (viii.), opened the gates and bade him enter in peace. And this stranger from the ends of the earth entered in friendly guise, as a father visits the house of his sons; but after he had secured himself, he broke down the walls with the

---

[1] Ps. xvii. 9: ἄνθρωπον ἀλλότριον γένους ἡμῶν (ἡοιτῶν, A). For the unmeaning ἡριτῶν Ewald would read ἡοώων, and explain "the race of heroes" to be that of Alexander.

[2] I here gladly acknowledge my obligations to M'Clintock and Strong's *Cyclopædia*, art. "Psalter of Solomon," to Hilgenfeld's edition of the Psalter in his *Zeitschrift*, 1868, pp. 133 ff., and to that of Geiger (Augsb. 1871); also to Langen's *Das Judenthum in Palüst.* (Freiburg, 1866), and to Wittichen's *Die Idee des Reiches Gottes* (Göttingen 1872), pp. 155 ff.

battering-ram (ii. 1), seized on the towers, poured out the blood of the inhabitants like water. Jerusalem was trodden down by the Gentiles, the altar profaned, of the prominent men some were put to death, many were made captives and sent as slaves into the far west. But retribution followed. The Dragon who took Jerusalem was himself slain in Egypt, his body cast forth on the shore, dishonoured and unburied.

Now, though isolated expressions in the Psalter suit events that happened at various dates of Jewish history, yet, taking the references as a whole, and especially regarding the mention of the chief oppressor's fate, we cannot forego the conclusion that the poet has before his eyes the actions and death of Pompey. On the decease of Hyrcanus I., B.C. 106, his son Aristobulus seized the supreme power and assumed the title of king. He was succeeded by Alexander Jannæus, his brother, who, attaching himself strongly to the Sadducaic faction, would be considered by the Pharisees (to which sect the pseudo-Solomon evidently belongs) as an enemy and a sinner. Besides this, being an Asmonæan, and not of the family of David, he had usurped a throne to which he had no just claim. A civil war ensued, and great atrocities were committed. Jannæus died B.C. 79; and then arose a contest for the sovereignty between his two sons, Hyrcanus II. and Aristobulus—the former a partisan of the Pharisees, the latter of the Sadducees. These intestine calamities might justly have been regarded as a punishment for the laxity which had been allowed and fostered of late. Gentile customs were introduced, mixed marriages permitted, and a general corruption of morals followed as a necessary consequence. In the midst of these domestic troubles, and when Hyrcanus, having defeated Aristobulus with the aid of Aretas, king of Arabia, was besieging him in the temple at Jerusalem, news arrived that the victorious Roman general, Pompey, was advancing on the city. Both brothers sent ambassadors to secure his aid; but Pompey deferred his decision, and Aristobulus, presuming that it would be unfavourable to his interest, shut himself up in the temple fortress and prepared for a siege. Hyrcanus, on the other hand, received the Roman with every demonstration of joy—throwing open to him the gates of the city, and putting it entirely at his disposal. Pompey sent for his military engines from Tyre, and besieged the temple. At the end of three months his battering-rams destroyed one of the largest towers, and he made his way into the fortress. A cruel massacre ensued; the priests were cut down even while ministering at the altar, and Pompey himself entered the sacred courts, and penetrated into the Holy of Holies. On his return to Rome, after demolishing the walls of Jerusalem, he took with him a large number of Jewish prisoners to grace his triumph ($\epsilon \grave{i}s \ \dot{\epsilon}\mu\pi\alpha\iota\gamma\mu\acute{o}\nu$, "for mockery"), among whom were Aristobulus and his two sons and daughters. Thus was the independence of Judæa overthrown. That the reference is not to Titus and his conquest of Jerusalem is evident from many circumstances, more especially from the fact that the destruction of the city and temple is nowhere mentioned. The man from a strange land, who carried away captives to the far west, is the same whose end is so exultingly told in the Psalter. This allusion cannot be doubted.

The manner of Pompey's death is well known. After his defeat at Pharsalia, he sought refuge in Egypt, but was treacherously murdered as he was landing on the shore; his head was cut off, and his body was left naked and dishonoured: "when," as pseudo-Solomon says (ii. 29 ff.), "the pride of the Dragon was disgraced, and he was stabbed in the mountains of Egypt, utterly despised by land and sea, and his body was left to rot on the shore, and there was no man to bury him."

It will be seen at once how close is the correspondence between the Psalter and this chapter of Jewish history. If we had space for further detail, that correspondence would appear still more striking; but enough has been said to show that some portion of the work, especially Ps. ii., was written after Pompey's death, and probably very soon after, while the event was still uppermost in men's minds. We may therefore fix the date of its composition at B.C. 48 at latest. Some of the Psalms are doubtless of earlier origin, dating probably from B.C. 63; and none exhibit any certain trace of Christian interpolations.

Taking then as proved the ante-Christian origin of the Psalter, we are prepared to find therein valuable intimations of the belief of the Hebrews in the age just preceding the time of our Lord. And we are not disappointed in our anticipations. It must be observed that the writer is a strict Pharisee, and that his notion of perfect religion is Pharasaic Judaism. Righteousness with him implies scrupulous performance of all legal and ceremonial enactments, and when he inveighs against transgressors, his ground for censure is that they have not observed the ordained prescriptions. The current opinions about the Messiah, the Resurrection, the Future Life, are plainly set forth. The way in which these subjects are introduced is briefly this :—-The notion of the writer throughout is that God is a righteous judge, both of His own people and of the heathen. He punishes the former as a tender father chastises the son of his love ; the heathen meet with the stern correction which their wilful sins deserve. These two aspects of corrective and vindictive discipline are shown by an appeal to history. The fate of the Maccabæan dynasty, the usurpation of the Asmonæans, the invasion and supremacy of the Romans, are regarded as the punishment of national sins ; the fate of Pompey is a specimen of the destruction which awaits paganism. This leads the writer to look forward to a day when Israel's supremacy shall be assured by the appearance of Messiah, and to express his belief in the resurrection and reward of the righteous and the future punishment of sinners. This premised, let the Psalmist here speak for himself. The following are some of his utterances concerning the Messiah and His kingdom :—

Behold, O Lord, and raise up for them their King,
The Son of David, at the time which Thou, our God, knowest,
That Thy Servant ($\pi\alpha\tilde{\iota}\delta\alpha$) should reign over Israel ;
And gird Him with power to beat down unrighteous rulers . . .
And He shall gather together the holy people which He shall guide
  in righteousness,
And shall judge the tribes of the people hallowed by the Lord His
  God.
And He shall not suffer unrighteousness to dwell in the midst of
  them,
And no wicked man at all shall abide with them ;

For He will know them that they are all the children of God,
And He will distribute them in their tribes upon the land.
And the stranger and the foreigner shall no more sojourn among them;
He shall judge the peoples and nations in the wisdom of His righteousness.
He shall have the peoples of the Gentiles to serve Him under His yoke,
And he shall glorify the Lord by the submission of all the earth.
And he shall cleanse Jerusalem with sanctification as from the beginning,
That Gentiles may come from the ends of the earth to see his glory,
Bringing as offerings her way-worn children,[1]
Yea, to see the glory of the Lord wherewith God hath glorified her.
And He is the righteous King over them, taught of God.
There is no injustice in His days in their midst,
For they shall all be holy, and their King shall be Christ the Lord.[2]
He shall not trust in horse or rider or bow,
Nor multiply to Himself gold and silver for war,
Nor gather hope from arms in the day of battle;
The Lord Himself is His King, the hope of the Mighty One is in the hope of God,
And He will set[3] all the nations before Him in fear;
For He will smite the earth with the word of His mouth for ever,
And bless the people of the Lord in wisdom with gladness.
He Himself is pure from sin that He may govern a great people,
Rebuke princes, and remove sinners by the power of His word.
And, trusting upon His God, He shall not be weak in His days
Because God hath made Him mighty by His Holy Spirit,[4]
And wise in the counsel of prudence, with power and righteousness.
And the blessing of the Lord shall be with Him in power,
And His hope in the Lord shall not be weak;

---

[1] Referring probably to such passages as Isa. xlix. 22, lxvi. 20; Zeph. iii. 10.

[2] Χριστὸς κύριος, as Lam. iv. 20. In Isa. xlv. 1, some of the Fathers read τῷ χριστῷ μου κυρίῳ instead of Κύρῳ. See Barnab. Ep. xii. 11; Tertull. *Adv. Jud.* vii.; Cypr. *Testim.* i. 21; cf. St. Luke ii. 11.

[3] The MS. has ἐλεήσει, which seems plainly wrong. Fr. and Hilg. read στήσει. Whiston: "will grind." I would suggest ἀλοήσει, "will thresh." Geiger retains ἐλεήσει, and translates: "has mercy on all people who fear before Him." But this is inappropriate.

[4] Ἐν πνεύματι ἁγίῳ. Cf. Isa. lxiii. 10, 11.

And who shall prevail against Him?
Mighty is He in His works, and strong in the fear of God.
Tending the flock of the Lord in faith and righteousness,
He will let none among them in their pasture to be weak.
He shall lead them all in holiness,
And there shall be among them no arrogance to oppress them. (xvii. 23 ff.)
May God purify Israel against the day of mercy by His blessing,
Against the day of their election in the presence [1] of His Christ.
Blessed are they who live in those days,
To see the good things of the Lord which He will do in the generation to come,
Under the rod of the correction of Christ the Lord in the fear of His God,
In the wisdom of the spirit and of righteousness and power.
A good generation shall there be in the fear of God in the days of mercy. (xviii. 6–10.)

From these passages we may gather the writer's sentiments. He is deeply afflicted by the calamities of his people. The oppression of the heathen, the ruin of his city, the pollution of the temple, the reign of paganism, the supremacy of unrighteousness, have broken his patriotic heart; and while he owns that his countrymen are justly punished for past iniquities, iniquities shared by prince and priest and people, he all the more looks forward to the coming Messiah, who shall bring salvation unto Israel. From their lost independence, from their present weakness and insignificance, he turns his longing gaze to better times; he hopes for supernatural help; he glows with anticipations of the glories of Messianic

---

[1] Ἐν ἀνάξει Χριστοῦ αὐτοῦ. The word ἄναξις seems to be wholly unknown. Ecclesiastical Greek recognises σύναξις—communion. Geiger translates: "in the kingdom of His anointed." It may mean "exaltation." In a fragment of Æschylus ἀναξία occurs in the sense of "kingdom."

victories. This hope is based on God's promise to David of eternal dominion, which, though for a time diverted into another channel (the Asmonæan dynasty), should be restored in due time under David's greater Son. The time is come for the revelation of God's mercy to His chosen nation; Israel is at its lowest point of misery; this is the Lord's opportunity. Let Him send Messiah to expel the unrighteous rulers, to cleanse the holy city from the heathen, yea, to drive them out of the holy land, and to gather together in one the dispersed of the people. But the large promises of God are not satisfied by Messiah's reign over Israel alone. His kingdom is over all the earth. He unites all peoples under His rule, and magnifies the name of God by extending His dominion wherever man has his dwelling-place; and this, not for a time only, but for ever.

Thus far the poet has exhibited only the earthly aspect of Messiah's kingdom, His conquests and power, obtained without weapons of war, by the word of His mouth. But lest this idea of Christ should seem too worldly, he hastens to show the significance of this universal sway, and its moral and religious effects. Messiah is Himself sinless, and reigns in a sinless kingdom. All unrighteousness shall be abolished; there shall be no iniquity in the restored Israel. Peace shall reign, and holiness shall triumph. Violence and injustice shall be found no more; the pride of sinners shall be extirpated. So grand an idea of wisdom and purity shall be exhibited in Israel, that distant nations shall flock to Jerusalem to see her glory and to learn her ways.

All this is to happen in God's good time, which,

in the author's view, is not far distant, even as the apostles of the Lord thought that the end was near, and expected to see the great consummation in their own days.

The Messiah, in this pseudo-Solomon's conception, is not very and eternal God. It is indeed not always clear whether God or the Christ is the subject of some of his paragraphs; but, taking one passage with another, we conclude that he regarded Messiah as the agent and organ of God, but not God Himself. He is God's deputy and executes His will; but Jehovah is the supreme King, and appoints Him as ruler and judge. Here we see the defective view of the nature and work of Messiah which meets us in the Jews of the New Testament. The faith is strong, the expectation is immediate, but the idea is erroneous, worldly, carnal, very far inferior indeed to that in the Book of Enoch, which is much more spiritual and nearer the truth.

To turn to another point. The writer has a strong faith in the Resurrection of the righteous in the time of Messiah, though he does not give expressly his notion of the sequence of events at that period. That sinners shall rise again does not enter into his view; nor does he state what shall be the fate of the unbelieving portion of the Gentile world in the great future; though he probably held with his contemporaries that exclusion from the kingdom of Messiah was equivalent to eternal death or annihilation. But the righteous are to rise again in order to share the blessings of the Messianic reign, and to shine with an everlasting light, and, as another pseudo-Solomon says (Wisd. iii. 7), "to run to and fro like sparks among the stubble." In the other world retribution is to fall upon the sinners; they shall be condemned in the day of judgment, and be destroyed as by fire. And sinners, in his view, are not merely those who are guilty of moral offences or vulgar wickedness; he calls by this name the hypocrites and menpleasers (ἀνθρωπάρεσκοι) of his own nation. Against these he inveighs in the bitterest terms. They are profane, unclean as the very heathen whose vices they imitated; their heart is far from the Lord; they have provoked the God of Israel to anger, so that He has grievously afflicted His people for their sake. And he calls for vengeance upon them in this world as well as in the next. May their life, he prays, pass in poverty and distress; may their sleep be vexed with pain and their waking with misery; may the work of their hands never prosper; may their old age be childless; may their dead bodies be cast forth dishonoured, and may ravens pick out their eyes. "So may God destroy all those who work iniquity; for the Lord is a Judge, great and mighty in righteousness" (Ps. iv.).

While thus uncompromising in his denunciation of iniquity and in his assurance of God's inflexible justice, the writer is not insensible to the hope that exists for sinners when they repent. If a man is ashamed of his sins and confesses them, God will forgive him and cleanse his soul. But he must be patient under the rod, and take the chastisement as the merciful correction of his error: "He that prepareth his back for the scourge shall be justified from iniquity; for the Lord is good to those who endure discipline" (Ps. ix., x.).

These are the Psalmist's words concerning the resurrection:—

> They that fear the Lord shall rise again (ἀναστήσονται) to life everlasting.
> And their life shall be in the light of the Lord, and shall fail no more. (iii. 16.)
> For the Lord will spare His holy ones,
> And will blot out their offences by chastisement;
> For the life of the righteous is for ever;
> But sinners shall be taken away for destruction,
> And their memorial shall no more be found;
> But the mercy of the Lord is upon the holy,
> And His mercy upon them that fear Him. (xiii. 9-11.)
> The holy of the Lord shall live in Him for ever;
> The Paradise of the Lord, the trees of life, are His holy ones.
> The holy of the Lord shall inherit life in gladness. (xiv. 2, 7.)

Thus also he speaks concerning the retribution that awaits the unrighteous:—

> Not so are sinners and transgressors. . . .
> Who have not remembered God,
> That the ways of men are always known unto Him,
> And He understandeth the treasure-chambers (ταμιεῖα) of the heart before they are made.
> Therefore their inheritance is Hades, and darkness, and destruction;
> And they shall not be found in the day of the mercy of the righteous. (xiv. 4-6.)
> He raises me up unto glory,
> But He lays the proud to sleep[1] unto eternal destruction in dishonour,
> Because they knew Him not. (ii. 35.)

---

[1] Κοιμίζων, which Fritzsche alters into κομίζων unnecessarily, for the Psalmist has the authority of Euripides for this use of the word :

. . . γενεάν
τὰν Ζεὺς ἀμφιπύρῳ
κοιμίζει φλογμῷ Κρονίδας.   Hec. 472 ff.

Cf. too in the Hebrew, 1 Kings iii. 20; 2 Kings iv. 21.

The mercy of the Lord is upon them that fear Him, while He
  executes His judgment,
To sever between the just and the sinner,
To repay sinners for ever according to their works,
And to have mercy on the righteous while the sinner is humbled,
And to repay the sinner for what he did to the righteous. (ii. 37–39.)
He fell; because evil was his fall and he shall not rise to life again;
The destruction of the sinner is for everlasting,
And God shall not remember him when He visits the righteous;
This is the portion of sinners for everlasting. (iii. 13–15.)
They who do iniquity shall not escape the judgment of the Lord,
They shall be seized as by skilled enemies;
For the mark of destruction shall be upon their foreheads,
And the inheritance of sinners shall be destruction and darkness,
And their iniquities shall pursue them unto Hades beneath;
Their inheritance shall not be found for their children,
For their iniquities shall make the house of sinners desolate;
And sinners shall perish in the day of the Lord's judgment for
  ever,
When God shall visit the earth in His judgment,
To repay sinners for everlasting. (xv. 9 ff.)

It will be seen that the destiny of a man is made to depend entirely upon his doings during life. He has the power of deciding upon his own course. "O God," it is said (Ps. viii.), "our works are at our choice, and we have power over our soul to do righteousness or iniquity with the works of our hands."

The Psalter ends with a hymn of praise to God as the Creator, Preserver, and Ruler of all things, who, as the writer has already said, from present confusion and calamity evolves harmony and peace.

Great is our God and glorious, dwelling in the highest,
Who hath ordained lights in the path of heaven to divide the time
  from day to day,
And they have never strayed from the way which Thou commandedst
  them.

In the fear of God hath been their way every day,
From the day in which God created them, and shall be for evermore ;
And they have wandered not from the day in which God created them,
From the generations of old they have never forsaken their way,
Save when God bade them at the command of His servants.[1] (xviii. 11–14.)

---

[1] The tautology in my version is a close rendering of the Greek, which, we must remember, is not the original.

II.

APOCALYPTICAL AND PROPHETICAL.

THE BOOK OF ENOCH.[1]

IN the Epistle of St. Jude the following passage occurs (vers. 14, 15): "And to these also, Enoch, the seventh from Adam, prophesied, saying, Behold, the Lord came with ten thousands of His holy ones, to execute judgment upon all, and to convict all the ungodly of all their works of ungodliness which they have ungodly wrought, and of all the hard things which ungodly sinners have spoken against Him." The question immediately arises, Is the apostle quoting from some writing extant in his day, or citing merely a prophecy preserved by tradition? The language does not help to a solution of the inquiry. Jude writes: "Enoch

---

[1] In compiling this account, I have availed myself of Bishop Laurence's translation of the Book of Enoch, Dillmann's *Das Buch Henoch*, Drummond's *The Jewish Messiah*, the Cyclopædias, English and German, and the able Dissertation in Dr. Gloag's *Introduction to the Catholic Epistles*. I have also used Ewald's *Abhandlung über d. Æthiop. Buches Henokh Entstehung*; Köstlin's "Ueber die Entstehung d. Buches Henoch," in Baur and Zeller's *Theolog. Jahrbuch*. 1856, Heftt 2 and 3; and Volkmar's "Beiträge zur Erklärung des B. Henoch," in *Deutsch, morgenl. Zeitschr*. 1860.

προεφήτευσε . . . λέγων." This might be said equally of an actual quotation or of a traditional report. But when it was discovered that the Fathers and other early writers often referred to a writing of Enoch and quoted sentences therefrom, it was obvious that they were acquainted with some document which bore the patriarch's name, and which was extensively known in early Christian centuries.[1] Thus, in the Epistle of Barnabas (as it is called), a work composed at the end of the first Christian century, we read (iv. 3): "The final stumbling-block hath approached, concerning which it is written, as Enoch[2] says, For to this end the Lord hath shortened the times and the days, that His beloved may hasten and come into the inheritance." In the Testaments of the Twelve Patriarchs and in the Book of Jubilees, the words of Enoch are frequently cited, and the resemblances to passages in our work are numerous. In the former, at least, nine passages contain distinct references to Enoch's prophetical writings; and in the latter not only is the book often used without acknowledgment, but it is also expressly mentioned. Justin Martyr does not quote it by name, but his views concerning the angels and their connection with man are plainly identical with and derived from this book.[3] That Irenæus made use of it is evident. Thus he says:[4] "Enoch also, pleasing God without circumcision, man though he was, discharged the

[1] The quotations are to be found in Fabricius, *Codex Pseudepigr. Vet. Test.* i. 161 ff.

[2] One Latin MS. of the Epistle gives "Daniel" instead of "Enoch." The sentence does not occur in the text of Enoch which we possess.

[3] *Apol.* ii. 5. [4] *Adv. Hær.* iv. 30 ; comp. iv. 16. 2.

office of legate towards the angels," a fact nowhere mentioned but in our work; "and was translated, and is preserved still as witness of the just judgment of God" (chaps. xiv., xv.). Tertullian seems to have regarded it as inspired. "These things," he writes,[1] "the Holy Ghost, foreseeing from the beginning the future entrance of superstitions, foretold by the mouth of the ancient seer Enoch." He adopts Enoch's story of the fall of the angels (which, indeed, is common to other of the Pseudepigrapha), and their introduction of mechanical arts, sorcery, and astrology; and while acknowledging that it was not received into the Jewish Canon (*armarium Judaicum*), he endeavours to show how it could have been preserved in the Deluge and handed down to Christian times, and that it was rejected by the Jews because it too plainly testified of Christ. Origen took a lower view of its authority, but he refers to it more than once,[2] using its language and adopting the ideas, as emanating from one of the greatest of prophets. Clement of Alexandria[3] regards it with a certain respect while denying its inspiration. "I must confess," says St. Augustine,[4] "that some things of Divine character were written by Enoch, the seventh from Adam, since this is testified by the Apostle Jude in his canonical Epistle; but they are deservedly excluded from the Jewish Scriptures, because they lack authority and cannot be proved genuine." In the *Apostolic Constitu-*

---

[1] *De Idol.* xv. Comp. *ibid.* iv. *De Cult. Fœm.* i. 3, ii. 10.
[2] See *De Princip.* i. 8, iv. 35; *Hom. in Num.* xxviii.; *Contr. Cels.* v. 54, p. 267.
[3] *Strom.* p. 550.   [4] *De Civit.* xv. 23; comp. *ibid.* xviii. 38.

tions the book is reckoned among Apocrypha, and it is placed in the same category in the *Synopsis Athanasii* and the Catalogue of Nicephorus. By the fifth century the book seems to have sunk out of sight, and little or nothing more was heard of it till Scaliger (1540–1609) discovered some fragments of it in an unpublished MS. of the *Chronographia* of Georgius Syncellus (A.D. 792), and printed them. The extracts are given by Fabricius, by Laurence and Dillmann, and of them all but one are found in our present text of Enoch. The exception is a short passage about the doom pronounced on the mountain where the angels made their impious conspiracy, and on the sons of men involved in their crime. The extracts in Syncellus' work tend to show that the Book of Enoch was extant in the Eastern Church for some time after it had practically disappeared from the Western. That the book was also in the hands of the Jews of mediæval times has been proved by references in the *Zohar*, a kind of philosophical commentary upon the law, which contains the most ancient remains of the Cabala.[1] Thus we read: "The Holy and the Blessed One raised him (Enoch) from the world to serve Him, as it is written, 'For God took him.' From that time a book was delivered down which was called the Book of Enoch. In the hour that God took him, He showed him all the repositories above; He showed him the tree of life in the midst of the garden, its leaves and its branches. We see all in his book." And again, "We find in the Book of Enoch, that after the Holy and Blessed One had

[1] Laurence, *Prelim. Dissert.* xxi.; Dillmann, *Einleit.* lvii.; Gloag, pp. 389 f.

caused him to ascend, and showed him all the repositories of the superior and inferior kingdom, He showed him the tree of life, and the tree respecting which Adam had received a command; and He showed him the habitation of Adam in the Garden of Eden." Further traces of the book have been discovered in other Rabbinical writings, but we need not linger on these.

From the above and similar allusions it was clear to all scholars that a book extant under the name of Enoch had been well known in earlier days; but for some centuries nothing more certain came to light; the appetite of critics had nothing more definite to feed upon. It remained for the great traveller Bruce to satisfy the long-unappeased desire for further information. In the year 1773, Bruce astonished the learned world by claiming to have secured in Abyssinia, and brought safely home, three copies of an Ethiopian version of the Book of Enoch. An idea, indeed, had long prevailed (whence originating it is hard to say) that such a version did exist; and it was thought at one time that a certain tract, transmitted from Egypt, and purchased by Peiresc for the Royal Library at Paris, was the identical work. This was found not to be the case; and warned by former disappointment, scholars awaited the examination of Bruce's MSS. with some anxiety. Of the three copies brought to Europe, one, a most magnificent quarto, was presented by the finder to the Library at Paris, and another to the Bodleian at Oxford; the third, kept in his own possession, was included in a MS. of the Scriptures, where it is placed immediately before the Book of Job, assuming an unquestioned position among the canonical books. On hearing that Paris possessed this treasure, Dr. Woide, librarian of the British Museum, immediately set out for France, armed with letters to the ambassador desiring him to procure the learned scholar access to the work. This was done, and Dr. Woide transcribed the whole book, and brought the transcript with him to England. His knowledge of Ethiopic was not sufficient to enable him to attempt a translation. He might have spared himself much trouble had he been aware that Oxford possessed a copy of the work; but the University itself received the present very quietly, and let it rest undisturbed on its shelves for many years. The Parisian MS. was noticed in the *Magasin Encyclopédique* by the Orientalist, De Sacy, who published therein a translation of certain passages. But it was not till the year 1821 that the book was fully brought before the world. In that year Dr. Laurence, then Professor of Hebrew at Oxford, and afterwards Archbishop of Cashel, published a translation of the whole, with preliminary dissertation and notes. This has been more than once reprinted, and was supplemented in 1838 by the publication of the Ethiopic text. The discovery of five different codices enabled Dillmann to put forth a more correct text; and his edition, with its German translation, introduction, and commentary, is now the standard work on the subject. There is another German version by Hoffmann, for the latter part of which he had the benefit of a MS. in the library of Frankfort-on-the-Maine, lately brought from Abyssinia; and there is also an English translation by Professor Schodde, of America, printed at Andover in 1882; but nothing seems likely to supersede Dillmann's edition, unless, indeed, the discovery is some day made of the original text from which the Ethiopic version was rendered. There was indeed at one time a hope of some additional light from Mai's discovery of a small fragment in Greek among the manuscripts of the Vatican Library. But further investigation led to the mortifying fact that no more was to be found; and as the portion extended only from ver. 42 to ver. 49 of chap. lxxxix., it was of little practical utility.

As to the language of the original work, there is no reason to doubt that it was Hebrew or Aramæan. It is true that the fragments of Syncellus and those found by Mai in the Vatican Library are all in Greek, and it was from Greek exemplars that the quotations in the Fathers were made; but a critical examination of these extracts and of the Abyssinian version leads to the conclusion that they are derived from a Hebrew source. To favour this verdict, critics are induced by such evidence as the following: there are in the version a great number of Hebrew idioms and expressions equally foreign to Greek and Ethiopic, and all capable of being easily rendered back into Hebrew; the writer or writers were thoroughly acquainted with the Scriptures in the original, and did not employ the Septuagint version; the names of the angels and archangels are of Hebrew etymology, viz. Uriel, Raphael, Raguel, Michael, Sarakael, Gabriel; the appellations of the winds can only be explained by a reference to the Hebrew, the east wind being so called because it is *the first*, according to Hebrew etymology, and the south, because *the Most High there descends*, the Hebrew term being capable of this interpretation. The names of the sun, Oryares and Tomas, are Semitic; so are those of the conductors of the months, Melkeel, Helemmelek, Meleyal, Narel, etc.; and, as Dr. Gloag observes, *Ophanim*, mentioned in connection with the cherubim and seraphim, is the Hebrew word for the "wheels" in Ezekiel. We are, then, tolerably secure in assuming the hypothesis of a Hebrew original. We have no criteria to enable us to judge when it was translated into Greek. The Ethiopic version was made directly from the Hebrew, subsequently to the translation of the Old Testament into Ethiopic; but the date is undetermined. If it keeps as close to the original as the rendering of Holy Scripture does, it may be regarded as a faithful and accurate representation of the text.

In the Ethiopic MSS. the work is divided into twenty sections; but the chapters are not uniformly arranged. Dillmann has retained the twenty sections, and subdivided them into 108 chapters, marking the verses of each chapter for greater distinctness of reference. This distribution is now generally followed.

We will first give a sketch of the contents of the work before discussing its date and authorship, and gathering the lessons which it teaches.

The book may be said roughly to consist of five parts, with an introduction and a conclusion. The general introduction, which is contained in the first five chapters, commences thus: "The words of blessing of Enoch, wherewith he blessed the elect and the righteous who shall exist in the time of trouble, when the wicked and ungodly shall be removed. Enoch, a righteous man, whose eyes God had opened, so that he saw a holy vision in the heavens, which the angels showed me, answered and spake." The account proceeds in the first person; but throughout there is no consistency shown in this matter, changes from the first to the third person being frequent, and marking the hand of an editor or interpolator. The vision was for future generations, and in it he learned that God would come down on Mount Sinai with all His hosts to execute judgment, punishing the wicked, rewarding the righteous. Then occurs the original of the passage quoted by St. Jude: "Behold, He comes with myriads of saints to sit in judgment on them, and will destroy the ungodly, and contend with all flesh for everything which the sinful and ungodly have done and committed against Him." Enoch observed the regular order of everything in heaven and earth, which obeyed fixed laws and never varied, and he contrasts the fate of the good and the evil; the latter shall find no peace and curse their day, while the former shall have light, joy, and peace for the whole of their existence. The above prelude affords a glimpse of the nature of the Book, with its allusions to natural phenomena and its eschatological views.

The first division is contained in chaps. vi.–xxxvi., and is subdivided into three sections.[1] Section i. (chaps. vi.–xi.) narrates the fall of the angels and its immediate consequences. Seeing the beauty of the daughters of men, two hundred angels under the leadership of Semyaza bound themselves by an oath to take wives from among mortal women. For this purpose they descended on Mount Hermon, and in due time became

[1] I use Dillmann's divisions throughout.

parents of giants of fabulous height and size. These monsters devoured all the substance of men, and then proceeded to devour men themselves; they also taught mankind all kind of destructive arts, and vice flourished under their instruction. And men cried aloud to heaven, and the four archangels heard them, and appealed to God in their behalf. And God sent Uriel to Noah, the son of Lamech, to warn him of the flood, and ordered Raphael to bind Azazel, and lay him in a dark cleft in the wilderness, there to remain till the fire received him at the day of judgment. Gabriel had to set the giants one against the other that they might perish by mutual slaughter; to Michael fell the duty of punishing the evil angels; they were to witness the destruction of their offspring, and then be buried under the earth for seventy generations till the judgment day, when they should be cast into eternal fire. Then when all sin and impurity shall be purged away "at the end of all generations," the plant of righteousness shall appear, and a new order of things; the saints shall live till they have forgotten a thousand children, and shall die in peace; the earth shall be fruitful, and be planted with all manner of trees; no corruption, or crime, or suffering shall be found therein; "in those days," saith God, "I will open the store-chambers of blessing which are in heaven, that they may descend upon the earth, and on the work and labour of men. Peace and righteousness shall join together, in all the days of the world and through all the families of the earth."

Section ii. (chaps. xii.–xvi.). After it has been said that Enoch was hidden from men's sight, being wholly engaged with the holy ones, he himself tells how the good angels sent him to the fallen angels, whose intercourse with heaven was entirely cut off, to announce their doom. Terrified, they entreat him to write for them a petition to God for forgiveness; he complies with their request, leaves their unholy neighbourhood, and, retreating to the region of Dan, falls asleep, and has a vision of judgment, which he afterwards is commissioned to unfold to the disobedient angels. Their petition is refused now and for ever. And the dread answer was given to him, as he relates, in a vision, wherein he was rapt to the palace of heaven and the presence of the Almighty, of which he gives a very noble description.

Section iii. (chaps. xvii.–xxxvi.) gives an account of Enoch's journeys through heaven and earth under the guidance of angels, in the course of which he is made acquainted with the wonders of nature hidden from man, with places, powers, and beings which have relation to revealed religion, Messianic hopes, and the last days. He is taken to the place where the storm-winds dwell, and the sun obtains its fire, and the oceans and the rivers of the nether world flow; he saw seven luminous mountains in the south-east, formed of precious stones, and the place where the disobedient stars were suffering punishment,[1] and that which, though now untenanted, shall be the penal-prison of the rebel angels after the final judgment when they are released from their present chains. On inquiring for what crime the stars (regarded as living beings) were thus sentenced, he is informed by Uriel

[1] These are probably the ἀστέρες πλανῆται, "wandering stars," of Jude 13.

that they had transgressed the commandment of God and came not forth in their proper season. He next passes to the west, where is Hades, the region where the souls of the dead are kept till the judgment; it is divided into four places, unto one of which all souls are assigned. In the course of his journeys he comes again to the seven fiery mountains, and in a beautiful valley finds the tree of life, whose fruit shall be given to the elect. Then going to the centre of the earth, he sees the holy land and the city Jerusalem, described as "a blessed and fruitful place, where there were branches continually sprouting from the trees planted therein." Here, too, he was shown the accursed valley (Gehenna), where the wicked shall suffer their eternal penalty in the sight of the righteous, who shall reign in Zion, and praise the Lord for His just vengeance on the evil-doers. He proceeds from Jerusalem eastward to the earthly Paradise, planted with odorous and fruit-bearing trees, lying at the very ends of the earth, and containing the tree of knowledge, of which Adam and Eve ate. Here, where the vault of heaven rests on the earth, he beholds the gates whence come forth the stars and the winds, and, instructed by the angel, writes their names and order and seasons. And, arriving at the north, he sees the three gates of the north-wind, and, going westward and southward, the three gates of these winds. Conducted again to the east, he praises the Lord who created all these wondrous things for His glory.

The second division, contained in chaps. xxxvii.-lxxi., is called "The second Vision of Wisdom," and consists of three parables, allegories, or similitudes, through the medium of which Enoch relates the revelations which he received concerning the ideal future and the secrets of the spiritual world. Many of the matters which he mentions we should treat as physical phenomena; in his view they assume a higher relation, and are therefore differentiated from the objects described in the preceding division which concerned only this earth and the lower heavens. The first similitude or figurative address (chaps. xxxviii.-xliv.) speaks first of the time when the separation between the righteous and sinners shall be made, and the angels shall dwell in communion with holy men. Then Enoch relates how he was carried to the extremity of heaven, and saw the celestial abodes prepared for the righteous, where they bless and magnify the Lord for ever and ever, and the special seat ordained for himself. He beholds the innumerable hosts of angels and sleepless spirits who surround the throne of God, and particularly the four archangels, Michael, Raphael, Gabriel, and Phanuel, to whom are assigned special duties. He is shown the secrets of heaven, the weighing of men's actions in the balance, the rejection of sinners from the abodes of the just, the mysteries of thunder and lightning, winds, clouds, dew, hail, mist, sun, and moon. Of these heavenly bodies the regular course and motion are their praise of God for creation and preservation, and this ceaseless praise is their rest. He finds the habitation of Wisdom in heaven, as man on earth would not receive her, but welcomed only iniquity. And lastly, he observes how the stars are called by name, and their courses weighed and examined, and recognises in their regularity and obedience a picture of the life of the righteous on earth.

The second similitude (chaps. xlv.–lvii.) describes the coming of "the Chosen One," the Messiah, and the operations of His judgment on the good and the evil. Sinners shall be taken from the earth and sent down to hell to await punishment; the righteous shall dwell with Messiah in peace and happiness. Enoch proceeds to give further description of the person and office of Him whom he calls "Son of man." To this important delineation we shall have to refer in detail hereafter; suffice it here to give a mere outline of the representation. He sees this Personification of righteousness in company with the Ancient of Days, and he is taught that He alone shall reveal all mysteries; He shall overthrow all worldly powers, among which are included sinners who scorned and refused to praise the Lord, and shall put an end to all unrighteousness. The glorification of the elect after the final judgment is further revealed, how they shall drink of the fountain of wisdom and righteousness, and hold full communion with the saints and angels. The Son of man existed before the world was created, and shall be in the presence of God for ever, and shall bring light and healing to the people. In Him all wisdom and righteousness dwell, and at His presence iniquity passes away like a shadow. In Messiah's days shall be made the great change in the condition of the good and evil, and even then it will not be too late for the evil to repent, for great is the mercy of the Lord of spirits. At this time, too, shall occur the resurrection of the dead, the righteous rising with their bodies to enjoy Messiah's kingdom, the souls of the wicked being consigned to the place of punishment. There shall then be no use for metals; gold, silver, copper are needed no longer; no earthly riches can save one from judgment. A further vision shows the place and instruments of punishment. In the midst of this account is inserted an interpolation concerning the Noachic Deluge, which is of later date than the visions, and is derived from a different source. Then follows a prophetical view of the last battle of the worldly powers against the Theocracy, and their overthrow before Jerusalem; and the final vision displays the Israelites returning to their own land from all countries whither they have been dispersed, and falling down before the Lord of spirits.

The third address (chaps. lviii.–lxix.) contains a further description of the blessedness of the righteous contrasted with the misery of sinners in Messiah's kingdom. In it are inserted many particulars concerning the Deluge, of which Noah, not Enoch, is the narrator. Probably these portions have been introduced by a later editor desirous of showing how the earlier judgment was a figure and an anticipation of that in Messiah's days. Likewise, there is in this address a recapitulation, with some differences, of those physical details which have been previously noticed. The blessedness of the saints is comprised in light, joy, righteousness, and everlasting life. Amid the intimations of the future thus given, Enoch also obtains some curious lore concerning thunder and lightning, the manner and object of their operation. Here follows the interpolation concerning the Flood, which introduces Noah receiving the vision " in the five hundredth year, on the fourteenth day of the seventh month, of the life of Enoch." This is evidently out of place and disconnected with the immediate subject. While showing to Noah the course of the coming judgment, the angel unfolds various meteorological secrets, attributing all the forces of nature to the agency of spirits. Then the narrative returns to the Messianic revelation, and the seer is shown the new Jerusalem, the abode of the elect; he sees the judgment of the saints, he hears their praise and worship of Almighty God in union with all the host of heaven; he hears the sentence passed on the mighty of this world, who shall in vain supplicate the mercy of the Son of man. Five chapters now succeed, containing a further account of revelations made to Noah concerning the Flood, and his deliverance therefrom, and concerning the fall of the angels and their punishment, and the warning thence derived for the mighty of later times. The names of these angels are given, and the special evil which each effected. One of these is called Penemue, and his sin was that he taught men "the art of writing with ink and paper, whereby many have gone astray from that time to the present."

The Book of Similitudes concludes with some personal details about Enoch himself. An interpolated paragraph relates that he was taken up to Paradise; but the genuine text describes how in an ecstasy he was raised to heaven, and God promised to give him a seat among the saints in the future Messianic kingdom.

The third division of the book, comprised in chapters lxxii.–lxxxii., is entitled "The Book of the Revolutions of the Lights of Heaven," and is occupied greatly with astronomical details, which do not give a high idea of the scientific attainments of the writer. The attempt to bring into a system the notions concerning such phenomena scattered throughout the Old Testament, in the popular ignorance of science, could not fail to produce much error and confusion, and has little interest for the theologian, unless we conceive that they have been introduced in order to oppose current heathen ideas, in which case they would have a certain historical use. This portion of the work falls conveniently into three sections. Section 1 treats of the courses of the sun, moon, and stars. The regular revolutions of the sun are explained, and the varying duration of day and night at different seasons; the waxing and waning of the moon are described and accounted for; it is shown how four intercalary days are rendered necessary, and how the luminaries go forth from the twelve gates of heaven. In section 2 the abodes and operations of the winds are noticed. Three of them proceed from each quarter, and occasion various effects, healthful or pernicious. At the end is an allusion to seven mountains, rivers, and islands, which cannot be identified. The third section reverts to the subject of the sun and moon, and gives the names by which they are known and further particulars respecting their connection with one another. All these matters, which Uriel showed to Enoch, the seer divulges to his son Methuselah. The angel likewise revealed to him the changes in the order of nature which shall occur in the days of sinners, in punishment of whom all seeming irregularities are sent. Before his spirit returned to earth, Enoch is bidden to read the heavenly tablets wherein all the future was written, even "all the deeds of men, and all the children of flesh upon earth, unto the remotest generations." On perusing this record, Enoch breaks forth in praise of God; he is then conducted by "three holy ones" (*i.e.* probably the three archangels inferior to Michael) to his own home, and informed that he should be left there for one year, during which he should teach what he had learned to his children; and the section concludes with his address to Methuselah, directing him to preserve with all care the writings committed to him, and to note the importance of correctness in matters connected with the reckoning of the year, and the revolutions of the heavenly bodies, and the changes of the seasons.

The fourth division of the book (chaps. lxxxiii.–xci.) recounts two visions which Enoch saw before he was married, while sleeping in the house of his grandfather Malalel (Mahalaleel). The first vision relates to the Flood; he sees the earth sinking into a great abyss, and prays that God will not wholly destroy the whole race of man, satisfying His just wrath by punishing only the evil. The second vision is more comprehensive and important; it embraces the history of the world from Adam until the establishment of the kingdom of Messiah. The account is derived almost entirely from the canonical Scripture, a transparent symbolism being used throughout. Men are represented under the image of animals, the patriarchs and chosen people being denoted by domesticated animals, as cows and sheep, while heathen and oppressive enemies are designated as wild beasts and birds of prey. The fallen angels are called stars; and the colours of the animals are symbolical—white for purity and righteousness, black for wickedness and disobedience. Thus concerning primitive man we read, a white bullock (Adam) sprang forth from the earth, and then a white cow (Eve), and afterwards there came a black bullock (Cain) and a red (Abel). The black bullock slew the red which vanished from the earth. And this black bullock begat many black cattle. And the white cow gave birth to a white bullock (Seth), which in turn begat much white cattle. In this way the history is allegorised. The offspring of the intercourse of the angels with the daughters of men is adumbrated as elephants, camels, and asses. The archangels' defeat of these sinful spirits Enoch beholds from a high place where he remains till the day of judgment. Thence he sees the advance of the Flood, and Noah's preservation in the vessel; his three sons are respectively white, red, and black, and the severance of the Shemites from the others is distinctly noticed. The history of the Israelites is traced from Abraham to Moses, then to the settlement in the Holy Land; then we have the time of the Judges, and the annals are continued on through the Kings to the Exile. The restoration is duly chronicled, and oppressions under the Greeks and Syrians are darkly foreshadowed. In chap. lxxxix. the Lord delivers the sheep into the power of lions, tigers, and other beasts of prey, which began to tear them in pieces. He Himself forsook their house and tower, which, however, were not now destroyed. The seer's words in the following paragraph have proved a *crux* to all interpreters. The Lord commits the punishment of the chosen people, represented as sheep, to seventy shepherds, who rule successively in four series, in the proportion of twelve, twenty-three, twenty-three, twelve. "I saw until three and twenty shepherds overlooked the herd, and they completed in their time fifty-eight times. Then were little lambs born of those white sheep, and they began to open their eyes and to see and to cry out to the sheep. And the sheep hearkened not unto them. And the ravens flew upon the lambs, and took one of them, and tore and devoured the sheep. And I saw horns grow upon those lambs, and the ravens threw down the horns, until one great horn grew, one from those sheep, and then their eyes were opened. It looked upon them, and cried unto them, and the youths (the lambs) saw it and ran unto it." Then comes an account of a terrible conflict between the birds of prey and the lambs; but the former could not prevail against the horn. "He (the horn) struggled with them, and cried out for help. And there came the man who wrote the names of the shepherds and laid them before the Lord of the sheep, and he came to the assistance of the youth; and the Lord Himself came in wrath, and all who saw Him fled away before His face; while the birds assembled together, and brought with them all the sheep of the field to break the horn of the youth." But their efforts are vain, and in the end they are themselves destroyed by the Lord. This defeat introduces the Messianic epoch, when Israel shall rise superior to the heathen, and Messiah shall judge all sinners, whether angels or men, and shall establish the new Jerusalem, which shall be filled with a holy people gathered from all quarters.

This portion of the work closes with an address of Enoch to his children, exhorting them to lead a holy life, founding his lecture on the certainty of the future which the preceding visions have delineated.

The fifth division of the book (chaps. xcii.–cv.) is called "An Instruction of Wisdom," and contains the practical application of the four preceding portions, addressed by Enoch primarily to his own family, and then to all the inhabitants of the earth. He opens the subject by predicting the resurrection of the righteous and the destruction of sinners. "The righteous," he says, "shall arise from sleep and advance in the way of righteousness, and his whole walk shall be in eternal goodness and grace. Mercy shall be shown him; he shall receive dominion, and walk in everlasting light; but sin shall perish in darkness for ever, and shall no more be seen from this day forward." Before he begins his exhortation, he recounts in brief what he had seen in visions and had read in the heavenly tablets concerning the ten weeks of the world, of which seven belong to the historical past, three to the apocalyptical future. The first week is concerned with Enoch, the second with Noah, the third with Abraham, the fourth with Moses, the fifth with the building of the temple, the sixth with its destruction, the seventh with the introduction of an apostate generation. He intimates that he himself lived at the end of the first week. This would be in due accordance with the personification. The eighth week is the commencement of the Messianic era, when the sword of the righteous shall overcome the oppressors, and the new Jerusalem shall be established. In the ninth week the knowledge of Jehovah shall be spread over the world, and all men shall be forced to acknowledge His power and equity. The tenth and last week ushers in the final judgment on angels and men: the old world shall pass away, and a new heaven shall appear, and earthly life shall be merged in the heavenly. After this preliminary apocalyptical address, the hortatory portion follows, the admonitions to the righteous and to sinners being intermixed. The former are exhorted to continue stedfast in their integrity, and woe is denounced on various classes of the latter. The seer weeps to think of the oppression of the good at the hands of the evil, but is comforted by the knowledge of the final victory of the saints at the coming of Messiah, and the punishment of the unrighteous. Then he sternly reproaches sinners, detailing their folly in many instances, and showing what judgment shall be awarded them. Finally he turns again to the righteous, comforts them in their tribulations, exhorts them to hope and patience by exhibiting their future happy lot and blessedness. They can die in peace, because for them death is the entrance to a better life. And to enforce his words he solemnly adds: "I swear to you, ye righteous, by His mighty power and glory, by His kingdom and majesty, I comprehend this mystery, and have read the heavenly tablets, and have seen the book of the holy ones, and have found written therein that all goodness, joy, and honour are prepared for the spirits of those who have died in righteousness, and that with much good shall ye be recompensed for your troubles, and your lot shall be better than that of the living."[1] And these books of his shall be handed down to posterity and translated

---

[1] The passage inserted in chap. xci. 12–17 plainly belongs to chap. xciii., and has been rightly introduced there by Laurence.

into different languages, and shall be to the good a source of joy, righteousness, and wisdom, and all who believe in them and have learned the lessons there taught shall receive the reward. The section ends with the Lord's own words: "I and my Son will unite Ourselves with them for ever, because they have walked in the paths of uprightness. And peace shall be upon you; rejoice, ye children of righteousness, in truth."

The book might naturally terminate here, but, apparently by another hand, two sections are added, one concerning the supernatural circumstances attending the birth of Noah and the prediction of the Flood (cvi.–cvii.); and the other consisting of a writing of Enoch respecting the reward of the righteous and the punishment of the wicked, composed, as he says, "for his son Methuselah, and for those who should come after him, and observe the law in the last days" (cviii.). Here he mentions how in his journeyings he has seen the place of torment, which he describes as a waste outside the earth, and a bottomless sea of fire. The work thus concludes with God's promise to the righteous: "I will bring into brilliant light those who love my holy name, and set them each on his throne of glory; and they shall shine for endless ages; for righteous is the judgment of God, and to the true will He give truth in the habitation of uprightness. And they shall see how those who were born in darkness shall into darkness be cast, while the righteous shine. And sinners shall cry out, and shall see how these glow with light, and shall continue in their punishment all the times prescribed for them."

The uncritical receptivity of primitive Christianity

regarded the name attached to this book as a sufficient attestation of its genuineness. Thus, as we have seen, Tertullian, while acknowledging that some in his day declined to accept the work, because it was not included in the "Armarium Judaicum," the Hebrew canon, himself opined that it was written by Enoch, and either preserved in the time of the Flood, or restored by Noah under Divine inspiration. Nor have there been wanting some good people in our own times, with more credulity than critical ability, who have freely accepted the antediluvian authorship and endeavoured to prove that the writer was inspired to predict events down to modern times. I have seen some passages in our book distorted even to enunciate the claims and operations of the British and Foreign Bible Society and the sinister actions of Russian politics. But leaving these dreams, let us come to something more practical. No one nowadays believes that the patriarch Enoch had any hand in the composition of the book which bears his name. This appellation is only another example of the pseudepigraphic idea which dominated so many writers in the period immediately preceding and succeeding the commencement of the Christian era. The sanctity and remarkable destiny of Enoch, the hoar antiquity with which he was associated, designated him as a fit personage to be the mouthpiece of revelations designed for a special purpose and needing the authorisation of a great name. One who himself had been admitted to immediate intercourse with the Most High was peculiarly fitted to reveal Divine mysteries. That no allusion to the production is made in the Old Testament is obvious; that some portion of it was extant in the first Christian century is certified by the quotation in St. Jude's Epistle. But this certainty will carry us but a little way, as no one can read the work without concluding that it is not the composition of one author or one age, but exhibits difference of origin and date; and if the section from which Jude took his extract presupposes a Jewish and pre-Christian source, other parts may be of quite another character and have no pretension to any such claim. It is a difficult matter (even when we have distributed the work into its several sections) to determine the relation of these parts to each other, and to assign to them their proper position in the treatise. There is no external testimony to appeal to, and we must be guided in our conclusions entirely by internal considerations.

Now in all these writings occurs this marked characteristic. There is past history given in the form of revelation, combined with hopes and predictions of the future. In the former case events are pretty accurately represented, either actually or symbolically; in the latter the seer allows himself free latitude for the display of imagination and the possible development of previous prophetic hints. The difficulty consists in exactly defining the point where history terminates and prediction commences. Usually no hint is given of any such interchange; one phase passes into the other with nothing to mark the passage. If in any particular instance we could say with certainty, here the author writes of contemporary events, and here he crosses from the actual to the ideal, we should at once possess a criterion for determining the date of the composition. Some such opportunity is supposed to be found in chap. xc., where at ver. 16 the emblematical account of past history merges into the expectations of the future. The vision to which we refer (chaps. lxxxv.–xc.) traces the annals of Israel from Adam to the great consummation of mundane affairs. If our readers will refer to the previous account of the contents of the book, they will see that in this Apocalypse the chosen people are represented under the image of domesticated animals, while heathens and enemies are denoted by wild beasts and birds of prey. The allusions are fairly intelligible unto the Captivity; but now comes the paragraph which has exercised the ingenuity of interpreters, and upon the exposition of which the determination of one date depends. About the time of the destruction of Jerusalem the Lord commits the punishment of the chosen people to seventy shepherds, who are told which victims they were to allow to be killed by the wild beasts, and how many, at the same time intimating that they will exceed their commission and destroy many more than the appointed number. Likewise He ordered "Another" to note the number of sheep thus destroyed. These shepherds executed their commission, and delivered the sheep into the hands of the lions and tigers, who burnt the tower and demolished the house. But the shepherds gave over to the beasts many more than they were ordered to do. And when they had ruled for twelve hours, three of the sheep returned and began to rebuild the house and tower. But the sheep mingled with the beasts, and the shepherds rescued them not. When thirty-five shepherds had fed them, birds of prey attacked them; and when twenty-three shepherds had tended the flock, and fifty-eight times were completed in all, then little lambs were born with the results of which we read above. These seventy shepherds are divided into four series, consisting respectively of 12, 23, 23, 12 members. The last of these members would bring us to the author's own time. Can we with any probability elucidate this riddle? The explanations have been as numerous as the commentators, and we might easily refute their theories by simply comparing one with the other. Out of the confusion thus created we may thank Dillmann and Ewald for helping to deliver us. They and others[1] have seen that an attempt was here made to give a new interpretation to the seventy years of which Jeremiah had spoken as the period of the Captivity, and which had not been followed by that complete restoration which had been anticipated. Hereupon the literal exposition was surrendered; and another theory was started which would account for the partial failure and point to its remedy. The seventy shepherds, according to these interpreters, are foreign and heathen rulers, represented in the prophets as seventy weeks; and they continue to oppress the chosen people till overcome by the great horn, whose victories herald the advent of the Messiah. There is great difficulty in defining the seventy rulers, and it is only with much accommodation that history can be forced into agreement with the writer's supposed idea. Hence it has been proposed to see in these shepherds, not kings, but angels appointed to superintend the chastisement of Israel at the hands

[1] Especially Drummond, Stanton, and Schürer.

of her enemies. As Drummond points out, these shepherds receive their commission at the same time, which would hardly have been the case had they represented successive monarchs. And further, at the judgment in the delectable land they are placed with the fallen angels; and the one who is deputed to write down the number of sheep destroyed is called "another" (angel); while the duty of protecting the flock from the wild beasts could not have been entrusted to Gentile powers.[1] If, however, we held the usual interpretation of the vision, we should have to explain it in the following way:—The first group of twelve shepherds comprises five Assyrian kings, three Chaldæan and four Egyptian, from Necho II. to Amasis, under whom, more or less, the Israelites suffered injuries. The second group of twenty-three consists of Persian monarchs, from Darius and Cyrus. These 12 + 23 make up 35, the half of the seventy. The next group, consisting also of twenty-three, is composed of Græco-Macedonian kings, from Alexander to his successors, the Ptolemies, Seleucidæ, down to Antiochus Epiphanes. The final twelve range in the Syrian line, from this Antiochus to the close of the reign of Demetrius II. This lands us at B.C. 125. The attempt, however, at *exact* interpretation is eminently unsatisfactory, while the general features of the scheme are clear enough; and following Schürer's lucid explanation, we may arrange the matter thus. The seventy shepherds are angels entrusted with the superintendence and punishment of Israel, who neglected their duty and

---

[1] See chaps. lxxxvii. 2, xc. 20 ff. Drummond, p. 40; Schürer, p. 64.

were doomed to hell. The time of the Gentile supremacy is divided into four periods, two of shorter and two of longer duration, as we have seen above. The first period begins from the date of the earliest Gentile invasion (*e.g.* Assyrian) to the return in the days of Cyrus, the three returning sheep being Zerubbabel, Ezra, and Nehemiah. The second period reaches from Cyrus to Alexander the Great, the substitution of birds of prey for wild beasts (xc. 2) marking the transition from Persians to Greeks. The third extends from Alexander to Antiochus Epiphanes, the lambs symbolising the Maccabees. And the fourth extends from the commencement of the Maccabæan to the author's own time. This brings us to the "last third of the second century B.C." The stirring events of the previous twenty or twenty-five years are symbolically depicted. The little lambs of the vision are the pious who rose against the Syrian tyrants, the ravens who tore and devoured them; the sheep with horns are the Maccabæan leaders, who at first had but little success; and one of them in particular was carried off by the enemy. This is Jonathan, the son of Mattathias,[1] who, B.C. 143, was treacherously murdered by Tryphon in Gilead. In similiar figures are represented the defeat and death of Judas and Simon. The great horn which afforded refuge to the persecuted is John Hyrcanus, and the account of the terrible conflict between him and the enemies of Israel merges here into

---

[1] This Mattathias was the youngest brother of the great Judas Maccabæus. The "great horn" is by some supposed to represent Judas himself, but the particulars of the vision do not well suit this theory. See Dillmann and Stanton.

the apocalyptical future. So it is at this point that we may place the meeting of history and revelation, and consequently the composition of this portion of our book.

But our task is by no means ended even if we have satisfactorily determined the age of one section. Were the work one whole, and evidently the production of one author, to fix the date of one portion would be sufficient to determine the approximate date of the rest. But we have every reason to see in the various divisions different authors and different times of composition. Without entering minutely into details, we may say that it is now generally agreed that at least three authors have contributed to the work. The earliest portion, and that which forms the ground-work of the whole (omitting certain interpolations), is found in chaps. i.–xxxvi. and lxxii.–cv. If the author of the historical vision were the writer of this portion, the date of the greater part of the whole work would be determined. There is nothing to guide one to the date in the first thirty-six chapters, but in the latter part of this section there are plain intimations of the same conclusion that has already been reached. The writer in chaps. xciii. 1–14 and xci. 12–17 (which has been displaced) gives another sketch of the world's history divided into ten weeks, or periods. In agreement with the personification, Enoch intimates that he himself lived at the close of the first epoch. The next five weeks are marked with tolerable distinctness as the epoch of Noah, of Abraham and Isaac, of Moses, of Solomon, of the Captivity. At the end of the seventh week comes the vision of Messiah's kingdom.

We have to determine the duration of this last period. It is impossible to affix any definite number of years to each week, as the duration of each plainly varies most considerably; it has therefore seemed expedient to reckon by generations, counting seven to a week in the earlier times and fourteen in the later periods.[1] This looks like an arbitrary proceeding, one of those accommodations to which critics resort in order to confirm a foregone conclusion. But there are substantial grounds in this case for the notion. It will be seen that seven generations each will cover the first five weeks, the first being from Adam to Enoch, the last from Salmon to Rehoboam. The sixth, according to Drummond's calculation (omitting, as in St. Matthew, Ahaziah, Joash, and Amaziah), consists of fourteen generations from Abijam to Salathiel. The seventh, taking the series of high priests, and excluding Jason, Menelaus, and Alcimus, as Philo-Græcists, ends with Jonathan, Simon, and John Hyrcanus — thus landing us at the result previously obtained by another road. Of course, there is a doubt concerning the conclusion of the series; but in any case the discrepancy will amount to little more than twenty years, and the date of composition of this portion of the work may be fixed between B.C. 153 and 130, or in the latter half of the second century before Christ.[2]

If we are satisfied with the results thus obtained (and

[1] Drummond, p. 42.
[2] There is an allusion in this vision which seems to imply that the book was composed in this seventh week. It is said (chap. xciii. 10) that in this week to the just "shall be given sevenfold instruction concerning every part of His creation." This, doubtless, refers to the portion of our work which treats of natural phenomena.

nothing more reliable is to be discovered), we have settled the approximate age of two considerable portions of our book. Another section (chaps. xxxvii.–lxxi.), containing the three parables or similitudes, affords little internal help for determining its date. It is evidently a section distinguished from the rest in character and treatment. There is a difference in the use of the names of God, who is called in this part "Lord of spirits," in the angelology, the eschatology, and especially in the doctrine of the Messiah, which is much more prominent and definite than in the other divisions. Another peculiarity to which Köstlin directs attention is, that contrasted with the pious are not the ungodly in general (as commonly elsewhere), but Gentile rulers and the mighty ones of earth. Ewald finds herein a reason for considering this to be earlier than the rest, because the enemies denounced are foreign and heathen, while in the other parts the sinners are faithless and renegade Israelites, such as were not heard of till the time of Antiochus Epiphanes. But on the same ground Hilgenfeld concludes that it was written after the fall of Jerusalem; so that no argument can be securely based on this peculiarity. There is one historical allusion which has been supposed to give a hint in this direction. In chap. lvi. we are told that the Parthians and Medes shall work destruction in the Holy Land, and shall in turn suffer vengeance at the hand of the Lord, turning upon and destroying one another; and it is argued hence that an incursion by them had recently happened, as in B.C. 40, when they overran Phœnicia and Palestine,[1] or

---

[1] Joseph. *Antiq.* xiv. 13; *Bell. Jud.* i. 13.

that at any rate they were the enemies most dreaded in the author's time. But the inference is wholly unwarranted. The writer is not referring to any historical events that had come under his own cognisance, but is giving expression to his predictive anticipations based on the revelation of Ezekiel, chaps. xxxviii., xxxix. A surer criterion is found in the Messianic references, which show marked development when compared with the statements in the former part, as we shall see later on. It is also noted that, while the Book of Jubilees (which we suppose to have been written at the earliest in the century preceding the Christian era) shows acquaintance with other portions of our work, it never makes any allusion to the marked peculiarities of these three parables. From this we gather that this section was unknown to the writer of the "Jubilees," or was then not extant. The language used at the commencement of the section implies the existence of other books of Enoch. We here read, "The second vision of wisdom, which Enoch saw;" and the "similitudes" which succeed are evidently the complement of the preceding revelations, introducing themes of higher character, and rising from mundane and material elements to matters of heavenly and spiritual signification. We may reasonably conjecture that it was composed some few years later than the preceding portion.

There remain the Noachian sections which are introduced often most inappropriately, and are now found in chaps. liv. 7–lv. 2, lxv.–lxix., cvi.–cvii., and scattered confusedly in some other places.[1] In chap. lxviii. 1, the

[1] *E.g.* xxxix. 1, 2, lx., and perhaps xvii. and xix.

Book of the Allegories of Enoch is expressly mentioned, so that these paragraphs must be of later date. They are probably derived from some lost Apocalypse of Noah, and have been inserted by some late editor, who, without much critical skill, wove the materials into a form which would give a *quasi* unity to the whole. The last chapter (cviii.) is probably the latest of all, though there is nothing in it to determine its date accurately.

The great fact which seems most surely ascertained is that the Book of Enoch is, with the exception of some few possible interpolations, of pre-Christian origin. It was written certainly before the Romans had obtained possession of Palestine, as throughout the whole work there is no mention whatever of them, and they never appear as the enemies of Israel. No knowledge of the New Testament is anywhere exhibited; the name of Jesus never appears; His death and resurrection are not mentioned;[1] all that is of Christological import might fairly be gathered from the Old Testament. The writer especially had studied the prophecies of Daniel, and derived much of his language and matter therefrom, amplifying what he found in previous utterances, and colouring it with his own poetical and often crude fancies.[2]

As to the place where the authors lived, we have good reason for asserting this to be Palestine. This situation

---

[1] It is curious that in the Testaments of the Twelve Patriarchs, under *Levi*, occurs an allusion to a prediction of Messiah's rejection, death, and resurrection, stated to be found in the Book of Enoch. No such passage is now extant in that work, and if it ever existed, it was probably a Christian interpolation.

[2] See Dr. Pusey's *Lectures on Daniel*, pp. 382 ff.

best accords with the circumstances revealed in the various treatises. Here we find individuals and the nation oppressed by foreign influence, and fervent aspirations for relief and freedom, showing a state of things which could only be experienced in the Holy Land itself. The attempts which have been made to determine the writers' locality by reference to the astronomy and geography of the treatises are quite futile. In both sciences the seers were far from being adepts, and to guide oneself to a decision through the fog of imaginary and erroneous details is a hopeless task.

Nothing can be determined concerning the names of the authors. Does the Apostle Jude, by quoting a passage in the book as the production of "Enoch, the seventh from Adam," authorise the attribution of the work or of this section to the patriarch? Such has been the contention of some, who hold that the passage in question at any rate was a fragment handed down by tradition from antediluvian times. But the verse is manifestly an integral part of the paragraph in which it appears, exactly suitable to and connected with the existing context, and it must meet with the same treatment at our hands as the rest of the section. We have seen to what date we must relegate this book, and that it has no pretension to any such hoar antiquity as the critics above would assign to it. Doubtless it was well known in early Christian times, and Jude and his contemporaries were familiar with it. Without any idea of giving a decided opinion concerning its authorship, and citing the words merely in illustration of his statement (as St. Paul quoted Menander and Aratus), Jude cursorily appeals to a work with which his readers were familiar, and gives it that title by which it was generally known. By using this quotation for a special purpose, Jude does not give his sanction to the whole contents of the work in which it is now contained. All that he endorses with his authority is this particular passage; and in attributing it to Enoch, he is speaking either from direct inspiration, or, as is more probable, merely repeating current tradition. We may confidently affirm that of the authors who more or less have contributed to the book in its entirety we know nothing; nor, indeed, have we any grounds for conjecturing their identity. That they were more than one is proved by the different uses and expressions which obtain in the several portions; *e.g.* (as we have already observed) the title Lord of spirits, applied to God so commonly in one section, is not found elsewhere; the angelology differs; the Messianic presentation is not identical, nor the eschatology. The attribution of the work to Enoch is doubtless owed to the fact that popular tradition assigned to him the reception of revelations concerning the secrets of nature and other mysteries, the discovery of the alphabet, and the writing of the earliest books that the world ever saw.

We have now to speak of the teaching of this book and the lessons to be drawn from it. Granting that it is of pre-Christian origin, these are of great interest and importance, as bearing on Jewish opinion in days immediately preceding the appearance of Christ. But there is one preliminary question to settle, and that is whether any or what use of this work was made by subsequent Christian writers. A reader at a late Church Congress astonished and scandalised many of his hearers by boldly asserting that St. John in the Apocalypse had merely plagiarised from certain extant productions of a similar nature. This profane theory was not altogether novel, and it requires mention here since the Book of Enoch has been appealed to as strongly confirming the idea of Christian writers' indebtedness to previous apocryphal literature.

The author of *The Evolution of Christianity*, in republishing Lawrence's translation of our book, endeavours in his introduction to prove that Enoch's work is the source of many Christian opinions and mysteries, primitive Christianity having "freely appropriated his visions as the materials of constructive dogmas." The writer accepts without question the Archbishop's views of the origin, date, and locality of the work, except that he is inclined to think that the compiler of the Book of Daniel borrowed from Enoch rather than *vice versâ*. He proceeds to give instances of the influence of Enoch on subsequent writers and opinions. A few of these we will cite. The theory of the immobility of the earth, for denying which mediæval physicists were condemned to the stake, is traced to a statement in Enoch (chap. xviii.) concerning the stone which supports the corners of the earth, and the four winds which uphold the earth and the firmament. But the idea is found in Job xxxviii. 6 ; Ps. xxiv. 2, etc.; and concerning the winds carrying the earth, we may compare Job xxvi. 7 with ix. 6 and Ps. lxxv. 3. The fate of the fallen angels and the happiness of the elect are described in the Book ; therefore the Christian view of these matters is derived thence. To this source is traced the teaching concerning the Messiah prevalent in the age immediately preceding and succeeding the appearance of Christ. Then we have a series of passages from the New Testament paralleled by extracts from Enoch which are supposed to have been in the Christian writers' minds when they spoke or composed the utterances which we now possess. Most of these citations are of very insignificant similarity; many are such as might be found in any works treating of analogous subjects, without any notion of plagiarism, and many more are simply derived from the canonical books of the Old Testament. The "meek shall inherit the earth," says our Lord in the Sermon on the Mount (Matt. v. 5); "the elect shall inherit the earth," says Enoch v. 7. "Woe unto you which are rich; for ye have received your consolation" (Luke vi. 44). "Woe to you who are rich, for in your riches have you trusted; but from your riches you shall be removed" (Enoch xciv. 8). "The things which the Gentiles sacrifice, they sacrifice to devils and not to God" (1 Cor. x. 20). "So that they sacrificed to devils as to gods" (Enoch xix. 1). The same idea is found in Bar. iv. 7, and in the Sept. Version of Ps. xcv. 5, cv. 37; Deut. xxxii. 17. The "great gulf fixed" between the souls in Hades (Luke xvi. 26) is paralleled by a passage (Enoch xxii. 9), mistranslated, "Here their souls are separated by a chasm;" the correct rendering being, "Thus are the souls of the just separated; there is a spring of water above it, light" (Schodde); and our Lord in the parable gives the prevalent opinion without comment. The rapture of St. Paul (2 Cor. xii.) and St. John (Rev. xvii., xix.) is similar to what befell Enoch (chap. xxxix.) in some respects; but one is not dependent on the other in details or description. Enoch hears the angels calling on God, as Lord of lords and King of kings (chap. ix. 3, 4); did St. John therefore borrow the expression (Rev. xvii. 14, xix. 6) from him? The apostle speaks of the tree of life (Rev. ii. 7, xxii. 2, 14); Enoch also (xxiv., xxv.) tells of such a tree, which is plainly derived from Gen. ii. 9, iii. 22, and is alluded to elsewhere, as Prov. iii. 18, xi. 30, etc.; 4 Esdr. viii. 62; "Testament. Levi." xviii. The tribulations of the last days as delineated in Matt. xxiv. are not unlike the predictions in Enoch lxxx.; but no one reading the two would gather that they were borrowed one from the other, the variations being numerous, and actual identity not appearing anywhere. There is a book connected with the judgment in Enoch (chap. xlviii.), as in Rev. xx.; but so there is in Ex. xxxii. 32; Ps. lxix. 28; Dan. xii. 1, etc. In Rev. v. 11 the number of angels is called "ten thousand times ten thousand, and thousands of thousands;" so in Enoch (chap. xl. 1) we read of "a thousand times thousand, and ten thousand times ten thousand beings, standing before the Lord," which is merely like Dan. vii. 10; Deut. xxxiii. 2. The new heavens and the new earth, adumbrated in 2 Pet. iii. 13 and Rev. xxi. 1, are expected by Enoch (chaps. xlv., xci. 16). The latter passage is perhaps an interpolation, and the former is based on Isa. lxv. 17, lxvi. In 1 Tim. iv. 1, 2 we read, "The Spirit speaketh expressly, that in the latter times some shall depart from the faith, through the hypocrisy of men that speak lies;" and St.

Paul is thought to have plagiarised from Enoch civ., "and now, I know this mystery that the words of rectitude will be changed, and many sinners will rebel, and will speak wicked words, and will lie and make great works, and write books concerning their words" (Schodde). Of this character and of no nearer identity are all the passages adduced by the critic as parallel; and, relying on such citations, we are asked to believe that our Lord and His apostles, consciously or unconsciously, introduced into their speech and writings ideas and expressions most decidedly derived from Enoch. Few unprejudiced persons will agree with the author of this opinion, whose aim seems to be to throw discredit upon the superhuman origin of Christianity, and to trace it to merely human development. According to him, "the work of the Semitic Milton was the inexhaustible source from which evangelists and apostles, or the men who wrote in their names, borrowed their conceptions of the resurrection, judgment, immortality, perdition, and of the universal reign of righteousness under the eternal dominion of the Son of man." Yet the same ideas run through all the pseudepigraphic writings, a fact of which our flippant author seems to be wholly unaware. The writer, as he deems, puts orthodox believers in a dilemma: either Enoch was an inspired prophet and the New Testament writers were justified in using his words as Divine utterances, or he was a visionary and fraudulent enthusiast, whose illusions were erroneously accepted by apostles and evangelists, who thus lose their claim to inspiration. Happily, there is a third alternative: the New Testament writers have not borrowed from Enoch, save in the single quotation by St. Jude.

But enough of this. Let us see what is the Christology of our book, and its Messianic utterances.[1] First, as to the names applied to the Messiah. He is called The Anointed One, the Christ (chap. xlviii. 10, lii. 4); The Righteous (xxxviii. 2); The Elect (xl. 5, xlv. 3, 4); The Son of man (xlvi. 2); Son of the Woman (lxii. 5). This last title occurs only once, and seems intended to accentuate the fact that He is very man. Of the Christian verity, that Jesus was incarnate by the Holy Ghost of the virgin, there is no trace. But to this Christ is attributed pre-existence with other Divine attributes. Thus in the second similitude we read (chap. xlvi. 1–3), "There I saw one who had a Head of days (age-marked), and His head was white as wool (Dan. vii. 9); and with Him was another, whose countenance resembled that of man; and full of grace was His countenance, like one of the holy angels. And I asked one of the angels, who went with me and showed me all the hidden things, about that Son of man,[2] who He was, and

---

[1] Drummond looks with suspicion on most of these allusions to Messiah as interpolations by a Christian or semi-Christian editor. There is really nothing to show the reasonableness of this notion; and were it true, it would be difficult to account for the vagueness of the statements, the reticence concerning the facts of Christ's life, and the apparent inconsistency in some of the expressions used and actions attributed to Him. A writer who desired to propagate Christian ideas among his countrymen would not have contented himself with statements concerning Messiah's advent in glory, and have omitted all notice of His previous humiliation.

[2] "Son of man" was probably currently used as a title of the Messiah at the time of the composition of the Allegories, as it was

whence He was, and why he went with the Head of days? And he answered me, and said to me: "This is the Son of man, who has righteousness, with whom righteousness dwells, and who reveals all the treasures of that which is hidden, because the Lord of spirits hath chosen Him, and His lot before the Lord of spirits hath surpassed every other through righteousness for ever and ever." The angel goes on to say that this Son of man will raise up kings and mighty men from their thrones, and hurl those that obey not to destruction, and break the teeth of sinners, and terribly punish those who extol not the name of the Lord of spirits. Before sun and moon were created, or the stars were made, His name was named before the Lord of spirits; and, being chosen to do great things hereafter, He was hidden, and revealed only, till He came into the world, by imparting treasures of wisdom to the elect. For in Him dwells the spirit of wisdom, and the spirit of Him who gives insight, and the spirit of instruction and power, and the spirit of those who are fallen asleep in righteousness.[1] He has not yet appeared on earth, but in due time He will come to execute vengeance on sinners, and to receive homage at the hands of the mightiest in the world. To Him all judgment is committed; He sits on the throne of Divine glory, and judges both dead and living, and even fallen angels themselves. He will be the joy of the righteous; it will be their high privilege to hold close communion with Him. In all that is said of the glory of the

in our Lord's own days. See John xii. 34, and ix. 35 in some MSS.; also Matt. xvi. 13.

[1] Chaps. xlviii., xlix.

Messiah, He is plainly not conceived of as God; His power is delegated; He is a creature subordinated to Almighty God, joining in the universal worship offered to the Lord of all; clothed indeed with highest attributes, but set at a distance from the supreme Lord. The writer indeed has assimilated the teaching of Daniel and the Prophets, but he is far from realising the doctrine of St. John.[1]

The eschatology of the book is somewhat confused, owing partly to the vagueness of the writer's own opinions, and partly to the variety of authorship. Speaking generally, we may say that the author anticipated the immediate development of Messiah's kingdom. The one object of the production, so far as unity can be traced therein, is to assert the great truth that retribution awaits transgression; this is confirmed by the history of the past, and emphasises the announcement of the events of the later days which are matters of prediction. In one passage [2] we are told that the eighth week of the world's history shall be one of righteousness, when vengeance is executed upon sinners at the hands of the godly. At the end of this period occurs a time of happiness and prosperity; the righteous shall inherit a new Jerusalem and erect a new temple. In the ninth and tenth weeks the everlasting judgment will take place, the present heaven and earth will vanish away, and be succeeded by a new heaven and a new earth, which shall exist eternally in goodness and righteousness.

---

[1] Chaps. li., lv., lxi., lxix.
[2] Chap. xci. 12-17. The passage belongs properly to chap. xciii., and is inserted there by Dillmann.

In other passages [1] referring to the same period there is no mention of this time of peace preceding the judgment; rather the Messianic reign is to be ushered in with war and calamity and desolation, and rest is not won till the evil angels and the wicked rulers are cast into the fiery abyss, and the Messiah, "the white steer," is born. There is no definite statement in this passage concerning the general resurrection as preceding the universal judgment.[2] But from other places we gather that in this matter a different mode awaits the wicked and the righteous. The spirits of the former shall be removed from Sheol, and sent into the place of torment,[3] but the spirits of the righteous shall be united to their bodies, and live on the new earth, sharing the ineffable blessings of Messiah's kingdom.[4] The resurrection of the body is a boon that belongs to the just alone, who were thus compensated for the evil times which they had passed while formerly in the flesh. The final judge is not Messiah, but God Himself, who shall descend from heaven to pass the sentence upon men and angels.[5] This view is common to all the apocalyptic literature of the period, so that our Lord's statement, "The Father judgeth no man, but hath given all judgment unto the Son," [6] was a novel idea to His hearers, even to those of them who had learned some portion of the truth concerning Christ's nature and attributes.

[1] *E.g.* chap. xc.
[2] A similar omission occurs in the description given in St. Mark xxv.
[3] Chaps. ciii. 8, cviii. 2–6.
[4] Chaps. li. 1, 2, lxi. 5, xcii. 3, c. 5.
[5] Chaps. i. 3, 4, xxv. 3, c. 5.
[6] John v. 22.

Of the intermediate state the description is somewhat obscure. Enoch (chap. xxii.) is shown a place in the far west where the souls of the righteous dead are collected, different abodes being assigned to them according to a certain classification; those who suffered wrong being separated from those who died from other causes. Near them is the locality where the spirits of sinners wait. Here also a division is made between those who had been punished on earth for their sins and those who hitherto had escaped retribution. These transgressors suffer pain in this abode, even as Dives in the parable speaks of being tormented in the flame.[1] Here they have to wait till the day of judgment, when their fate is decided for ever. But some highly favoured souls do not dwell in this western abode. They are taken to Paradise, which is the Garden of Eden in the north country, and whither Enoch himself was translated. This is their temporary home.[2] One sees here a trace of the distinction between the destiny of the souls of the good and those of the highest saints, which is found in some mediæval and in some Catholic theology; and in accordance with which, while some rest in Hades or Paradise, others are raised to heaven at once and enjoy the beatific vision.

As regards angelology, in some parts of the work there is a somewhat strict classification of these heavenly beings. They are innumerable, but among them are distinguished seraphim, cherubim, and ophanim, angels of power and angels of lordship. The ophanim ("wheels")

---

[1] Chap. ciii. 7, 8; Luke xvi. 23-25.
[2] Chap. lx. 8, lxi. 12, lxx.

are so named from the representation in Ezekiel i. and x. There is one called the Angel of Peace (chap. xl. 8) who seems to be the highest of all, and to have the direction of things in heaven and earth. The four archangels, Michael, Raphael, Gabriel, and Phanuel, have separate functions assigned to them in connection with Messiah's kingdom. Michael leads the ceaseless praise of God; Raphael presides over the sick and suffering; Gabriel is mighty to assist the oppressed; Phanuel aids the repentant and those who hope for life eternal.[1] As regards evil spirits, these are sometimes supposed to be the fallen angels, whose transgression is continually coming in view; sometimes the spirits of the giants born from their illicit connection with mortal women. Others are called Satans, and at their head is Satan himself, who is represented with his followers not only as leading men astray, but as the agent of God in inflicting punishment on sinners. In this view he is allowed, as in Job, to visit heaven and prefer accusations against men. Whence these Satans came, and whether they were originally good angels, Enoch reveals not; but he denounces their fate in Messianic times, when they shall be cast into a blazing furnace and tormented eternally.[2]

The Book of Enoch shows its variety of authorship by the inequality of literary skill which is found in it. If some passages are of high eloquence, and redolent of piety and reverence and noble aspirations, others are characterised by wild speculation and empty bombast. But with all its faults and shortcomings, it is of great

---

[1] Chaps. lxi. 10, lxxi. 3, 7, 8, 13, xl. 1 ff., ix.
[2] Chaps. xv. 8, xl. 7, liii. 3, liv. 6.

value as introducing us to the views and feelings of Jews, their hopes and convictions, at the period immediately preceding the Christian era, and helping us to estimate the moral, religious, and political atmosphere in which Christ lived. Hence the work is to be regarded, not as a mere literary curiosity, but as offering a substantial aid to the understanding of the most important period of the world's history.

THE ASSUMPTION OF MOSES.

In the Epistle of St. Jude we read (ver. 9): "Michael the archangel, when contending with the devil he disputed about the body of Moses,[1] durst not bring against him a railing judgment, but said, The Lord rebuke thee." Hereupon two questions arise. Whence did the apostle derive the story to which he refers? And what was the occasion of the dispute? To the latter question a conjectural answer alone can be given. Taking into consideration the circumstances of the burial of Moses, we see that it was intended to be a secret transaction. The Lord, we are told (Deut. xxxiv. 6), "buried him in a valley of the land of Moab, over against Beth-peor; but no man knoweth of his sepulchre unto this day." Doubtless there was a good reason for this secrecy. The proneness of the Jews to idolatry, the likelihood that the

---

[1] An attempt has been made to read 'Ιησοῦ instead of Μωϋσέως, and to refer the occurrence to Zech. iii. 2; but there is no authority whatever for such change of the text.

body of their great leader might become an object of adoration, even as the brazen serpent drew their hearts away in later time, the tendency to follow the creature-worship and to pay that undue reverence to relics which they had seen in Egypt,—these considerations may have led to the concealment of the body of Moses. And the devil wished to frustrate this purpose. He saw an opportunity of using the mortal remains of Moses to draw away the Israelites from true religion. He would have no mystery about the burial. The people should be shown their leader's resting-place; of the result he had no doubt whatever. And Michael, the appointed guard of the grave, as the Targum says, resisted this evil attempt of Satan, and firmly carried out the purpose of God. Using the words which God Himself had employed when the wicked spirit endeavoured to withstand His act of clothing Joshua, the high priest, in festal garments (Zech. iii.), Michael answered, "The Lord rebuke thee." And in the unknown spot the body rested; or, at any rate, it was seen no more till it appeared to the wondering three on the Mount of Transfiguration fourteen hundred years later.

The former question, as to the origin of the narrative to which St. Jude refers, is answered by Origen,[1] who

[1] *De Princ.* iii. 2. 1: "In Genesi serpens Evam seduxisse describitur, de quo in Adscensione Mosis, cujus libelli meminit in Epistola sua Apostolus Judas, 'Michael archangelus cum Diabolo disputans de corpore Mosis,' ait a Diabolo inspiratum serpentem 'causam exstitisse prævaricationis Adæ et Evæ.'" *Opp.* i. 138. The title of the work is given as Assumtio Moysis, sometimes as Ascensio or Receptio M., both being translations of the Greek ἀνάληψις M., and this not in the sense of ascension of body and soul, as in the case of Christ, but with the meaning that while his body was buried his

intimates that it is derived from a book which he calls the Ascension of Moses, Ἀνάληψις Μώσεως. That St. Jude should refer to a work current in his day, though not appertaining to the canon of Holy Scripture, is quite supposable, as there is good ground for believing that in another place (ver. 14) he cites the apocryphal Book of Enoch. The existence of this Assumption or Ascension of Moses is testified by many other early writers. In the remarkable use of the word μεσίτης in the Epistle to the Galatians (iii. 19) some have seen a reference to, or evidence of acquaintance with, our book. Certainly the term is applied to Moses in the first chapter, where the dying lawgiver says: "Itaque excogitavit et invenit me, qui ab initio orbis terrarum præparatus sum ut sim *arbiter* testamenti illius." Referring to this, and having the Greek original before him, Gelasius of Cyzicum [1] gives the latter words of Moses as εἶναί με τῆς διαθήκης αὐτοῦ μεσίτην. But we cannot lay much stress on the use of that expression, as it is employed in this connection by Philo [2] and the Rabbinical authors, and was probably applied to Moses by writers antecedent to Christianity in agreement with Deut. v. 5, where he says: "I stood between the Lord and you at that time, to show you the word of the Lord." It is also asserted

soul was conveyed by angels to heaven. Moses himself in one passage (*Assumt.* x. 14) speaks of sleeping with his fathers, and in another dates an event from his reception ("a receptione mea," x. 12). More indefinitely it is termed "Secreta M." (Didym.), and βιβλία ἀπόκρυφα M. (*Const. Apost.*).

[1] *Comment. Act. Syn. Nic.* ii. 18. (Mansi, *Concil.* ii. p. 844.) The passage in Heb. ix. 15 is translated in *Cod. Claromont.*: "et ideo novi testamenti arbiter est," where the Vulgate has "mediator."

[2] *Vit. Mos.* iii. 19: οἷα μεσίτης καὶ διαλλακτής. Vol. ii. p. 160 M.

that Clemens Romanus quotes our book when, speaking of Moses (xvii. 5), he says: " He, though greatly honoured, magnified not himself, but answered when the revelation was made to him at the bush, ' Who am I, that Thou sendest me? I am slow of speech, and of a slow tongue.' And again he saith: ' I am as smoke from the pottery.' "[1] The last clause is deemed by Hilgenfeld to be cited from the Assumption. This is possible, but the existing fragments do not contain it. The earliest reference which can be relied on is found in the works of Clemens Alexandrinus,[2] who, describing the death of Moses, says it is probable that Joshua saw Moses in twofold form when he was taken up ($\dot{a}\nu a\lambda a\mu\beta a\nu\acute{o}\mu\epsilon\nu o\nu$), one with the angels, and one honoured with burial in the valley. This curious opinion is shared by Origen,[3] who asserts that in a certain uncanonical book mention is made of two Moses' being seen, one alive in the spirit, the other dead in the body. Evodius,[4] a contemporary of St. Augustine, has the same gloss, derived from the same source : " When he ascended the mountain to die, the power of his body brought it to pass, that there should be one body to commit to earth,

---

[1] Ἐγὼ δέ εἰμι ἀτμὶς ἀπὸ κύθρας. Lightfoot's references to Jas. iv. 14 and Hos. xiii. 3 are not satisfactory.
[2] *Strom.* vi. 15 (p. 806, Potter), cf. i. 23, 153.
[3] In *Libr. Jesu Nave*, Hom. ii. 1 : " Denique et in libello quodam, licet in canone non habeatur, mysterii tamen hujus figura describitur. Refertur enim quia duo Moses videbantur, unus vivus in spiritu, alius mortuus in corpore."
[4] Augustin. *Ep.* 158 (ii. p. 426, Ben.): " Quamquam et in apocryphis et in secretis ipsius Moysi, quæ scriptura caret auctoritate, tunc cum ascenderet in montem ut moreretur, vi corporis efficitur ut aliud esset quod terræ mandaretur, aliud quod angelo comitanti sociaretur."

and another to be the companion of his attendant angel." Another legend, traced to the same origin,[1] recounts how at Moses' death a bright cloud so dazzled the eyes of the bystanders that they saw neither when he died nor where he was buried. Other writers give a different reason for the dispute with Michael from that suggested above, still, however, referring to the tradition contained in the Assumption. Thus (Ecumenius[2] writes, that the archangel took charge of Moses' body, but the devil claimed it as his own, being the body of a murderer in that he had killed the Egyptian; and an old Scholion[3] on the passage in St. Jude adds: "that it was when Satan asserted this claim and blasphemed, Michael replied, 'The Lord rebuke thee.'" Epiphanius[4] gathers from this book how the angels buried the body of Moses without washing it, for they had no need to wash it; nor were they defiled by contact with so holy and pure a body. Didymus of Alexandria,[5] who lived in the fourth century A.D., informs us that some persons in his day raised an objection against the Epistle of St. Jude, as also against the Assumption of Moses, on account of the passage concerning the dispute with Satan; just as, according to Jerome,[6] the same Epistle was rejected for its reference to the apocryphal Book of Enoch. Mention is made of

[1] *Caten. in Pent.* ap. Fabric. *Cod. Pseud. ep. V. T.* ii. p. 121.
[2] *In Ep. Jud.* p. 340.
[3] *Caten. in Ep. Cath.* ed. Cramer, Oxon. 1840.
[4] *Hæres.* ix. p. 28.
[5] *In Ep. Jud. enarrat.* (vi. p. 326, Galland. B. Patr.): "Licet adversarii hujus contemplationis præscribunt præsenti epistolæ et Moyseos Assumtioni propter eum locum ubi significatur verbum archangeli de corpore Moysis ad angelum (*al.* diabolum) factum."
[6] *Catal. Script. Ecclesiast.*

the Assumption in some catalogues of the books of Scripture. Thus in the Catalogue of Nicephorus it is placed, with the Book of Enoch, the Testaments of the Patriarchs, and some others, among the Apocrypha of the Old Testament; and reference is made to it in the so-called *Synopsis* of Athanasius. Apollinaris[1] says: "It is to be noted that in the times of Moses there were also other books, which are now apocryphal, as evident from the Epistle of St. Jude, where he teaches about the body of Moses, and where he cites as from ancient Scripture the passage, 'Behold, the Lord cometh,'" etc. In the Acts of the Second Nicene Council[2] some passages are cited from the *Analepsis* which are not now extant. Thus we read that in the dispute with Satan, Michael said: "Of His Holy Spirit we all were formed;" and again: "From the face of God went forth His Spirit, and the world was made." Another fragment of the same Acts[3] already mentioned gives the chief contents of the work: "Moses the prophet, when he was about to depart from life, as it is written in the Book of the Assumption of Moses, called Joshua unto him, and spake, saying: 'God looked upon me before the founda-

---

[1] *Niceph. Catena*, i. 1313, Lips. 1772.

[2] *Comm. Act. Conc. Nic.* ii. 20: ἐν βίβλῳ 'Αναλήψεως Μώσεως Μιχαὴλ ὁ ἀρχάγγελος διαλεγόμενος τῷ διαβόλῳ λέγει· ἀπὸ γὰρ πνεύματος ἁγίου αὐτοῦ πάντες ἐκτίσθημεν. καὶ πάλιν λέγει· ἀπὸ προσώπου τοῦ Θεοῦ ἐξῆλθε τὸ πνεῦμα αὐτοῦ, καὶ ὁ κόσμος ἐγένετο. To this the philosopher answers: Περὶ δὲ τῆς ῥηθείσης 'Αναλήψεως Μωϋσέως, περὶ ἧς ἀρτίως εἰρήκατε, οὐδὲ ἀκήκοά ποτε εἰ μὴ νῦν, ὅθεν αἰτῶ ὑμᾶς σαφεστέραν μοι τῶν λεχθέντων παραστῆσαι τὴν σύστασιν. Mansi, *Concil.* ii. 857. These and other passages from ancient writers are cited by Volkmar, Hilgenfeld, and Fritzsche in their editions of the book.

[3] C. xviii. p. 28.

tion of the world, that I should be the mediator of His covenant.'" The *Apostolical Constitutions* mention among those writings that are without the canon "The apocryphal Books of Moses,"[1] referring doubtless to our work. It seems also certain that it was well known to the Rabbinical writers, who raised a crop of legends on its foundation.[2]

Thus we see that the Assumption of Moses was a book known and quoted up to the twelfth or thirteenth century of our era. But from that time till some twenty years ago it has been wholly lost. Commentators on St. Jude were forced to content themselves with a vague reference to this unknown composition; and the words of Dean Stanley in Dr. Smith's *Dictionary of the Bible* (art. "Moses"), written in 1863, accurately represent the amount of acquaintance with the subject possessed by most people. Speaking of the passage in Jude, he concludes thus: "It probably refers to a lost apocryphal book mentioned by Origen, the *Ascension* or *Assumption of Moses*. All that is known of this book is given by Fabricius, *Codex Pseudep. V. T.* i. 838–844." The fragments, however, printed by Fabricius are very insignificant, and quite insufficient to give any idea of the character and contents of the work. But Dr. Stanley was unconsciously inaccurate when he made the statement just mentioned. Already in 1861 A. M. Ceriani, the learned librarian of the Ambrosian Library at Milan, had published a Latin version of a large portion of the Assumption which he had found in a palimpsest of the

---

[1] Βιβλία ἀπόκρυφα Μωϋσέως.
[2] Volkmar, *Mose Prophetie u. Himmelfahrt*, p. 10.

sixth century.[1] It is curious that nearly forty years previously Amedeus Peyron had edited from the same manuscript some hitherto unknown orations of Cicero,[2] but the "Assumption" remained still undiscovered. It was therefore with the utmost satisfaction that the learned world received the news that fresh fragments of this apocryphal work had been suddenly disinterred. The MS., indeed, was without title, corrupt and imperfect, and in places illegible; but these circumstances only augmented the interest which was centred upon it. Here was a nodus which demanded solution at the hands of scholars. "Liber enim," as Erasmus says,[3] "prodigiosis mendis undique scatens, crux est verius quam liber." That it was the same book as the old *Analepsis Mos.* was proved by its containing the passage in the Acts of the Nicene Council quoted above. The discovery appears to have passed almost unnoticed in England, but in Germany it stirred the minds of savants with an excitement as great as that lately aroused by the "Teaching of the Twelve Apostles." Professors set themselves the task of correcting, explaining, and supplying the gaps in the very imperfect publication of Ceriani. First Hilgenfeld, with the aid of other scholars, put forth a critical edition[4] containing a corrected text, which threw much light on the many dark places, and afforded a readable whole. A year or two later he took the pains to translate the Latin

---

[1] *Monumenta Sacra*, tom. I. Fasc. i., Mediol. 1861.
[2] *Ciceronis Orationes*, Stutg. et Tübing. 1824.
[3] *Ep.* 1203, vol. iii. p. 1420.
[4] In his *Novum Testamentum extra Canon.*, Lips. 1866. Afterwards in *Messias Judæorum*, Lips. 1869; and in his *Zeitschr.* for 1868, etc.

into Greek, no very difficult task, as the version had been most slavishly rendered from the original, retaining everywhere Greek phraseology and often Greek words. This he published with valuable notes. Then Volkmar [1] printed a neat little edition with a German translation and commentary. This was followed by that of Schmidt and Merx,[2] whose conjectures and corrections are remarkable rather for audacity than probability. Fritzsche,[3] the last editor, speaks somewhat slightingly of his predecessors' labours, but has largely availed himself of them. In his very useful edition he prints on one page the text as originally published by Ceriani, and on the opposite side gives an amended text with the *lacunæ* mostly supplied, and with copious critical notes. The work has never, I believe, been published in England. A useful dissertation on the book, which combines the latest information, is appended to Dr. Gloag's *Introduction to the Catholic Epistles*.

There is another work which is sometimes confounded with the Assumption, but is entirely different in scope and treatment. This is an *Apocalypse of Moses* in Greek, written by a Christian, and belonging to the class of Adamaic books, wherein is given a history of Adam's life and death as revealed to Moses. It has been published by Tischendorf and Ceriani.

---

[1] *Handbuch d. Einl. in d. Apokr.* vol. iii., and separately under the title of *Mose Prophetie und Himmelfahrt*, Leipz. 1867.
[2] *Archiv. für wissensch. Erforsch. des A. T.*, Halle 1868.
[3] *Libri Apocryph. Vet. Test.*, Lips. 1871. He says in his preface: "Arduum sane et magni erat negotii hunc libellum mirum quantum corruptum emendare; feci tamen quod potui. Omnia virorum doctorum consilia, vel etiam commenta et opinionum monstra referre nihil attinuit." P. xxxiv.

Whether the Assumption was originally written in Hebrew cannot now be determined.[1] If its birthplace was Palestine, it is most probable that it was composed in Hebrew or Aramaic. It is evident that it was known only in a Greek form to those early writers who mention it; and it is also certain from internal evidence that the old Latin version which has survived was made from the Greek and not the Hebrew. The use of such words as "prophetiæ," "scene testimonii," "allophyli," proves this incontestably. The Latin of the translation is beyond measure barbarous and anomalous, the vulgar dialect of country peasants, and resembling the old *Itala* rather than any classical form which we possess. It appears, too, to have been transcribed by an ignorant writer, who has accordingly introduced many blunders of his own manufacture. As the MS. came originally from the Abbey of Bobbio, near Pavia, whence also issued the famous Muratorian Canon (the language of which is very similar to that of the Assumption), it was probably copied by one of the inmates of that establishment, "stronger," as Colani says, "in caligraphy than Latin." Of the place and date of the original composition we can form only conjectures. We might do more if we had the whole before us; but, unfortunately, both the beginning and the end are missing. At the commencement probably only a few lines are lost, but at the conclusion a very serious deficiency is to be lamented. Nicephorus

---

[1] Merx, Schmidt, and Colani assert strongly that the work was written originally in Aramaic, which they think will account for most of the obscurities of the Latin text. See *Revue de Théologie*, 3e. ser. vol. vi. p. 68.

states that the original work consisted of 1400 stiches, assigning similar dimensions to the Book of Revelation. We are thus led to the conclusion that little more than half has been preserved, and important passages, wherein some guide to the chronology would naturally have been introduced, are lost or mutilated beyond hope of replacement. Our *data*, therefore, are much limited, and we possess but scanty foundations on which to construct a theory. With regard to the locality of the treatise, we may at once exclude Alexandria from being its birthplace. The author shows no trace of the Alexandrian school; he never allegorizes, never indulges in mystic speculations, but keeps to pure history, whether he is relating the past or predicting the future. His standpoint is unadulterated Judaism, and there is good reason, as will be seen, for classing him among the Zealots. Hilgenfeld considers that the author was a Jew sojourning at Rome; but his arguments are very far from decisive, and we shall have most critics with us in determining that the work was written in Palestine. The author shows such accurate acquaintance with the parties of the Jews in Palestine, and the events which happened there, that it can scarcely be doubted that he is writing amid the scenes and characters which, under the disguise of prophecy, he depicts, either in Galilee or in the country east of Jordan, where the party of Zealots was strongest. As to the date of the composition, scholars have long had important differences, Wieseler fixing it at 2 B.C., and Volkmar at 135–138 A.D. Between these two extreme dates many variations occur; thus Ewald assigns it to A.D. 6, Hilgenfeld to A.D. 44, Merx to

A.D. 54–64. Fritzsche traces it to the sixth decade of the first century A.D., and Langen (mistaking the application of chap. viii.) assigns it to a period shortly after the destruction of Jerusalem by Titus. Most of these critics found their opinions upon the unintelligible fragments of numbers in chap. vii. But it is absurd to employ the hopelessly mutilated text for this purpose; and, in truth, we can only be certain of these facts, that the book was written before the destruction of Jerusalem, of which no mention is made, and before the death of Herod's two sons, Philip and Antipas, probably towards the commencement of their reign; for the author predicts for the sons a shorter reign than their father's, which could be said truly of Archelaus alone, for Antipas reigned 43 years, Philip 37, and Herod the Great only 34 years.[1] The concluding clauses of chap. vi., which speak of the arrival of a powerful western chieftain who should take captives, and burn the house, and crucify some, point to the war of Varus, B.C. 4;[2] and when the writer goes on (chap. vii.): "ex quo facto finientur tempora," it is natural to conclude that he wrote after this little war. If we knew accurately the date of St. Jude's Epistle, we might have another criterion; but too much stress must not be laid upon the supposed quotation from the Assumption, as the passage referred to is not extant, and both Jude and pseudo-Moses may have used some

---

[1] Archelaus reigned only nine years, and was then banished by Augustus. The passage of the MS. above referred to is the following: "et . . . roducit natos . . . ecedentes sibi breviora tempora donarent." As treated by Fritzsche the passage reads: "et producet natos, qui succedentes sibi breviora tempora dominarent."

[2] Josephus, *Antiq.* xvii. 10.

tradition current among the Jews of the period.[1] On the whole, we shall not be far wrong if we attribute the composition to the early part of the first Christian century, *i.e.* between A.D. 6, the time of the banishment of Archelaus, and A.D. 33, the date of Philip's death.[2] Before offering a sketch of the contents of the little work, I will transcribe a few lines of the manuscript with a view of showing its corruptions, and the difficulties that stand in the way of interpreters. I should premise that the MS. is a palimpsest of the fifth or sixth century, written in two columns to the page, each line containing from twelve to eighteen letters without division of words, and with very rare punctuation. The following is the commencement of the existing fragment: ". . . qui est bis millesimus et quingentesimus annus a creatura orbis terræ nam secus qui in oriente sunt numerus . . . mus et . . . mus profectionis fynicis cum exivit plebs post profectionem quæ fiebat per moysen usque amman trans iordanem profetiæ quæ facta est a moysen in libro deuteronomio." This passage is thus manipulated by the latest editors: "[Anno Moyseos centesimo et vigesimo] qui est bis millesimus et quingentesimus annus a creatura orbis terræ, nam secus [= secundum eos] qui in oriente sunt numerus est cccc mus et vii mus et xxx mus profectionis Phœnices,[3]

---

[1] Some German writers have assigned a very late date to our book, and then have used this assumption as an argument for attributing the Epistle of St. Jude to post-apostolic times. See Volkmar, *Mose Prophetie und Himmelfahrt.*

[2] See Wieseler's article in *Jahrh. für deutsche Theol.* xiii. 622 ff., 1868. Of the contents of this article I have gladly made some use in my paper. See also Schürer, p. 79.

[3] A great controversy has been raised over the words "profectionis fynicis." The latter word is explained by the best commentators to

cum exivit plebs post profectionem quæ fiebat per Moysen usque Amman trans Jordanem, profetiæ factæ sunt a Moyse in libro Deuteronomio." It would lead us too far were we to attempt to solve the many questions which are raised by this brief extract; rather let us confine ourselves to an endeavour to obtain a general view of the contents and object of the work.

✗ The work, as we have it now, is divided into two parts—first, the charge of Moses to Joshua his successor, in which is given a sketch of Jewish history, mingled with prophecies of future events up to the restoration of the pure theocracy. This is followed by a humble, self-depreciating speech of Joshua, to which Moses makes an encouraging reply, broken off short by the mutilation of the manuscript, which ends thus: "exivit enim deus qui prævidit omnia in sæcula, et stabilitum est testamentum illius et jurejurando, quod" . . . The remainder, which gave its name to the work, doubtless contained the account of the death and burial of Moses, and the dispute about the body to which St. Jude refers; but this will probably now be never brought to light.

be the Greek Φοινίκης; but they differ in its interpretation, some contending that "the journey of Phœnicia" means the migration of Canaan, *i.e.* the Israelites into Egypt; others, with more reason, affirming that it signifies "the journey into Phœnicia," *i.e.* the removal of Abraham to Canaan. Certainly Canaan is so called by Eusebius (*Præp. Ev.* ix. 17. 2): τοῦτον διὰ τὰ προστάγματα τοῦ Θεοῦ εἰς Φοινίκην ἐλθόντα. Others, again, think that the fabulous bird Phœnix is meant, which is said to have reappeared A.D. 34, and to whose reappearance Moses' death and revival are compared. Wieseler makes this into an argument for attributing to our book a locality on the east of Jordan, as the Arabians used the Phœnix-period in their computation of dates.

It will, perhaps, be most satisfactory to give a free translation of part of Moses' speech, adding such remarks as seem to be necessary for its elucidation, or to show its bearing on the Messianic doctrine.[1] We must keep in mind the fact (for a fact it seems to be) that the book is written by a partisan of a section of the Zealots, whose standpoint was that no mortal man ought to rule Israel, be he priest or king, of the line of Aaron or of David,— that Jehovah alone is King. This tenet, coupled with an energetic and fanatical zeal for the law, led to the outburst of Judas of Galilee, and to the excesses of the sect in later times. We shall see this ruling dogma continually appearing in the Assumption. The author at the same time seems to be inimical to the Pharisees, as being too dogmatical in their religion and undecided in their politics.

This, then, is the last charge of the great lawgiver: "The Lord prepared me before the foundation of the world to be the mediator of His covenant. And now that I am about to be gathered to my fathers, I commit to thee this writing, which thou shalt preserve safely [2] unto the day of visitation." This prophecy of Moses was to be kept in the holy place till the last time of judgment. "And now thou shalt lead the people into the land promised to their fathers, and shalt settle them there. And it shall come to pass that after they have been in possession for five [3] years, they shall be governed

---

[1] I use generally Fritzsche's amended text as the most probable and most available form.

[2] "Quos ordinabis et chedriabis"—*i.e.* κεδρώσεις, "shalt smear with oil of cedar." So κεδροῦν is used by Diod. Sic. v. 29.

[3] The MS. has a blank where the number ought to be; "V." is

by princes and tyrants[1] eighteen years; and ten tribes shall revolt for nineteen years." The eighteen years represent eighteen rulers, as in the Book of Enoch, viz. fifteen judges ("principes") from Joshua to Samuel, and three kings ("tyranni"), Saul, David, and Solomon; the "nineteen" are the kings of Israel from Jeroboam to Hoshea. "But two tribes shall come and remove the tabernacle of testimony; and God shall make a resting-place for His sanctuary among them (2 Sam. vi.; 1 Kings viii. 4). And they shall offer victims for twenty years." This refers to the reign of the twenty kings of Judah, including Athaliah. "And seven shall fortify the walls, and nine will I watch over, and they shall maintain the covenant of the Lord." Seven kings improved the condition of the people, viz. Rehoboam, Abia, Asa, Jehoshaphat, Joram, Ahaziah, and Athaliah; and nine God defended, viz. Joash, Amaziah, Uzziah, Jotham, Ahaz, Hezekiah, Manasseh, Amon, Josiah. "But the last four kings shall worship false gods, and defile the temple with their idolatries. And then from the East shall come a mighty king (Nebuchadnezzar) who shall destroy the city, and burn the sanctuary, and take their precious things, and carry all the people and the two tribes into captivity. Then the two tribes shall call the ten to repentance, acknowledging the justice of their punishment; and all together shall invoke the God of their fathers, and humbly confess that that chastisement which Moses

supplied from Josh. xiv. 10, and Joseph. *Antiq.* v. 1. 19. Wieseler thinks that the date 2500 A.M. was here repeated.

[1] "Principibus et tyrannis." In calling them "tyranni" rather than "reges," the seer means to convey his disapproval of this invasion of the pure theocracy.

predicted has righteously fallen upon them. At the end of seven and seventy years one of their princes shall pray for them." This refers to the intercession of Daniel; the seventy years of exile are extended by seven according to the Jewish predilection for that number, traces of which we see in Matt. xviii. 22, and in the genealogy of our Lord in St. Luke. "And God shall look upon them, and put it into the heart of the prince (Cyrus) to restore them unto their own country. Some portions of the tribes shall return to their appointed place and rebuild the city walls; but the two tribes alone shall remain true to the Lord, yet lamenting that they are now unable to offer acceptable sacrifices." The notion of the writer is, that the temple having been restored under heathen auspices, and the officiating priests being friendly to the pagan supremacy, the services therein were illegitimate and inefficacious.[1] As for the ten, they shall thrive in the foreign land, and shall some day rejoin the others in the day of restoration.[2] And now the times of trial shall draw near,[3] and vengeance shall arise because of the wickedness of princes given for their punishment; for ministers who are not priests, but slaves and born of slaves, shall defile

---

[1] A similar notion is found in the Book of Enoch, chap. lxxxix. 73, where it is said, in reference to the same period, that "all the bread offered on the table was impure and defiled."

[2] This is one of the many difficult passages in the work. The MS. gives "et x tribus crescent et devenient apud natos in tempore tribum." "Tribum" plainly ought to be "tribuum;" "apud natos" is = "ad natos, posteros;" and "the time of the tribes" must mean the era of the restoration of Israel. Very different explanations are offered by commentators; the above is substantially that of Fritzsche.

[3] "Adpropiabunt tempora arguendi."

the altar;[1] and those who are their doctors of the law shall pervert justice and fill the land with iniquity."[2] The writer makes no definite reference to the persecution of Antiochus or the gallant struggles of the Maccabees, but hurries at once to the later time of the decadence of that great family and the consequent corruption of religion and morals. The scribes and Rabbis of the Asmonæans were doubtless Sadducees, to which party John Hyrcanus had attached himself (Joseph. *Antiq.* xiii. 10. 6).

In the view of the seer, which, as I have said, is that of the sect of Zealots, the holy people were to be governed by no earthly king, not even by a prince of Jewish birth. Jehovah alone is their Ruler. From this standpoint he regards the rule of the Asmonæan princes as usurping the authority of the Lord. He proceeds: "Soon shall

[1] The seer seems here to acknowledge the legitimacy of the worship of the second temple, which he before denied. This is, doubtless, because he considers the Jews as independent under the Maccabees. But this worship was marred by its ministers. "Non sacerdotes, sed servi de servis nati." Thus John Hyrcanus was taunted by the Pharisee Eleazar with being the son of a captive woman, and therefore disqualified for the priesthood (Joseph. *Antiq.* xiii. 10. 5).

[2] MS.: "Et ideo implebitur colonia et fines habitationis eorum sceleribus." By "colonia," which is frequently used in the book, is probably meant Jerusalem, as though regarded as a settlement among the heathen Jebusites,—pseudo-Moses taking Joshua's point of view. See Josh. xv. 63; Judg. i. 8, 21. The MS. proceeds: "a domino qui faciunt erunt impii judices inerunt in campo judicare quomodo quisquæ uolet." The scribe himself has attempted to correct this unintelligible passage, but without success. Fritzsche reads: "a Domino qui deficiunt erunt impii judices, et erunt in campo judicare quomodo quisque volet." Wieseler: "a deo qui faciunt (those who are on God's side, the Pharisees), erunt impii judices in ea (colonia), a domino qui faciunt (the king's party, the Sadducees), erunt impii judices, hi erunt in campo, judicare, quomodo quisque volet."

ruling kings arise,¹ calling themselves priests of the Most High God, and shall profane even the Holy of Holies. To them shall succeed an insolent king, not of the family of priests, a man rash and shameless,—and he shall judge them as they are worthy. He shall slay their chieftains with the sword, and strangle them in secret places,² so that their bodies shall not be found; he shall kill old and young, and spare not; there will be great dread of him throughout the land, and his tyranny shall continue for four and thirty years." This is a fine and true description of Herod the Great, and the notorious cruelties practised in his reign. The mistake concerning the length of the reigns of Herod's sons has been already noticed. "He shall beget sons, who shall reign a shorter time than their father; until a mighty king of the West shall come, and shall utterly defeat the people, lead some away into captivity, crucify others around the city, and burn part of the temple." The mention of the *partial* destruction of the temple by fire forbids us to see here an allusion to the final conquest of Titus, and compels us to look to another event for an explanation of the prophecy. That event is doubtless the defeat of the Jews by Varus, when, as Josephus narrates,³ the porticoes or cloisters of the temple were

---

¹ "Tunc exurgent illis reges imperantes." This was a grievous reproach in the eyes of a Zealot.
² The MS. has the unintelligible words: "Et locis ignotis singuli et corpora illorum ut nemo sciat ubi sint corpora illorum." For "singuli et," Fritzsche proposes "strangulabit;" Hilgenfeld "sepeliet." Cf. Joseph. *Antiq.* xv. 10: "And many, carried off either openly or secretly into the castle, Hyrcania, were put to death."
³ *Bell. Jud.* ii. 3. 1 ff.; *Antiq.* xvii. 10. 1 ff.; *ibid.* 10.

burnt, the sacred treasures plundered, and two thousand of the insurrectionists were ruthlessly crucified.

Up to this point the history has been tolerably clear; but now (chap. vii.) comes a passage which is most obscure, and has given rise to many interpretations and great controversies.[1] The seer is evidently speaking with studied ambiguity, and as we do not know what he means by "the last times," nor by what intervals he divides them, it is impossible to arrive at any sure solution of the enigma here presented. He seems to have regarded the victory of Varus as a token of the subjection of Israel to the heathen yoke and the virtual

[1] As some readers may like to exercise their ingenuity upon this crucial passage, I give it as it stands in the MS., premising that the *italics* represent the probable letters, now too faint to be deciphered for certainty: "Ex quo facto finientur tempora momento ... etur cursus *a* ... horæ ·iiii· *ueniant* coguntur secu*n* ... ae ... pos ... initiis tribus ad exitus ·viiii· propter initium tres septimæ secunda tria *in* tertia duæ *h* ... *ra* ... *tæ*." The various attempts to rectify the grammar and to supply the *lacunæ* in this paragraph may be seen in Fritzsche's note. He himself leaves it as hopeless. The following is Wieseler's version: "Ex quo facto finientur tempora, momento finietur cursus annorum. Horæ iiii venient; cogentur seculi septimæ (diræ?) postumæ in initiis tribus ad exitus viiii; propter initium tres septimæ, secunda trias, in tertia duæ horæ peractæ." "Then shall press on the nine last fearful weeks (year-weeks, as in Dan. ix. 24) of the age with three beginnings unto the end; next to the beginning (the subjugation of Judea by Pompey) are three weeks, a second triad (of year-weeks), in the third triad are two hours accomplished." Pompey took Jerusalem A.U.C. 691; the nine weeks, or 63 years, at the close of which the age shall come to an end, coincide with A.U.C. 754, which is a little after the time of the war of Varus. The insurrection of Judas, which the Jews dignified with this name, occurred A.U.C. 750, the date of our Saviour's birth. An explanation of this mysterious chronology may be seen in Wieseler's article; but it is all guess-work, and more curious than profitable.

overthrow of the theocracy. "Ex quo facto finientur tempora." "When this shall come to pass the times shall end. In a moment the course of years shall end, when the four hours come." The "four hours" may possibly be the "time, times and a half" of Dan. xii. 7, and the following paragraph probably defines more exactly the various stages of the epoch which culminated in the erection of the supremacy of Rome. More than this we are unable to affirm. Next we have a description of the Herodian princes under Roman rule, and the parties then prevalent: "among them shall reign pestilent and godless men, boasting themselves to be just,[1] zealous indeed, but crafty, self-pleasers, hypocrites. These are gluttonous and wine-bibbers; they devour the substance of the poor, saying that they do it for pity's sake; their language is: Let us eat and drink luxuriously as princes. Their hands work iniquity, and their tongue speaketh proud things: Touch me not lest thou defile me."[2] One cannot help seeing here a reference to the Herodians, and, in the latter part, to "the scribes and Pharisees, hypocrites," who were so sternly de-

[1] MS.: "docentes (? dicentes) se esse justos." Some commentators see here a reference to the Sadducees and a play on their name, Tsedhûkîm, the Righteous, as they are called in the Mishna.

[2] Comp. Mark vii. 1 ff. It is noteworthy that a contemporary of our Lord uses very similar terms to those which He employed in censuring these professors of religion. The clause above: "They devour the substance of the poor," etc., is in the MS.: " . . . *rum* bonorum com *e* stores dicentes se *hæc* facere propter misericordiam." Editors make . . . *rum* stand for "pauperum;" it might equally well represent "viduarum," and then the likeness to the clause in Matt. xxiii. 14 would be very remarkable. In both passages the hypocrites are represented as teaching people to spend their substance upon them as putting it to a holy use.

nounced by our Lord in St. Matt. xxiii. The first portion of the description applies closely to the Sadducaic faction in Herod's half-pagan court, which really affected the doctrine of the Epicureans. Then falls upon them the punishment of their iniquity: "Lo, then shall come on them a wrath and a vengeance such as never before were seen. A mighty power shall be roused against them; those who confess circumcision shall be crucified, and they who deny it shall be tortured and imprisoned; their wives shall be given over to the heathen, and their children shall be made uncircumcised. Under pain of fire and sword they shall be compelled to carry the idols of their masters,[1] to offer on their altars, and to blaspheme the great name of God." The persecution here foreshadowed recalls, and is meant to recall, that under Antiochus Epiphanes.[2] Is there any parallel to be found within the limits of the period to which we attribute the composition of the Assumption? Colani[3] boldly says there is not, and affirms that the only persecution which answers to the one mentioned in the text, is that which took place under Adrian as a punishment for the rebellion of Bar-Cocheba, A.D. 136. But for an author, writing the history of the Jews (be it in a predictive form), to omit all mention of the destruction of Jerusalem under Titus, and to leap at once to the calamities which were consummated by the erection of Ælia Capitolina, is a proceeding so very improbable, that

---

[1] "Cogentur palam bajulare idola eorum inquinata." Comp. Bar. vi. 4. 26.

[2] Comp. 1 Macc. i. 22 ff., 43 ff.

[3] *Revue de Théol.* p. 75. See also Volkmar, pp. 58 ff.

we cannot admit it for a moment. The other alternative (if it be granted Adrian's persecution is meant) would be to endow Pseudo-Moses with the true spirit of prophecy, or at least to allow that he has made a most happy guess at the future which subsequent events fully justified. Of course, Colani and those who hold his opinion would say that the book was written after A.D. 136; but I have already given reasons for assigning it to a much earlier date, nor does this part of the "prophecy" alter this decision. Evidently the writer wished to announce in striking terms the chastisement which he saw coming upon his nation from heathen Rome. How could he better herald this than by recalling to mind the awful cruelties of Epiphanes, and using his acts as a type of the hostility of godless tyrants assailing the fallen Israel? What those cruelties were, and how in many particulars they answered to the description in our text, may be seen in the beginning of the First Book of Maccabees. That, as a fact, the atrocities of earlier days were repeated in after years, is only what might have been expected. Given similar victims, similar circumstances, similar perpetrators, the result was sure to be analogous also. Here, as elsewhere, history repeats itself, and we need seek no closer fulfilment of the prediction. By speaking, in the following paragraph, of "a second vengeance," the writer seems to desire to call to remembrance the persecution of Antiochus.

We now come to the great *crux* of the whole book (chap. ix.), at a satisfactory solution of which no commentator has yet arrived. "In that day, at his command (*illo dicente*) a man shall arise from the tribe of

Levi, whose name shall be Taxo. And he shall call his seven sons unto him, and thus address them: 'Behold, my sons, a second time has vengeance fallen upon this people, a cruel, foul punishment, and pitiless captivity. What nation or people has suffered for their iniquities as we have suffered? Ye see and know that we have never tempted God,[1] neither our fathers nor ancestors, so as to transgress His commandments. And herein lies our strength. Let us then do this: let us fast for three days; and on the fourth day let us go into a cave which is in the field, and rather die than break the commandments of our God. For if we do this and die, the Lord will avenge our blood.'" Now the question is, who is meant by "Taxo?" Is it a real name? Are we to take it as representing a certain numerical value, as the beast in the Revelation of St. John? And if so, is the name Greek, Latin, or Hebrew? Or is it a cypher, containing the same number of letters as the name intended? Into these and such like questions editors have entered at great length, with this conclusion, according to Fritzsche, with which I am forced to agree: "ut nemo adhuc inventus est, qui nomen satis probabiliter enuclearet, ita de ejus explicatione videtur desperandum." Among the various theories offered, that of Wieseler[2] seems in some respects reasonable. In his view the seer is again introducing details from Maccabæan history, such as occur in 1 Macc. ii. 29 ff. and 2 Macc. vi. 11 ff., or from the

---

[1] The MS. gives: "quia nunquam temptans deum nec patres," etc. Fritzsche corrects, "temptavimus;" Volkmar, temptantes;" Colani retains "temptans," referring, according to his interpretation, to Rabbi Jehouda-ben-Baba.

[2] *Jahrb.* 1868, p. 629.

deeds of that Matthias who was the ringleader in the disturbances which took place on the rumour of the death of Herod, and who, according to Josephus (*Antiq.* xvii. 6; *Bell. Jud.* i. 33), made much the same speech as Taxo, before pulling down the Roman eagle on the temple gate, urging his followers to sacrifice their lives in defence of the honour of God. As for the word "Taxo," it is probably the Low-Latin word meaning "a badger," equivalent to the Hebrew תַּחַשׁ, *tachash*, which is very similar to the German "Dachs," and has the same meaning; and it may be either a play on the badger skin which formed part of the covering of the tabernacle, or the appellation of the man who had to act the part of this animal by hiding in dens of the earth.[1] This man may be either Judas of Galilee, or some chief among the party of the Zealots, possibly the writer himself. Now the principal fact that militates against Taxo being Judas is the character of Judas himself. Though his followers saw in him the promised Messiah, he was by no means one who would have used the words attributed to Taxo. Non-resistance was not his policy. Certainly he taught that it was better to die than to break the law of God; but it was death with arms in their hands that he exhorted his followers to meet. His watchword, "We have no master but the Lord," led him to fight with earthly weapons, and the cruelties and excesses of his companions have stained the name of Zealots for all time.

There is so much more matter interesting and import-

---

[1] Comp. 2 Macc. x. 6: "They wandered in the mountains and in dens like beasts." Heb. xi. 38.

ant in this little work that we need not spend further time on the interpretation of "Taxo." Suffice it to say that Hilgenfeld affirms the original to have been τξγ′ = 363, *i.e.* numerically Messiah. But it is inconceivable that Messiah should be represented as hiding in a cave and there awaiting death. Volkmar writes ταξο, which he makes = 431, and deems that the person intended is Akiba, the comrade of Bar-Cocheba. Colani and Carrière pronounce that the translator has mistaken the original Aramæan word which meant "ordinance"[1] for a proper name, whereas the sentence really signifies, "there shall be a man of the tribe of Levi who shall promulgate an ordinance, or give an instruction"—the instruction being the address to the sons which follows, and the speaker being Rabbi Jehouda-ben-Baba, who, according to a Rabbinical tradition, acted somewhat in the manner of "Taxo" towards the end of the persecution of Adrian.[2] But the date of the Assumption renders this last theory utterly untenable. Perhaps, after all, the simplest solution is to regard the word as a corruption of the text.

To proceed: "Then shall His (Jehovah's) kingdom be manifested in all His creation, and the devil (Zabulus) shall find his end, and with him all sorrow shall vanish away.[3] Then shall power be given[4] to the messenger

[1] טכסא, found in Chaldee and Syriac in the sense of the Greek word τάξις.

[2] See *Revue de Théol.* pp. 80 ff.

[3] Comp. Isa. xxv. 8, xxvi. 21. The word Zabulus is merely another form of Diabolus, found in African Latin, *di* being pronounced as *z*, and *o* changed into *u*. See Rönsch's article in Hilgenfeld's *Zeitschr.* 1868, p. 100. The word is found in Cyprian and Lactantius.

[4] "Implebuntur manus," a translation of the Hebrew phrase for

who is set in the highest place,[1] who soon shall avenge them (Taxo and his comrades) of their enemies." This "messenger" seems to be the prophet like unto Moses of Deut. xviii. 15, 18, who himself is called "the great Messenger" in chap. xi. of our book. Nor can we be intended to see in this personage the Messiah. At the most, the expected One was an equal of Moses, superior to him neither in person nor in act. The same expectation of a *faithful* prophet ($προφήτης\ πιστός$) is found in 1 Macc. xiv. 41, where the epithet points to Moses, to whom it is specially applied.[2] The party among the Zealots, to which the writer belonged, looked for a heaven-sent Saviour and Deliverer to prepare the way for the visible reign of Jehovah; and when the multitude, who were miraculously fed by Christ (John vi.), exclaimed: "This is of a truth that prophet that should come into the world," they were expressing the vague expectation of the advent of a personage like unto Moses, possessed perhaps of some Messianic features, but not the Messiah Himself. We see the difference in the estimation in which our Lord was held by His contemporaries. "Some said," we are told (John vii. 40), "of a truth this is the prophet. Others said, This is the Christ." And although we know from Christ's own words[3] that Moses wrote of Him when he foretold the appearance of a prophet like unto himself, yet this was by no means the general view, and a distinction between

consecrating or appointing to an office. Comp. Ex. xxviii. 41; 1 Kings xiii. 33.

[1] "Nuntii qui est in summo constitutus."
[2] See Num. xii. 7; and in the New Testament, Heb. iii. 2, 5.
[3] St. John v. 46; comp. i. 45 and Acts xxvi. 22.

Christ and this prophet was generally recognised.[1] In the following eloquent passage which speaks of final triumph, Jehovah Himself comes to the rescue of His oppressed people:[2] "Then shall the Heavenly One arise from the seat of His kingdom, and come forth from His holy habitation, with wrath and indignation for His children's sake. And the earth shall tremble and quake to its utmost borders; and the lofty mountains shall be humbled and shaken, and the valleys shall sink. The sun shall give no light, and shall turn into darkness; the horns of the moon shall be broken, and she shall be turned into blood, and the circle of the stars shall be confounded. The sea shall retreat to the abyss, the springs of water shall fail, and the rivers shall be dried up; because the Most High, the Eternal, the only God,[3] shall arise and come manifestly to chastise the nations and to destroy their idols. Then shalt thou be happy, O Israel, and shalt mount on the necks and wings of the eagle, and thy days shall be fulfilled.[4] And

[1] See John i. 21, where, noting the use of the definite article, ὁ προφήτης, Theophylact mentions the error of the Jews in ignoring the identity between the prophet and the Messiah. See Acts iii. 22.

[2] Merx and Schmidt see in this portion of the Assumption an Essenic psalm. It certainly runs easily into a strophic arrangement. But the writer was not an Essene, for in that case, as Schürer has pointed out, he would not have jeered (as he does in chap. vii.) at the Pharisaical purifications (Joseph. *Bell. Jud.* ii. 8. 10).

[3] "Summus Deus, eternus, solus." There are passages parallel to this prophecy in 2 Esdr. (*e.g.* vi. 24), in the Book of Enoch (i. 6, xci. 9), and in the Psalms of Solom. xviii. 4. Comp. Joel ii. 10, 31, iii. 15.

[4] "Et ascendes supra cervices et alas aquilæ, et implebuntur" (dies tui). The last words are a conjecture of Fritzsche. There is evidently something omitted in the MS. With this reference to the eagle we may compare 2 Esdr. xi., xii.; but there is no need, with

God shall exalt thee that thou shalt cleave to the starry heaven, over the place of their habitation.¹ And thou shalt look from above and see thine enemies on earth, and shalt know them, and rejoice, and give thanks, and acknowledge thy Creator."

The triumph over the heathen power of Rome, here, as in the Book of Esdras, represented under the symbol of the eagle (which had twelve feathered wings and three heads), is ascribed to the direct intervention of Jehovah, the signs that are to accompany His presence being adopted from the imagery of the Old Testament prophets. There is no hint of a conquering Messiah, a Son of David, who should restore the dominion of Israel, and reign a mighty King over an innumerable people. The Zealot could not contemplate the accession of any earthly monarch to the government of the chosen nation; his hopes centred in the restoration of the theocracy and the visible rule of Jehovah. It is with this grand expectation that he comforts the stricken hearts of his brethren. Then he proceeds to define the time of this epiphany. Addressing Joshua, he says: "Keep these words and this book; for," he continues, "from my death and assumption unto His appearing shall be two hundred and fifty

---

Volkmar, to conclude that Pseudo-Moses borrowed the symbol from Esdras. The profane introduction of the Roman eagle into the temple led to the insurrection repressed by Varus; and the symbol would be naturally used by any writer of the period. Joseph. *Antiq.* xvii. 6.

[1] "Et faciet te hærere cœlo stellarum, loco habitationis eorum." If "eorum" is correct, it must refer to the heathen who are to suffer chastisement, and the place of their dwelling must be Rome. The idea is that the Israelites shall see and exult in the overthrow of their pagan enemies. Comp. Isa. lxvi. 14, 24.

times." At the commencement of the book, if the revised reading of editors may be trusted, the last year of Moses' life is said to correspond with the year 2500 A.M.; and, taking "the times" as weeks of years (250 × 7), we find that the great Parousia will occur in the year of the world 4250. This would be 45 A.D. according to the chronology of Josephus, as gathered from some portions of his writings; but no importance can be attached to this, as he is very inconsistent in his dates, and we have no reason to suppose that Pseudo-Moses followed the system of chronology used by that writer. Without attempting to solve the enigma of the number of years, I should be inclined to suppose that the seer had no definite date in his mind, and merely assigned this visible interposition of Jehovah to the distant future, using terms in his vaticination with which the prophets of old had made him familiar.

But it is time now to turn to the second part of the Assumption. When Joshua heard the words of Moses, we are told, he rent his clothes, and fell upon his face, addressing his leader with words of grief and fear: "What a word is this that thou hast spoken, full of tears and sorrow![1] Thou art leaving this thy people. What place will receive thee, and what will be the memorial of thy burial? Who will dare to transfer thy body hence as that of any other mortal man? Other

---

[1] "Quæ est plena lacrimis et gemitibus." Eurip. *Hec.* 230: πλήρης στεναγμῶν, οὐδὲ δακρύων κενός. The first words of Joshua's speech are: "Quid me celares, Domine Moyse? et quo genere celabo de quo locutus es voce acerba?" Volkmar and Wieseler read "zelares" and "zelabor" for "celares" and "celabo;" and the latter sees a reference here to the party of Zealots to which the seer belonged.

men are buried in the earth; but thy grave is from the rising to the setting sun, from the south to the north; the whole world is thy sepulchre. And thou wilt depart; and who will nourish thy people? Who will pity them and be their leader? And who will pray for them every day that I may bring them into the land of the Amorites? How shall I be able to lead them as a father guides his only son, or a mother her daughter now ripe for marriage? And how shall I give them food and water? For the people have so increased under thy prayers that they number now a hundred thousand men. The kings of the Amorites, when they hear that thou art departed, will war against us, thinking that there is no longer among us that sacred spirit (Moses) worthy of the Lord, manifold and inconceivable master of the word, faithful in all things, the Divine prophet throughout the world, the perfect teacher. And they will say: 'Let us attack them.[1] If our enemies have once sinned against their Lord, they have now no defender to pray for them to the Lord, as Moses was a mighty messenger,[2] who every hour, day and night, had his knees pressed to the earth, looking to the Almighty and praying Him to visit the world with mercy and justice, remembering the covenant of the fathers.' Yea, they will say, 'He is with them no

---

[1] This is an important passage, showing the regard in which Moses was held. "Sed et reges Amorreorum cum audierint expugnare nos, credentes jam non esse semet (secus, Fr.) sacrum spiritum dignum Domino, multiplicem et incomprehensibilem, dominum verbi, fidelem in omnia, divinnm per orbem profetem, consummatum in sæculo doctorem jam non esse in eis, dicent eamus ad cos." Chap. xi. Comp. Deut. xxxiv. 10 ff.

[2] "Magnus nuntius," as we have seen above, "the prophet like unto Moses" called "nuntius qui est in summo constitutus."

more, let us drive them from the face of the earth.' And what shall become of this thy people, my lord Moses?"

To this sorrowful appeal Moses answers with encouragement. He tells Joshua to fear nothing. All nations are in God's hands, who has predetermined all that happens, even to the least particular, and unto the end of time. "The Lord," he proceeds, "hath appointed me to pray for the people, and to make intercession for their sins. Not for my strength nor for my weakness hath this befallen me, but from His mercy and long-suffering. And I tell thee, Joshua, that it is not for the piety of this people that thou shalt destroy the nations. The vault of heaven and the foundations of the world were created and approved by God,[1] and are beneath the ring of His right hand.[2] They who keep the commandments of God shall be increased, and prosper in their way; but sinners and the disobedient shall have no part in the promised blessings, and shall be punished by the heathen with many torments. For it is not possible that He should destroy His people utterly. For God will come forth, who hath foreseen all things in every age, and His covenant is established, and with an oath, which" . . .

Here the manuscript ends, some ten or twelve leaves being lost. The missing fragment doubtless contained the conclusion of Moses' address, and then told how Joshua departed to his appointed work, and how Moses

---

[1] Gen. i. 31.

[2] MS.: "Sub nullo dexterae illius sunt." This has been rightly restored by editors to "sub annulo," etc. Comp. Hag. ii. 23.

took his Pisgah view of the promised land, died, was buried by the angels in spite of Satan's opposition, and received his "assumption"—his mortal body being laid to rest in the unknown valley, his immortal part being escorted by angel bands to heaven itself.

It is unfortunate that the only quotations of, and references to, the Assumption which have reached us from antiquity contain sentences and statements not now extant, though there can be no reasonable doubt that they were portions of the original document. From our present fragments we can gather enough, however, to teach us the importance and utility of the work.

Like many other apocalyptic productions, it is a combination of history and prophecy, partly a narrative of past events, partly an ideal view of the future. It is not so much an independent prophecy, wherein the seer, constrained by the overmastering spirit, pours forth a stream of rebuke, warning, and prediction, as an exposition and development of hints given in the Pentateuch, and especially in Deuteronomy, so that Wieseler has termed it "a prophetical Midrasch." Written, as it must have been, in the first half of the first Christian century, it contains no trace of Christian ideas, or of any acquaintance with the pretensions, the life and death of Jesus. That in some respects our Blessed Saviour would have corresponded to the notion of the coming prophet entertained by some of the Zealots, is obvious. As claiming no earthly sovereignty, He would have suited the sentiments of those who would own no lord but Jehovah; but the moral triumphs to which His kingdom aspired, the bloodless victories of religion, would have been very far from answering their hopes or fulfilling the desires of their fiery hearts. The prophet whom they had taught themselves to expect was merely the precursor of the restored theocracy, when, under the visible chieftainship of Jehovah, the heathen should be destroyed as the doomed Canaanites perished, and Israel should rise victorious by earthly arms wielded under the direction and with the assured assistance of God Himself. At the same time it is interesting to remember that one at least of Christ's apostles was a Zealot, and learned to see in his Master "the Prophet" and the Messiah. Now this sect, as an offshoot of the Pharisees, though in some respects opposed to them, doubtless shared with them the belief in the resurrection of the dead; but there is no direct statement of this doctrine in the Assumption. Writing in the character of Moses, who has left no teaching on the subject in the Pentateuch, the seer would naturally avoid dogmatising on this matter; but he uses the phrase "being gathered to his fathers," which perhaps in his time carried with it the hope of the resurrection. There is, indeed, no trace of Christian doctrine throughout the work; it is distinctly narrow and national. The earth is made for the chosen people, whose strength lies in obedience to the law, and whose transgressions shall be punished by the hands of the heathen. But the Lord will never wholly destroy the Israelites for His oath's sake and the promise made to their forefathers. The seer never looks to the salvation of the heathen. They are raised up merely as instruments of chastisement for sinning Jews; and when this purpose is fulfilled, they shall themselves be judged, and meet with the reward of their lawlessness and idolatry. He does, indeed, condescend to correct some of their prevalent errors concerning creation and religion, but this is done for the sake of his own people who might be led astray by the paganism of Herod's court. The selfish, narrow prejudice which so often appears in the Gospels, disdaining to hear of favours offered to non-Israelites, is found conspicuously in the Assumption. That side of the Messianic idea which promised light and grace to the Gentiles, was repugnant to the Zealot. His keen sense of injury at the hands of Rome blinded him to the possibility of the conversion and acceptance of those who were now aliens. Nor did he see the necessity of a Messiah such as we Christians receive. If we regard the description of Moses given above, we shall observe that the prophet usurps the place of Messiah; this "Divine" personage leaves no room for Christ; he is the mediator between God and the people, the appointed intercessor, and nothing higher or more heavenly is expected. The idea of the Son of God made man is wholly foreign to the seer's theology, and the only Messiah he looks for is "that prophet" who should herald the restoration of the theocracy. And that this "nuntius in summo constitutus" is not a Divine person, is shown by the very phrase used of him above: "his hands shall be filled." For this is an expression employed to designate the consecration of an earthly priest or prophet, and applies not to an angel or to Deity Incarnate. The hope of Pseudo-Moses is, as I have said, confined to the Parousia of Jehovah Himself displayed by some manifest sign as the Shekinah, when under His

I

guidance Israel should overthrow her enemies. In believing that this appearance was to happen soon, the Zealot's view was much the same as that of the primitive Christians, who could say with firm confidence, "the coming of the Lord draweth nigh," and expect that He would in their day restore again the kingdom to Israel. That this hope was a great support in times of distress and persecution may well be imagined; and it was to give definiteness to this expectation and to enforce its lesson that our book was written.

For showing the hopes and opinions of an influential party among the Jews at the beginning of the first Christian century few documents of greater interest than the Assumption of Moses have reached our times. And the particular point which the book illustrates, viz. that the expectation of a personal Messiah was not universal, is worthy of more study than it has received.[1]

THE APOCALYPSE OF BARUCH.

In addition to the Book of Baruch, a translation of which is contained in the Apocrypha of our English Bibles, there had from old time been known to exist a certain document in the Syrian language, called "The Epistle of Baruch the scribe to the nine-and-a-half tribes beyond the Euphrates."[2] This had been published in

[1] The same view is found in another Pseudepigraphic work, the Book of Jubilees.
[2] There exists also an Ethiopic work called by Dillmann, "Reliqua

the London and Paris Polyglots in Syriac and Latin, in Latin alone by Fabricius in his *Codex Pseudepigr. Vet. Test.*, and in English by G. Whiston in his *Authentic Records*. Later, a French rendering was given by Migne in the *Dictionnaire des Apocryphes*, and Lagarde put forth again the Syriac version in his Syriac edition of the Old Testament Apocrypha. Many questions resulted from the publication of this document. Was it a complete work or a fragment of some larger treatise ? What was its connection, if any, with the usuallly-received apocryphal work of Baruch ? What was its original language ? Who and of what country was its author ? Jew or Christian ? And when was the letter written ? These inquiries greatly exercised the minds of scholars abroad, and the theories evoked by the discussion show a wide divergence of opinion.[1] But many of these questions were answered by the discovery in 1866 of a Syriac version of the Apocalypse of Baruch, of which this Epistle formed the concluding portion. This interesting work was brought to light by the industry of A. N. Ceriani, the learned librarian at Milan, to whom we are indebted for the disinterment of that long-lost book, the Assumption of Moses. In a MS. of the sixth century, Ceriani found a complete copy of the Apocalypse, which he published first in a Latin translation, and then in the original Syriac, both in ordinary type, and later (1883) in a photo-lithographed facsimile. This Latin version has been reprinted by Fritzsche, with a few emendations,

verborum Baruchi haud apocrypha, quæ ad tempus quo in Babylonia captivi erant pertinent."—*Chrest. Æthiop.*, Lips. 1866.

[1] See Kneucker, *Das Buch Baruch*, pp. 190 ff.

and is commonly regarded as equivalent to the genuine copy.[1]

Before discussing the contents of the book, a few words must be prefixed on the subject of the author and matters connected therewith.

The earliest quotation of the book occurs in a lost work of Papias, the disciple of St. John, cited by Irenaeus (*Adv. Haeres.* v. 33. 3). Herein it is asserted that in Messiah's days the vine shall have a thousand branches, and each branch shall produce a thousand bunches, and each bunch shall have a thousand grapes, and each grape shall make a cor of wine. Before it was known whence this legend was derived, neologian critics, assuming it to have Christ as its author, found in it a subject of ridicule and offence. It is now shown to occur in the Apocalypse of Baruch, chap. xxix. That the saying was attributed to Christ is easily accounted for. Papias wrote his lost work between 120 and 130 A.D., by which time our book must have become well known among Christians. The mention of Messiah occurs just before the legend; and doubtless persons remembered the story of the vine in connection with the Messiah, and at last quoted it as spoken by Christ Himself.[2] Whether the Apocalypse is referred to in any of the catalogues of sacred books may reasonably be doubted. The term "Baruch," in Pseudo-Athanasius' *Synopsis*, and in the *Stichometria* of Nicephorus, belongs

---

[1] The most available comment on the book is that by Joseph Langen, *Commentatio qua Apocalypsis Baruch anno superiori primum edita illustratur*, Bonnæ 1867.

[2] Ewald, in *Gött. gelehrte Anz.* 1867, p. 1715.

probably to the book so called in the Septuagint version.
There are also other apocryphal books bearing this
name, some of Gnostic, some of Christian origin, and it
is possible that they were known to the writers of the
catalogues. But a portion of the work from early times
formed an integral part of the Syriac Bible, and to this
day is used among the Jacobites in their funeral service.[1]
Its real date, however, can only approximately be determined. Of course, the writer merely assumes the person
of Baruch, the son of Neriah, for literary purposes, not
with any idea of imposing upon the credulity of his
hearers. He announces at the commencement that the
word of the Lord came to him in the twenty-fifth year
of Jechoniah, king of Judah. This at once places the
revelation in an unhistorical region; for Jechoniah lived
eleven years before the destruction of Jerusalem, reigned
only three months, and then was carried captive to
Babylon. And the departure from historical fact is
continued in chap. vi., where it is said that on the next
day after this revelation was made the city was taken
by the Chaldæans. The clue to this apparent mistake is
to be found in the nature of the treatise. It is an
Apocalypse, and in it real events are introduced with
the special purpose of foreshadowing or delineating other
circumstances. Now this first destruction of Jerusalem
adumbrated its final destruction under Titus, and we
cannot doubt that the seer is referring to this latter
calamity under the figure of the first. If he means that
the vision came to him twenty-five years after the
Chaldæan invasion, he intends to affirm that he received

[1] Renan, *Journal des Savants*, April 1877.

the revelation so long after the ruin of the holy city, that is, about 95 A.D. Or the twenty-five years may be dated from the captivity of Jechoniah, which was some eleven years earlier, a mode of reckoning used by Ezekiel (*e.g.* chap. xxix. 17, xxx. 20, xxxi. 1) and the exiles in Chaldæa. This would make the date of our book to be about 84 A.D. That it was composed in early Christian times may be gathered from certain passages which bear evident marks of being no late interpolations, but portions of the original work. Omitting for the present those which contain Messianic teaching, we will quote a few which betray a Christian spirit or some acquaintance with the literature of the New Testament.[1] Chap. x. 13, 14: "Ye bridegrooms, enter not into your chambers; ye women, pray not that ye may bear children; for the barren shall rejoice, and they that have not sons shall be glad, and they that have sons shall be sorrowful" (comp. Matt. xxiv. 19; Luke xxiii. 29). Chap. xxi. 13: "If this were the only life which men have, nothing could be more miserable" (1 Cor. xv. 19). Chap. xxiv. 1: "Lo the days come, and the books shall be opened, in which are written the sins of those who have sinned, and the treasure-houses shall be disclosed in which is gathered the righteousness of those who were justified on earth" (Rev. xx. 12). Chap. xlviii. 34: "There shall be rumours many and messengers not a few; and mighty works shall be shown, and promises made of which some shall be vain and some shall be confirmed" (Matt. xxiv. 24–26). Chap. xx. 1, 2: "The days shall come when the times shall hasten more than

[1] Kneucker, p. 195.

of old, and the hours shall speed on quicker than before, and the years shall pass away more rapidly than now. For this I have sustained Zion, that I might rather hasten and visit the world in her time" ("For the elect's sake those days shall be shortened," Matt. xxiv. 22). Chap. liv. 10: "Blessed is my mother among them that bear children, praised shall she be among women" (Luke i. 42, xi. 27). "For what gain have men lost their life, and what have they who were once on earth given in exchange for their soul" (chap. l.). This is remarkably similar to Matt. xvi. 25, 26, especially as in both passages the pleasures of this life are contrasted with the joys of heaven. The many parallelisms between our book and the Revelation of St. John make it almost a certainty that the seer was acquainted with the latter work.[1] Thus it is said, chaps. xx., xlviii., that the end of the times draws near (Rev. i. 1, 3, xxii. 7); chaps. xxi., lix., that spirits stand before the throne of God like burning lamps (Rev. i. 4, iv. 5); chaps. ii., xiv., that the righteous intercede for sinners before God (Rev. v. 8, viii. 3); chap. xlviii., evil spirits and those who are inspired by them shall work miracles (Rev. xiii. 13, xvi. 14); chap. xxix., the hidden manna shall be given as a reward to the righteous (Rev. ii. 17). Chaps. lxxvii., lxxxvii., an eagle is sent to make a solemn announcement (Rev. viii. 13 ἀετοῦ); chap. xxviii., the number three and a half is used in mystic computation of time (Rev. iii. 9, etc.); chap. iv., the sacred city Jerusalem is taken up to heaven, which St. John sees descending (Rev. iii. 12, xxi. 2). Then there are many expressions which have a Christian

[1] See Langen, p. 4.

sound, as Faith, Faithful, Those who believe, The written law, Future judgment, Promise of the life to come, The new world, The mouth of hell, The place of hope, Saved in his works (Jas. ii. 14). These and suchlike terms do not necessarily imply that the writer was a Christian, which notion his views concerning the Messiah decidedly nullify; but they show that he was conversant with Christian ideas, and had some acquaintance with the new literature which had sprung up under the gospel. It is supposed that the book was written before the Second Book of Esdras (as it is called in our Bibles). That in many points the two works have a remarkable affinity cannot be disputed. The only doubt is, which of the two is prior to the other. Many critics have decided that Baruch borrowed from Ezra; but their arguments are very weak, and Schürer has given reasons for deciding the other way, and assigning priority of composition to our book. According to him, Esdras is of a much more finished character, and shows greater maturity of thought and more lucidity of style—points which intimate a later origin. But the point must be left undecided.

Why the writer has assumed the name of Baruch is not difficult to imagine. The fame of one so well known, and associated with the great prophet Jeremiah, would add an authority to a work which no other personality would have offered. Since, too, as must be allowed, the book has a close and remarkable analogy with what we call the Second Book of Esdras,[1] another reason may be found for the appropriation of the name Baruch. We

---

[1] The two works are compared by Langen, p. 6 ff. See also Ewald, *ut sup.* p. 1707.

need not, with Ewald, hold that the two works are the production of the same author (as indeed there are some facts which militate against this view); or that the Book of Baruch was intended to correct some erroneous opinions of Esdras concerning original sin; but let us suppose that the Second Esdras was well known to our writer. Not wishing to repeat the personification of his predecessor, and yet desirous of giving his composition an authorisation not inferior, he fixed on the follower of Jeremiah as the recipient of the Revelation which he purposed to publish. Whether in this he was consciously treading in the steps of the composer of the apocryphal Book of Baruch is a matter of doubt. Kneucker identifies the two. His view is, that, whereas in chap. lxxvii. the seer was to write two letters, one to the nine-and-a-half tribes to be conveyed by an eagle, and one to the brethren in Babylon to be taken thither by three men, and only the former of these is forthcoming in the Apocalypse, the other is the "Baruch" of the Septuagint. This is described in the Syriac MS. as "the Second Epistle of Baruch the Scribe," the first being that to the nine-and-a-half tribes. Opposed to this conjecture is the fact, that the Book or Epistle of Baruch, according to the Received text, is sent from Babylon to Jerusalem, not from Jerusalem to Babylon, and is generally allowed to be of a much earlier date than the Apocalypse, and of Hebrew origin. The Syriac inscription is probably an unauthorised interpolation intended to show a connection between the two treatises, but warranted neither by internal nor external evidence. That the work was written originally in Greek is evident from an examination of the Syriac version, wherein are found actual Greek words transliterated, as well as what were evidently paronomasias in the original, but which have lost their force in translation.[1] Besides this, the superscription in the Syriac MS. expressly notifies that the work is a translation from the Greek; and there is some evidence of the use of the Septuagint in the references to the Old Testament, as where Baruch is said to have received a revelation under the oak near Hebron (chaps. vi., xlvii., lxxvii.), which idea is probably derived from Gen. xiii. 18: παρὰ τὴν δρῦν τὴν Μαμβρῆ, ἣ ἦν ἐν Χεβρώμ. It is certain, too, that the author's locality is Jerusalem. "Your brethren," he says, chap. lxxx., "are carried captive to Babylon, we, a poor remnant, are left here." Only in Palestine or Alexandria could such a book have been composed in the Greek language. But there is no trace of Judæo-Alexandrian philosophy (such as meets us in Philo's writings and the Book of Wisdom) to be found in the Apocalypse. Like Ecclesiasticus, it takes its stand on the plain dogmatic teaching of the Scriptures and the traditions concerning Messiah then extant. To none but Palestinian Jews, who had seen their holy city destroyed, could this prophecy, which promised restoration and prosperity to their ruined capital, have been addressed. This point being settled, we may fix the date at about A.D. 90. We have noticed above an argument for this date from the author's own statement concerning the time that the revelation was made unto him. Another

---

[1] See Kneucker, p. 191, note 2, and Langen, § vii. We have in the Latin version, "agon et molestia in labore multo," which must be the equivalent of the Greek ἀγών τε καὶ θλίψις ἐν πολλῷ πόνῳ.

may be drawn from Papias' reference to the book. The lost work of this Father was written about A.D. 120–130. Now he quotes this Apocalypse as well known to his readers. Such an acquaintance could hardly have been obtained under thirty years or more. This lands us again at the same period. So does the inference (if legitimate) that it was written after St. Matthew's Gospel and the Revelation of St. John. Nor could it have been composed after the total overthrow of Jerusalem by Adrian (A.D. 135). The destruction of the city by Nebuchadnezzar and by Titus is mentioned, but no hint of a third and more effectual demolition is given. On the contrary, restoration is promised after the second ruin, and the people, groaning under this calamity, are comforted with the thought of speedy and most complete re-establishment. This will place the writing between A.D. 70 and A.D. 135, and help to confirm our previous conclusion.

The book is divided into two unequal parts, the first (chaps. i.–lxxvii.) containing the historical points and the revelation of past and future, the second being the letter to the nine-and-a-half tribes. The former is sent to Babylon, which we must consider to mean Rome; the latter, to the Jews dispersed in the Parthian kingdom, "across the river," as it is expressed, the Euphrates being the boundary line dividing the Eastern empire of the Parthians from the Western empire of the Romans. This distinction between the two great members of the dispersion is found in many other documents of this time, most of which, however, were written with reference to Rome.[1] The entire demolition of ancient Jerusalem,

[1] Ewald, p. 1713.

with all its calamitous consequences, under Adrian led to the loss of much of the literature of the period, the preservation of any portion being probably due to the care of Christians. These carried with them in their wanderings the books which have come down to us or were known to the early Fathers. The letter at the end of the Apocalypse, as being addressed to the Eastern Jews, was soon separated from the other part, and translated into Syriac and widely circulated; while the other section, comprising three-fourths of the whole, was so completely lost that it soon existed only in a Syriac version, which, as has been mentioned, itself remained unknown until quite recently.

In these and such like apocalyptic writings there is a certain similarity which greatly conduces to their correct interpretation. Under the general design of comforting his countrymen in times of trouble and defeat with the hope of the speedy appearance of the Messiah, the seer composes a prophecy which shall embrace the past, the present, and the future. He represents himself as receiving direct communication from God, and enjoined to make known the revelation to men. Placing himself in the distant past, he gives a summary of the history of his people up to the present time, touches lightly on the events that pass before his own eyes, and then in figure and type shadows forth a glorious future which shall abundantly compensate the distress and humiliation now prevalent. This is very nearly an outline of the Apocalypse of Baruch. The first portion, comprising chaps. i.-lxxvii., is divided into seven sections, the close of each section being usually marked by a fast of seven days.[1] *First Section:* In the twenty-fifth year of Jechoniah, king of Judah, it was revealed to Baruch that Jerusalem and her people should be destroyed, and the inhabitants of the land should be carried away captive. Upon his asking whether the end of the world should come then, he is told that the prophecies which spoke of the everlasting covenant referred to a new world and a new Jerusalem which should be eternal. On the next day the Chaldæans took the city; but first, that the enemy might not be able to vaunt their power, the angels destroy the walls, and hide in the earth the precious things of the temple. Zedekiah, the king, is taken captive to Babylon, while Baruch and Jeremiah are left in Jerusalem, and weep and fast seven days (i.-ix.). Then Jeremiah, by Divine command, is sent to Babylon, but Baruch stays amid the ruins of the city to receive a revelation, which comes to him after another seven days' fast (x.-xii.).[2] *Second Section:* As he stands on Mount Zion, a voice falls from heaven, telling him that his people are chastised in mercy in order to lead them to repentance: he complains that good men are no better off than sinners and the heathen, though this world was made for God's people;[3] and the Lord answers, that this

---

[1] So 2 Esdr. v. 13, vi. 31. In other works of this kind the fast is usually of three days' duration (three weeks in Dan. x. 2). Comp. Assumpt. Mos. ix. 6; 2 Macc. xiii. 12; Test. XII. Patr. *Test. Jos.* 3.

[2] Historical truth is here violated. Jeremiah was compelled to go to Egypt, while Baruch in the course of time, according to Jewish tradition, made his way to Babylon. The seer has manipulated facts to suit the requirements of his Apocalypse. Comp. Jer. xliii. and Bar. i.

[3] This notion is found, 2 Esdr. vi. 55, ix. 13; Assumpt. Mos. i. 12.

life is short and full of trouble, but the life to come
shall set right all present anomalies. And he bids
Baruch prepare himself for a new revelation (xiii.–xx.).
Third Section: At the end of seven days the seer comes
to the appointed place, and asks impatiently to know the
meaning and the issue of God's dealings with men. He
is told that he is ignorant, but is comforted with the
hope that the end is near, when good and evil shall meet
their reward; and the signs that shall precede this final
time are enumerated under twelve divisions, concluding
with the days of Messiah and His two advents—the
first to establish an earthly kingdom, the second to
manifest His eternal reign, when He shall raise up those
who have slept in hope, and reward them with heavenly
glory. To the question as to the extent of the tribulation which shall precede this time, the seer is told that
it will affect the whole earth. Then Baruch summons a
meeting of the elders, and announces to them that Zion
shall be destroyed, but shall be rebuilt again; yet again
it shall be ruined, and for the last time restored gloriously
so as to last for ever (xxi.–xxxiv.). *Fourth Section:*
Then the prophet, as he sleeps amid the ruins of the
Holy Place, sees in a vision on one side a mighty forest
girt by mountains, and on the other a vine, from whose
roots issued a placid streamlet. Anon this streamlet
became a great river, and it overthrew the mountain,
and tore up the forest, leaving of it nothing but one
cedar, which also at length it destroyed. And the vine
and the stream exulted over the fallen cedar, and the
vine grew more and more, and all the plain was filled
with flowers that fade not. The seer is told that hereby

is signified the fate of four kingdoms which have afflicted Zion, the last of which, the most powerful and most evil of them all, is to perish before the arms of Messiah. "Then shall be revealed the chieftainship of my Messiah, who is like a spring and a vine, and He on His appearing will annihilate that congregation. And that cedar which thou sawest is the last prince (*dux ultimus*) who is left alive. He shall be brought in chains before Messiah on Mount Zion, and there be put to death" (xxxv.–xlvi.). *Fifth Section:* After another seven days' fast Baruch tells the people of his approaching departure, and urges them to continue faithful to the law, explaining to them the retribution of the world to come. Another seven days' fast intervenes, and then Baruch, in answer to his prayer, is told of the tribulations that are to come upon the earth, and of the manner of the resurrection both of the evil and the good, and their punishment and reward (xlvii.–lii.). *Sixth Section:* After this, he sees a vision of alternate dark and bright waters, which is explained as a record of Israel's history from Adam to Messiah (xlviii.–lxxi.). The glories of Messiah's eternal kingdom are then unfolded. Baruch is informed that shortly he will be taken from earth, though not by death (liii.–lxxvi.).[1] *Seventh Section:* He again announces his departure to his friends, prays for their welfare, and on the twenty-first day of the eighth month writes two letters, one to the exiles in Babylon, which he sends by the hands of men, and one to the nine-and-a-half tribes beyond the river, which he entrusts to an eagle. The latter Epistle is given in full, and concludes the book.

[1] Comp. 2 Esdr. xiv. 9, 49 (Fr.).

In it he comforts his distant brethren under their trials with the remembrance that God has not cast off His love for them, but is only temporarily chastening them for their disobedience. Nebuchadnezzar indeed has been permitted to afflict them grievously, but it was the Lord who destroyed the forts and walls; and He also hid the sacred vessels that the heathen should not rejoice over them. All shall be changed ere long; the day is soon coming when the Gentiles shall be punished for their iniquity, and Israel shall be rewarded; only let them prepare for the life to come by virtue and obedience, and all shall be well with them (lxxvii.-lxxxvii.). The other Epistle is not given, and some, as I mentioned above, have considered the Septuagintal "Baruch" to be the missing document. But as this theory is inadmissible, we must deem either that the writing is wholly lost, or that the two Epistles were identical. There is nothing improbable in the latter supposition. Their tenor would naturally be similar, and it is difficult to see what more the seer could have said than he had already expressed in the extant letter. The conclusion of the book may have told how Baruch was taken from the earth, after he had seen in a vision all the regions of the world, as it had been promised him.

Such being a general view of the contents of the Apocalypse, we can now enter more particularly into some of the matters contained in it. And first, there are some puzzles connected with numbers which must be mentioned. Two such riddles confront us, a shorter and a longer.[1] The former concerns the end of the

[1] Ewald expounds them with zest, *Gött. gel. Anz.* pp. 170-8.

present world. This is to happen at the conclusion of "two parts weeks of seven weeks."[1] The seven weeks, which are probably derived from Dan. ix. 25, imply an interval of 49 years, which must be reckoned from the destruction of Jerusalem, A.D. 70. The expression "two parts" means two-thirds, as in Hebrew and Latin. Two-thirds of this period, say 33 years, would land us in the reign of Trajan (A.D. 98–117). In the chapter preceding this prophecy the seer foretells a course of twelve calamities, each more crushing than its predecessor, which should happen before the end. These may be well understood of events up to the death of Domitian (A.D. 96). But all this is pure speculation, and calculations founded hereon cannot be trusted. The longer riddle is on safer ground, being a history of past events in the form of prophecy (chaps. liii.–lxxiv.). The seer beholds a vast cloud rising from the sea, and discharging black and clear water alternately twelve times in succession. Under this image of dark and bright waters following each other in succession, the writer represents the history of man from Adam to the first destruction of Jerusalem. The alternation of light and shade, prosperity and adversity, reward and punishment, in human records, is compressed into twelve great periods, the character of which is marked by the changed appearance of the waters in the vision. "And it came to pass," says the

[1] "Mensura autem et supputatio temporis illius erunt duæ partes hebdomades septem hebdomadarum" (chap. xxviii.). This somewhat obscure sentence may be intended to signify that this time of tribulation is divided into seven parts which are weeks, and into two parts which are also of septenary dimensions. So Langen, p. 16.

seer, "that the cloud began to rain down upon the earth the waters with which it was charged. And I saw that the aspect of the waters was not one; for first they were black for a time, and then they became bright, but these were scanty; and afterwards I saw black waters a second time and then again bright; and this was done twelve times; but the black were always more abundant than the bright. Last of all, the cloud poured forth waters blacker than ever, and fire mingled with them. This fire was lightning, which gave shine to the whole earth, and healed the regions on which the dark waters had fallen. Then twelve streams arose from the sea, and subjected themselves to this lightning." Upon the seer praying for the interpretation of this mystery, the angel Ramiel is sent to explain it thus: "Whereas thou sawest first black waters descend upon the earth, this is the sin which Adam, the first man, sinned. For since by his transgression came into the world death, which was not in his time, and sorrow and pain, and labour, what could there be blacker than these things? Adam endangered his own soul and the souls of other men, so that all who lived on earth perished in the Flood. These are the first black waters. And whereas after these thou didst see bright waters, this denotes the advent of Abraham and his son and his sons' sons and those who are like unto them; because at that time, though there was no written law among them, yet the commandments were duly observed, and faith in the judgment to come arose, and the hope of a new world was then built up, and the promise of the life hereafter was planted in men's hearts. These are the first bright waters which thou sawest." And thus the angel expounds the signification of the vision unto the first destruction of Jerusalem and onwards to Messiah's time. Then we have the doings of subsequent sinful generations, especially the Egyptians, contrasted with Moses, Joshua, and the Sinaitic revelations; the works of the Amorites and magicians contrasted with the times of David and Solomon; the revolt of Jeroboam and the sins and punishments of his successors set against the piety of Hezekiah and his defeat of Sennacherib; the ungodliness of Manasseh against the integrity of Josiah. The eleventh downpour represents the tribulation in Baruch's own time; and the twelfth bright water adumbrates the restoration of Israel. The last dark water represents the tumult and tribulation which will come upon the earth before the final advent of Messiah. In this interpretation some points are noteworthy. There is a strange opinion about Manasses, king of Judah (chap. lxiv.). It is said that his impiety was so heinous that he was condemned to the penal fire. Ignoring the old tradition of his repentance and consequent acceptance with God (2 Chron. xxxiii. 12, 13, 19), of a belief in which the apocryphal "Prayer of Manasses" is an evidence, Pseudo-Baruch testifies that though his prayer was heard, he himself was lost. "When he was placed in the brazen horse," probably an image connected with the worship of Moloch, "the figure was melted with the ardent heat, and he perished therein, a sign of the end that awaited him. For he had not lived a perfect life, nor was he worthy; but by this sign he learned by whom he was to be tormented hereafter. For He who can reward is also able to punish." The legend found in the *Apostolical*

Constitutions and elsewhere[1] gives a very different result. According to these authorities, at his prayer, the image fell to pieces, and he escaped unharmed, returned to Jerusalem, and lived afterwards piously and prosperously. The opinion of Manasses' damnation in spite of his prayer is, as far as we know, peculiar to Pseudo-Baruch. Concerning the angels who "kept not their first estate," our seer holds the notion that they fell by their commerce with the daughters of men. "Adam," he says, "imperilled not only his own soul but the angels also. For at the time when he was created they had full liberty, and some of them descended and had intercourse with women; and then they who thus offended were tormented in chains. But the rest of the host of angels, an innumerable company, kept themselves pure." This interpretation of Gen. vi. 4 is, in the main, one that is common enough in Jewish, and indeed in Christian, commentaries. But it has a special feature which differentiates it from other glosses. The writer seems to teach that, as the tree of knowledge was the trial of Adam's faith and constancy, so the beauty of mortal women was appointed to be the probation of angels; and that the difference between good and bad angels consisted in the continence of the one and the unchastity of the other. The "tormenting in chains" reminds us of 2 Pet. ii. 4 and Jude 6, and is confirmed by many expressions in the Book of Enoch.[2]

---

[1] *Apost. Constit.* ii. 22; Suidas, *s.v.* Manasses; Fritzsche, *Exeg. Handb. zu d. Apokr.* i. p. 158.

[2] *E.g.* v. 16, x. 4 ff., xiv. 4, etc. Such passages as these substantiate the reading σειραῖς, *chains*, not σιροῖς, *dens*, in 2 Pet. ii.

There are some other peculiarities in this book which are interesting. The seer claims to have revelations made to him in two ways, by an angel, and by the voice of God. The angel he names Ramiel, "who presides over the visions of truth" (chap. lv.), and who tells him (chap. lxiii.) that he was the agent in the destruction of the host of Sennacherib in Hezekiah's reign. The name of this angel is not found elsewhere except in the Syriac version of 4 Esdr. iv. 36, v. 20, where the Latin has Jeremiel in most MSS., but in one (Turicensis) Huriel. Probably the name Ramiel is a corruption of Jeremiel, which word was formed from Jeremiah, who might well be called the prophet of truth, and give his name to the angel of the vision. The close connection between Baruch and Jeremiah makes this supposition very probable. In other passages of Esdras (iv. 1, v. 20, x. 28), Uriel is the heavenly messenger, which is in accordance with statements in the Book of Enoch (*e.g.* chaps. ix., xx., lxxiv.), where an angel of this name is often introduced. But it is very possible that the three names refer to the same heavenly being. Revelation by the direct voice of God seems to be an unusual claim on the part of Jewish apocalyptic writers. Inspiration by Bathkol, the daughter of the voice, indeed is asserted by the Rabbis up to the time of the composition of the Mishna; but this was never considered to be the voice of God Himself, but that of an angel, His agent or minister. Thus when the voice from heaven came to our Lord (John xii. 28), some of the people supposed that an angel spoke to Him; when God called to Moses from the bush, it was an angel who addressed him; and when the Law was uttered from Sinai, it was given "by the disposition of angels."[1] But Pseudo-Baruch especially distinguishes the heavenly voice from the revelation by the angel. "It came to pass after this," he says (chap. xxii.), "the heavens were opened, and I saw, and power was given unto me, and a voice from the highest was heard, and He said unto me." It is not till some time afterwards that Ramiel is said to interpret the vision of the waters. Langen supposes that the seer, being acquainted with St. Matthew's Gospel, took the hint of the narrative in chap. iii., and thus made the voice come immediately from God. I should think rather that the writer used the ambiguity of expression in the Old Testament to enhance the dignity of the revelation he was making. To do this he had no need to imitate St. Matthew's account.

On the subject of original sin our seer is thought to oppose the more orthodox doctrine enunciated by Esdras. Both writers speak of the evil introduced into the world by Adam's sin, but they diverge when treating of its effects on his descendants. While Esdras teaches that Adam communicated an infected nature to his posterity,[2]

---

[1] See Acts vii. 53; Heb. ii. 2. Joseph. *Antiq.* xv. 5. 3: ἡμῶν τὰ κάλλιστα τῶν δογμάτων καὶ τὰ ὁσιώτατα τῶν ἐν τοῖς νόμοις δι' ἀγγέλων παρὰ τοῦ Θεοῦ μαθόντων.

[2] "O thou Adam, what hast thou done? for though it was thou that sinned, thou art not fallen alone, but we all that come of thee" (2 Esdr. vii. 48). "Unto Adam Thou gavest commandment to love Thy way; which he transgressed; and immediately Thou appointedst death in him and in his generations" (iii. 7). "The first Adam bearing a wicked heart transgressed, and was overcome; and so be all they that are born of him. Thus infirmity was made permanent" (iii. 21, 22).

Pseudo-Baruch sometimes affirms that the sin of Adam is transferred to others by imitation alone. "If," he says (chap. liv.), "Adam first sinned, and brought untimely death upon all men; yet also they who are born from him, each one of them hath prepared future torment for his own soul; and again, each one hath chosen future glory for himself. Adam was the cause of guilt to his own soul only; but we, each of us, are the Adam to our own souls." It is curious to trace here indications of that doctrine which, developed into Pelagianism, became the cause of serious controversy in the Christian Church. The received maxim among the Jews was that the whole world was comprised in Adam and sinned in his sin. The expression in Job xiv. 4 ("Who can bring a clean thing out of an unclean? not one"), whether we take it interrogatively or optatively, comes to the same thing, and intimates that the old belief obtained: "Behold, I was shapen in iniquity, and in sin did my mother conceive me" (Ps. li. 5).

Let us turn now to the doctrine of the Messiah contained in our book. As we know that the apostles and early believers expected the second coming of Christ to happen shortly, so Pseudo-Baruch looks for the appearance of Messiah in the course of a few years. In their utter dejection and distress, seated amid the ruins of their beloved Jerusalem, the sorrowing Jews could find comfort in nothing but the hope of a speedy restoration under the leadership of Messiah. The actual time of this Parousia is concealed under a veil of symbolical words; but it is to be preceded by exceeding heavy calamities, confirming the saying "that man's extremity is God's opportunity." In his vision the seer beholds a kingdom (Rome), the power of which shall be greater and more evil than any before it; and it shall rule supreme for many ages and be highly exalted; in it truth shall not dwell, but all who are stained with crime shall find refuge therein, as evil beasts hide themselves in the forest. "And it shall come to pass when the time of its fall shall approach, then the dominion of Messiah shall be revealed, and He shall root up the multitude of that kingdom" (chap. xxxix.). But before that event, "the harvest of the good seed and the bad shall come, and the Almighty will bring upon the earth and its inhabitants and upon its rulers confusion of spirit and stupor of heart. And they shall hate one another and provoke one another to battle, and the base-born shall lord over those of high degree, and the mean shall be exalted above men of renown, and the many shall be delivered to the few, and those who were nothing shall rule the mighty, and the poor shall be more than the rich, and the wicked shall be raised above the heroic, and wise men shall hold their peace and fools shall speak: the thought of men shall then not be confirmed, nor the counsel of the Almighty, nor the hope of those that hope. And when what has been foretold shall come to pass, on all men shall come confusion, and some of them shall fall by the sword in battle, and some shall perish in great tribulation, and some shall be ensnared by their own friends. But the Most High shall reveal it to those nations whom He prepared before, and they shall come and fight with the leaders who shall then remain. And it shall come to pass that whosoever shall escape from the war shall die in the earthquake, and whosoever shall escape from the earthquake shall be consumed in the fire, and whosoever shall escape from the fire shall perish in the famine. And it shall come to pass that whosoever shall escape from all these evils, of the conquerors and of the conquered, shall be delivered into the hands of my servant Messiah. For the earth shall devour the inhabitants thereof" (chap. lxx.). Other signs are mentioned (chap. xlviii.), some of which, as we have seen above, have a striking similarity to those which our Lord foretold should usher in the last day. No safety shall anywhere be found except in the Holy Land, which "shall have pity on its own children and protect them in that day" (chap. lxxi.). And then shall Messiah begin to be revealed.

In his idea of the reign of Messiah, Pseudo-Baruch takes a different line from Esdras and other apocalyptical writers. The common notion of a great Leader, who by a course of uninterrupted triumph should restore and enhance the glory of the depressed Israelites, does not satisfy his hopes. This is only one and a partial view of the effects of this Divine interference. The Messiah has a twofold kingdom, an earthly one which passes away, and a heavenly one which is everlasting. Such a question as that of the apostles (Acts i. 6): "Lord, wilt Thou at this time restore again the kingdom to Israel?" spoke only of temporal restitution and sovereignty, and would not have intimated the full hope that we see to have been conceived by our seer. Of a suffering Messiah he has no notion; nor does he give any trace of the later belief in two Messiahs, a Messiah ben David of whom were predicted glory and triumph, and a Messiah ben Joseph to whose lot fell all the foretold sufferings and woe. His Messiah is one only person viewed at different times and under a different aspect. First He comes as the great earthly conqueror, who was to emancipate the people from the dominion of Rome, punish their enemies, and restore the Jews to more than pristine glory. In this earthly kingdom all the Israelites who are then alive shall have their part; and while those who have oppressed them shall perish, they who have never known them or had connection with them, and they who have joined themselves unto their God as proselytes, shall be saved, being in subjection to the ancient people. This dominion shall be established in the Holy Land, when the last leader of the enemy is brought in chains to Zion, and is there condemned and executed by Messiah. The glories of this kingdom, in accordance more or less with ancient prophecy, are thus described (chap. lxxiii.): "It shall come to pass when He shall have humbled whatsoever is in the world, and sat down in peace for ever upon the throne of His kingdom, then shall He be revealed in happiness, and a great calm shall ensue. Health shall descend like dew, and sickness shall pass away, and care and distress and groaning shall no more be found among men; and joy shall pace through all the earth. No one shall die before he hath filled his days, no sudden calamity shall happen to any. Trials, accusations, contentions, revenge, bloodshed, avarice, envy, hatred, and all such things shall be utterly abolished. For these are the things which have filled this world with evil and vexed the life of men. Then the wild beasts shall come forth from the forests and minister unto men; and asps and snakes shall issue from their holes to become a little one's plaything. Women shall be delivered without pain. The reaper shall not be wearied, the builder shall feel no fatigue, for all works shall co-operate with the labourers in that time of peace." Like other apocalyptic writers, Pseudo-Baruch represents the happiness of Messiah's kingdom under the figure of a splendid banquet, in which mighty animals shall be served up as the food of the righteous guests. The Lord says to him, chap. xxix.: "Behemoth shall be brought to light from his place, and Leviathan shall ascend from the sea, two great creatures which I made on the fifth day of the creation, and have reserved unto this time;[1] and then they shall be for food for them that are left. The earth also shall give her fruits, ten thousand for one." Then comes the passage about the vine (quoted by Papias) given above. He proceeds: "Those who have hungered shall be gladdened, and they shall again see prodigies daily. For spirits[2] shall go forth from my presence every morning to bring the odour of aromatic fruits, and at the close of day clouds dropping the dew of health. And then shall fall a second time the treasure of manna, and they shall eat thereof in those years, since these are they which have come to the end of the time."

Such is our seer's description of the earthly reign of Messiah. But we may note that in two points he differs from many of the writers of Apocalypses. First he

[1] See 2 Esdr. vi. 49, where instead of "Enoch," the Syr. and Ethiop. version, read "Behemoth." Book of Enoch, lix. 7 ff.
[2] *Spiritus;* or is it "winds"?

takes a more liberal view of the Gentile world than his contemporaries. While others were content to believe that salvation was of the Jews, and belonged to them exclusively, Pseudo-Baruch admits certain of the Gentiles to share the glories of Messiah's kingdom. Proselytes from the heathen, and any that had taken no active part in oppressing Israel, or from their remoteness of position knew nothing of God's people, would be allowed to participate in the blessings of the Messianic reign, provided that they came in humbly as subjects of the heavenly Prince. It is interesting to observe an abatement of that jealousy which so frequently meets us in the Gospels, where an extension of God's favour to the Gentiles is reprobated by the Jews as an opinion profane and detestable. Our seer has lighted upon a great truth, though he knew not its full import, how that the Christ should be not only the glory of Israel, but, as the aged Simeon believed, a light to lighten the Gentiles, and to be for salvation unto the ends of the earth.[1]

The other point in which our seer differs from many Hebrew writers is this: he allows a participation in Messiah's earthly kingdom to those Jews only who are alive at His appearing. The common opinion among the Jews was that the righteous dead should rise from the grave to inherit His glory: this was to be their privilege; they were to obtain part in the first resurrection which was quite distinct from the general resurrection at the day of judgment. Of this opinion Pseudo-Baruch makes no mention. "Messiah," he says,

[1] Luke ii. 32 ; Acts xiii. 47.

" shall protect the people who are found in the appointed place," *i.e.* Zion.[1]

How long this earthly kingdom is supposed to last is nowhere distinctly stated. The seer speaks of the time of Messiah's appearance being fulfilled (chap. xxx.), before He returns again in glory, but he does not assign any definite period to His earthly sojourn. The notion of a reign of a thousand years, which is generally supposed to have originated in Judaism and to have passed from thence to Christianity, does not appear in our book. There is a passage in Esdras[2] which reckons the duration at four hundred years. This is probably derived from the consideration that the period of affliction in Egypt was to be compensated by a similar period of refreshment and rest. But Pseudo-Baruch gives no confirmation to this opinion. Nor does he assert with Esdras[3] that Messiah shall die. He passes over this event in silence, and proceeds to picture His return in glory in the fulness of time. At His coming all men shall arise again, not Jews only, but all men; and not the righteous only, but sinners also. " To the dust it shall be said, Restore that which is not thine, and place thou here all that thou hast kept safe till now " (chap. xlii.). " And the storehouses [4] shall be opened wherein have been kept the souls of the righteous, and they shall

[1] Comp. 2 Esdr. vi. 25, ix. 8, xiii. 16 ff., 49.
[2] 2 Esdr. vii. 28. Comp. Gen. xv. 13 and Ps. xc. 15.
[3] 2 Esdr. vii. 29 : "After these years shall my Son Christ die." This clause is wanting in the Arabic version, and many doubt its genuineness.
[4] *Promptuaria.* The word often occurs in 2 Esdr. in the same connection.

come forth, and the multitude of souls shall appear in one concordant assembly, and the first shall rejoice and the last shall not be sad, for they shall know that the end of all the times has come. But the souls of sinners, when they shall see all things, shall pine away the more; for they know that their punishment has come and the hour of their damnation" (chap. xxx.). "The earth shall restore the dead which it had to keep, changing nothing in their form; but as it received them so it shall restore them, and as I [the Lord] have committed them unto it, thus shall it place them before me. And they shall recognise each other" (chap. l.). Here again Pseudo-Baruch is not in agreement with the usual opinion of his contemporaries. Josephus[1] asserts that the Pharisees believed that the souls of the righteous alone would rise again, while the wicked would remain in prison everlastingly, suffering there eternal punishment. This dogma probably could not be truly predicated of all Pharisees,[2] but it was undoubtedly held by a large majority of Jews. The Book of Enoch,[3] which represents the current belief, teaches that the souls of sinners shall suffer vengeance without being united again to their bodies, but the righteous shall be raised, body and soul, to participate in the blessings of Messiah's reign. And such, with certain modifications, was the opinion that generally obtained in these and later times; while Pseudo-Baruch teaches that synchronally with

---

[1] *Antiq.* xviii. 1. 3; *Bell. Jud.* ii. 8. 14.
[2] Comp. Acts xxiv. 15. Schoettgen, *Hor. Hebr. in* Matt. xxii. 29, and *in* Joh. vi. 36.
[3] See xcviii., ciii., cviii.

Messiah's return shall be the general resurrection, the judgment, and the eternal reign. Whether the period between the first and second advent of Messiah corresponds with the millennium of St. John in Rev. xx. is a question which we cannot now discuss. That no mention of the first resurrection is made in our book is a fact which separates it from Jewish and Christian speculations. One thing is plain, that what others call the second or general resurrection is the great event which Pseudo-Baruch foresees as appertaining to Messiah's second appearance in glory.

In presenting the details of this resurrection, the seer says, as St. Paul, that all will be changed, the aspect of the evil becoming more horrible, and that of the righteous more glorious; the one being transformed to the splendour of the angels, the other terror-stricken by fearful sights and visions; the one made bright and beautiful to receive the blessings of the eternal world, the other tantalised with the sight of the blessed and sent away to punishment.[1] On the subject of the happiness of the saved he enlarges in many passages. "They shall see the world which is now invisible to them; they shall see the time which is now hidden from them. And time shall never more grow old to them; for they shall dwell in the high places of that world, and shall be like unto the angels and equal to the stars, and shall be transformed into all the beauty that they can desire, and changed from light unto the radiance of glory. In their sight shall be unfolded the breadths of Paradise, and there shall be displayed before them the comeliness of the

[1] Chaps. xxxii., li.

majesty of the living creatures which are beneath the throne,[1] and all the hosts of angels who now are holden by my word from being seen, and holden by my command that they should stay in their own places till the time of their appearance is come. Thus the excellency of the righteous shall surpass that of the angels. For the first shall succeed the last, those for whom they waited, and the last those whom they heard to have passed by; and they have been delivered from this world of sorrow, and have laid down the weight of care." If it might seem an extravagant belief in the mouth of a Jew that, admitted to the life beyond the grave, he should be more excellent than the angels, yet his hope is far inferior to that of the Christian. We are told that we shall see God, behold "the King in His beauty." The Jewish prophet holds out no hope of this blessed vision. The righteous shall see highest orders of angels, and all the hosts of heaven, yea, the glory of God, the light in which He dwells; but Himself no eye of man, however holy and blessed, shall behold.[2]

The scene of this happiness is the new world which God shall create especially for His true servants. And that the prophecies of the glory of Jerusalem may be rightly understood, the seer is taught that the earthly city may be destroyed once and again, but it shall be renewed in glory, and receive an everlasting crown (chap. xxxii.). "Dost thou remember," says the Lord, "what that city is of which I said, 'I have graven thee

---

[1] These are elsewhere (chap. xxi.) called "the powers that stand before God," and seem to mean the highest angels, the seven mentioned Tob. xii. 15 and Rev. viii. 2.

[2] So in the Book of Enoch xiv. 8. 2 Esdr. vi. 64 (Fr.): "Primo vident in gaudio multo gloriam Altissimi qui assumit eas."

upon the palm of my hands'?" No earthly city this, but a heavenly, mystic one, prepared before the world was made, shown to Adam before he fell in Paradise, but withdrawn, as Eden itself, after he had sinned.[1] Abraham, too, beheld it when he kept watch between his victims slain; and to Moses it was revealed on Mount Sinai, when he received the communication touching the Tabernacle and its appurtenances. Since then it has been kept in the secret place of God till the time for its disclosure should arrive.[2] This glorious city shall be the abode of the righteous. But the seer, unlike St. John, attempts not to describe its splendours; no revelation of these particulars is made unto him, and he leaves it in its beauty a wonder and a mystery. The Paradise, in which he locates both the throne of God and the home of the blessed, is not the place in the other world where the souls of the just await the day of judgment, which was its usual signification among the Jews, but heaven itself, and, as one would suppose, the so-called third heaven. St. Paul, in the account of his own rapture (2 Cor. xii.), seems to make a distinction between Paradise and the third heaven, speaking of being on one occasion "caught up even to the third heaven," and on another, "being caught up into Paradise." But in this, as in some other points before noticed, Pseudo-Baruch does not adhere closely to the received opinion,

[1] In 2 Esdr. iii. 6, Paradise is said to have been created before the earth.
[2] 2 Esdr. vii. 26: "The bride (or city) shall appear, and she coming forth shall be seen, that now is withdrawn from the earth." xiii. 36: "Zion shall come, and shall be showed to all men, being prepared and builded." Comp. Rev. xxi. 2.

but follows another tradition, or takes an original view.

With regard to the punishment of the wicked, the seer holds this opinion. They shall first see the glory of the righteous, and then shall be led away to punishment,—their home shall be in the eternal fire (chap. xliv.). Of the annihilation of the condemned other writers have spoken;[1] but nothing of the kind is found in our book. Sinners are said, indeed, to waste away ("tabescere"), but this is only an expression to characterise their torment, which they are transfigured to endure.[2]

Such are the chief points of interest in this book; and they are useful in many ways, but chiefly as conveying instruction on the tenets and expectations of the Jews about the period of the first Christian century, and exhibiting the contrast between real and spurious revelations.

THE TESTAMENTS OF THE TWELVE PATRIARCHS.

The work thus named has a special interest for Englishmen, as having been first made known in this country, in the middle of the thirteenth century, by the celebrated Grosseteste or Greathead, Bishop of Lincoln, who, with the aid of a clerk of St. Albans, translated it from Greek into Latin. It had been

---

[1] Pseudo-Clem. *Hom.* iii. 6: εἶναι γὰρ εἰς ἀεὶ οὐκ ἔτι δύνανται οἱ εἰς τὸν ἀεὶ καὶ μόνον ἀσιβήσαντες θεόν. Thus also, Ascens. Isa. iv. 18.

[2] "Fiet enim aspectus eorum qui nunc impie agunt pejor quam est, ut sustineant supplicium."—Chap. li.

brought to his notice by one John de Basingstokes, Archdeacon of Leicester, who, while studying at Athens, had lighted upon this treatise, and thought so highly of it that he induced the bishop to obtain a copy of it from Greece. The credulous Matthew Paris, who supplies these particulars, asserts roundly that the document formed part of the sacred canon, but had been suppressed by the Jews on account of the evident prophecies of Christ contained therein.[1] This, of course, is a mistake. What is certain is, that it was well known in the early Church, was honoured and quoted by early Christian writers, and was named in some catalogues of sacred books. In the synopsis of Sacred Scripture which is found among the writings of Athanasius it is mentioned as one of the Apocrypha in conjunction with the Book of Enoch, the Assumption of Moses, and some others; and it is referred to in the *Stichometria* of Nicephorus of Constantinople. It is also probably named in the Acts of one or two minor Councils held in Rome and Spain in the fifth and sixth centuries. But there is no doubt that Tertullian and Origen knew and quoted the book. Thus the former[2] writes: "For to my mind Paul was promised even in Genesis. Among the tropes and prophetical benedictions on his sons, Jacob, turning

---

[1] Matt. Par. *Hist. Anglor.*, quoted by Mr. Sinker, whose most valuable and interesting work has supplied many of the materials of this paper. The title of this book is the following: *Testamenta XII. Patriarcharum: ad fidem codicis Cantabrigiensis edita: Accedunt Lectiones cod. Oxoniensis. The Testaments of the XII. Patriarchs: An attempt to estimate their Historic and Dogmatic Worth*, Cambridge 1869. Appendix, containing a collation of the Roman and Patmos MSS., and Bibliographical notes, Cambridge 1879.

[2] *Adv. Marcionem*, v. 1.

to Benjamin, said, 'Benjamin, a ravening wolf in the morning shall devour, and in the evening shall give victual.' For he foresaw that from the tribe of Benjamin would some day arise Paul, a ravening wolf in the morning devouring,—that is, at first laying waste the Lord's flock, as a persecutor of the Church,—and afterwards giving victual at evening,—that is, as time declined feeding the sheep of Christ as the Teacher of the nations." This is evidently a reproduction of the idea of a passage in the Testaments, where Benjamin thus addresses his children:[1] "I shall no longer be called a ravening wolf on account of your ravages, but a worker of the Lord, distributing food to them that work what is good. And one shall rise up from my seed in the latter times, beloved of the Lord, hearing His voice, enlightening with new knowledge all the Gentiles, bursting in upon Israel for salvation with the light of knowledge, tearing it away from it like a wolf, and giving it to the synagogue of the Gentiles; and until the consummation of the ages shall he be in the synagogue of the Gentiles and among their rulers as a strain of music in the mouth of all. And he shall be inscribed in the holy books, both his work and his word, and he shall be a chosen one of God for ever; and because of him my father Jacob instructed me saying, He shall fill up that which lacketh of thy tribe." Similarly in another place Tertullian says:[2] "Paul, from a persecutor becoming an apostle, who first shed the blood of the Church, and afterwards changing his sword for a pen, and turning his falchion into a plough, even Benjamin, a ravening wolf, then himself

[1] The translation is Mr. Sinker's.   [2] *Scorpiace*, xiii.

bringing victual, according to Jacob, he commendeth martyrdom and what he deems desirable." Origen cites the book by name.[1] "Nay," he says, "but in a certain little book, which is called the Testament of the Twelve Patriarchs, although it is not contained in the canon, we find the thought that by individual sinners we ought to understand individual Satans." This idea occurs in the Testament of Reuben (chaps. ii. and iii.), who warns his sons that all sins are the embodiment of the seven spirits of evil which he specifies. There is possibly, too, an allusion to our work in Jerome,[2] who writes: "And if so it please you, you may read the fictitious revelations of all the patriarchs and prophets; and when you have studied them, go and sing in the women's weaving shops." It is possible that the notion of Christ's descent from the tribes of Levi and Judah, found first in Irenæus, may have been derived from our book, where it occurs frequently. The passage alluded to is found in Iren *Fragm.* xvii. (ed. Harvey, ii. 487): "From them Christ was foreshadowed and acknowledged and born; for in Joseph He was foreshadowed; from Levi and Judah He was born according to the flesh as king and priest; and through Simeon He was acknowledged in the temple." These are nearly all the references to the book which occur. For many centuries it fell completely out of sight, and, indeed, nothing was heard of it till, as mentioned above, the Bishop of Lincoln took it in hand. But the Greek text did not profit by the invention of printing in its early stage, nor was it till quite the end of the seventeenth century that it was published in an

[1] *Hom. in Josuam*, xv. 6. [2] *Adv. Vigilant.* c. vi.

available form. In 1698 Grabe printed the Greek text entire in his *Spicilegium Patrum et Hæreticorum* from a MS. left to the University Library of Cambridge by Archbishop Parker, and containing that prelate's autograph. This is probably the original from which Grosseteste's version was made. It was reprinted by Fabricius in his *Codex Pseudepigraphus*, and by Gallandi in the first volume of the *Bibliotheca Veterum Patrum*, and later by Migne in his *Patrologia Græca*. There is only one other Greek MS. of the Testaments existing in England, and that is one in the Bodleian Library at Oxford—a paper quarto of the fourteenth century, presented to the University by its then Chancellor, the Earl of Pembroke, in 1629. Quite lately two other MSS. have been examined, one in the Vatican Library, of the thirteenth century, and one in a monastery at Patmos, belonging to the sixteenth century, which has been noticed by Tischendorf.[1] A careful collation of these MSS., and of some transcripts made from them, has been published by the Rev. Robert Sinker, and in his hands the text has assumed as great an accuracy as is likely to be attained till other aids are supplied from continental sources. Of versions, especially in the Latin language, there are numerous specimens. Mr. Sinker mentions no less than forty MSS. of the Latin version, and numerous published editions dating from 1510–1520. The work has been translated into most modern languages, including French, German, Dutch, Icelandic, etc. The first English version was printed by John Daye in 1577, long before the Greek text was published, the earliest

---

[1] *Aus dem heiligen Lande*, p. 341.

Latin translation having appeared some sixty years previously. This English edition was the work of A. G., the initials probably of Arthur Golding, and was continually reproduced in subsequent years. Another version, rendered from the text of Grabe and Fabricius, was put forth by W. Whitson in his *Collection of Authentical Records, belonging to the O. and N. Testaments*, 1727. Of late years a new version has appeared in the second volume of Clark's *Ante-Nicene Christian Library*. This translation is the work of Mr. Sinker.

The language of the original work was certainly Greek; that is, the writing which we now possess is probably that which came from the hand of the author. It is at the same time quite possible that a Hebrew document may have existed on which the present was more or less based. But of this no trace has ever been found; nor does the present writing bear any of the characteristics of a version, though it is thoroughly impregnated with Hebrew thought. In it we find an employment of the Septuagint: and there are certain *paronomasias* which could not have been derived from a Hebrew original, and many expressions which appertain to Greek philosophy, and have no equivalent in the Hebrew. We may conclude that the work as we have it is essentially Greek, and can be traced to no other source.

Having thus sketched the literary history of the Testaments, we may next glance at its contents, and shall then be able to consider its origin and date, and to mention some of the features most noteworthy in points of history and doctrine. The name indicates the nature of the treatise. The twelve sons of Jacob herein give their final instructions to their children. With the account more or less extended of their lives, wherein are often contained facts not found in the canonical Scriptures, they combine moral injunctions for the guidance of their descendants, forecasts of future backslidings, and revelations concerning the coming of Messiah's kingdom, which shall triumph over sin, and bring universal peace and happiness. Thus in each section three elements are distinguishable, Haggadean history, appropriate exhortations, and predictions of the future. Each Testament is supposed to embrace some chief topic, more or less apposite to the particular patriarch's life and character. Thus that of Reuben is concerning Thoughts, Simeon concerning Envy, Levi concerning Priesthood and Arrogance, and so on, through the whole twelve. But let us take the sections in the order in which they occur, and give a short statement of the subjects contained in each Testament. Further details will be presented when we come to analyse these contents.

Reuben—Concerning Thoughts.

Reuben, before he died in the 125th year of his life, two years after Joseph's death, gathering his children and grandchildren around him, gives his last instructions. He confesses his great sin, and urges them to avoid his error, for which he had been sorely punished. Man has seven spirits given him wherewith to carry on his work in the world, viz. life, sight, hearing, smell, taste, speech, reproduction, and an eighth, sleep. With these Beliar (Satan) has intermingled seven spirits of error, which are these: fornication, greediness, fighting, fraud, arrogance, lying, injustice, and sleep, which belongs to both classes. In forcible language the patriarch denounces fornication. Women from the first have been seducers; they caused the fall of the Watchers (ἐγρήγοροι) before the Flood; it behoves men to be wary in their converse with them. He ends by commanding his children to give heed to Levi, to whom with Judah is entrusted the chieftainship. For Levi shall know the law of the Lord, and shall judge Israel and offer sacrifices, until the consummation of the times of Christ the High Priest whom the Lord hath declared.

SIMEON—CONCERNING ENVY.

He was fierce and unfeeling, and the most inimical to Joseph of all the brethren; but Joseph bore no malice. His example should be followed, and brotherly love cherished. The writing of Enoch foretold that the Simeonites should corrupt themselves, and attempt to injure Levi; but they shall not prevail. If they repent, they shall flourish and blossom like the rose. The Canaanites, Philistines (Καππάδοκες), and Hittites shall perish; peace shall be established, Shem shall be glorified, because Messiah shall come. "Obey, Levi!" he concluded, "and in Judah ye shall be redeemed; for from these two tribes salvation shall arise."

LEVI—CONCERNING PRIESTHOOD AND ARROGANCE.

This is the most important of all the Testaments, professing to tell all that shall happen to the tribe till the day of judgment. Other patriarchs indulge freely in moral and religious warnings; here the apocalyptic element is much more conspicuous. Levi narrates how that the Lord showed him two visions; first of the heavens, seven in number, which he was privileged to see, because he was appointed to minister in sacred things, and to announce the coming of Him who was to redeem Israel. It was at this time that he was enjoined to take vengeance on the Shechemites. In the second vision he is invested by seven angels with the insignia of the priesthood. The first angel presents him with the holy oil and the rod of judgment; the second washed him with pure water, and gave him bread and wine, the holy of holies, and clothed him in glorious robes; the third indued him with a linen ephod; the fourth with a purple girdle; the fifth gave him an olive branch; the sixth put a crown on his head; the seventh gave him a diadem and incense. And it was announced that his seed should be divided into three powers, which are obscurely explained. Jacob, knowing by revelation the office of Levi, taught him much lore concerning sacrifice, tithe, first-fruits, etc. He foretells the rejection of the Messiah, and the consequent dispersion of the nation. Levi then sketches his own family history, mentioning among other facts that Amram married his daughter Jochabed. He deduces from the prophecy of Enoch that the active iniquity of the people will last seventy weeks, and their punishment shall continue "until He Himself shall again visit you, and pitying, shall receive you in faith and water."

JUDAH—CONCERNING FORTITUDE, AVARICE, AND FORNICATION.

He was keen and bold when young, loving and obedient to his parents, and won the favour of the Lord. His heroic deeds are recounted, many details being given which are not found in Scripture. He urges his children to avoid drunkenness and uncleanness, sins of which he had been guilty in the matter of Tamar; and covetousness, which is pernicious. "Love ye Levi," he enjoins, "that ye may live long. To me the Lord hath given the kingdom, and to him the priesthood; and He hath subjected the kingdom to the priesthood. On me He bestowed things of earth, on him things of heaven. For as the heaven is above the earth, so is the priesthood above every earthly kingdom. And the Lord hath chosen him above thee to come near unto Himself, and to eat of His table and the first-fruits of the dainties of the children of Israel." He predicts wars and commotions which shall last till Messiah comes. After this the patriarchs shall rise again, and they that suffered on earth shall be recompensed by a happy life.

ISSACHAR—CONCERNING SIMPLICITY.

He begins by narrating the story of the mandrakes, amplifying the briefer account of Gen. xxx., and then sketches his own character and life. He was a husbandman, simple, quiet, industrious, faithful, scrupulous in payment of tithes and offerings. He enjoins his sons to practise agriculture and to be simple in their lives, so that Beliar may not seduce them to luxury and irreligion.

ZEBULON—CONCERNING COMPASSION AND MERCY.

This patriarch asserts that he has no sin to recall but that against his father when he connived with his brethren in concealing from him the fate of Joseph, though he grieved bitterly for it. He gives a long account of the transaction, and as a lesson from this incident, urges his sons to be kind and merciful, not only to brethren, but even to irrational animals, remembering that as a man deals with his neighbours, so the Lord will deal with him. He was the first to make a boat and go a-fishing, and with the produce to feed the poor. He admonishes concerning the duty of forgiveness of injuries, and love and unity; and he concludes by predicting the evils which dissension and unbelief will bring upon them, and which will only be terminated when the Lord, the light of righteousness, shall Himself appear among them, and he, Zebulon, should some day rise again.

DAN—CONCERNING ANGER AND LYING.

He had tried all his life long to avoid anger and lying, and to please God; but was guilty of envy and malice in the case of Joseph. Let his sons beware of these sins, or they will bring on themselves destruction. In the last days, he knows that they will oppose Levi and Judah, and be grievously punished for it. But a time will come when, from these tribes the salvation of the Lord will arise, and wage victorious war against Beliar; and the saints shall rest in Eden, and the righteous shall rejoice in the new Jerusalem, which shall be unto the glory of God for ever and ever! "Therefore draw ye nigh unto God and to the angel that intercedeth for you (τῷ παραιτουμένῳ ὑμᾶς), for He is the Mediator between God and man for the peace of Israel."

Naphtali—Concerning Natural Goodness.

He was the son of Bilhah, daughter of Rutheus, brother of Deborah, Rebecca's nurse. Rutheus himself was a Chaldæan of Abraham's kindred, a worshipper of God, who had been carried away as a captive and bought by Laban. Naphtali, being remarkably active, was his father's messenger. When forty years old he saw a vision on the Mount of Olives, towards the east of Jerusalem. The sun and moon stood still; Isaac called his sons to run and seize them; Levi laid hold of the sun, Judah of the moon, and both were raised aloft with them. Levi received twelve palm branches, Judah had twelve rays beneath his feet. Then appeared a bull with two horns, and on its back the wings of an eagle. All tried to seize it, but Joseph alone was successful, and was carried up on high. And the holy writing came in sight which spake of the captivity of Israel. In a second vision Naphtali sees Jacob and his sons standing by the Sea of Jamnia; and, lo! a ship appeared full of dried flesh, inscribed *The Ship of Jacob*, but without crew or pilot. Jacob and his sons embark, a tempest arises and carries away the father; the ship is almost engulphed, and finally dashed to pieces. Levi prays, and the twelve are saved on pieces of wreck, and, reaching home, find their father safe and sound. The usual prediction concerning the punishment of sinners and the advent of Messiah closes the Testament.

Gad—Concerning Hatred.

He boasts of his courage in defending the flocks from wild beasts, and tells how he was incensed with Joseph for repeating to his father the evil deeds of the brethren, and desired his death. He and Judah sold him for thirty pieces of gold, but kept ten for themselves, concealing the real amount received. He confesses his sorrow for this sin, and urges his children to beware of hatred and covetousness, on which subjects he dilates at considerable length. "For," he says, "as love wishes even to revive the dead, and to recall those who are sentenced to death; so hatred would like to slay the living, and desires the destruction even of those who have but little erred. The spirit of hatred by reason of faintheartedness ($\mathit{\dot{o}\lambda\iota\gamma o\psi v\chi i a\varsigma}$, ? hastiness of spirit) co-operateth with Satan in all things unto the death of men; but the spirit of love co-operateth with the law of God unto men's salvation." As the other patriarchs, he enjoins his sons to honour Judah and Levi, because from them the Lord shall raise up a Saviour for Israel.

Asher—Concerning two Faces of Vice and Virtue.

He begins in much the same way as the *Didaché*: "Two ways hath God given to the sons of men;" and he proceeds in words which recall the dictum of Ben-Sira:[1] "All things are two, one over against the other. There are two ways, of good and evil, and withal two counsels in our breasts distinguishing these paths." He admonishes his sons to be single-minded, and not to wear two faces; and he gives various examples of double-mindedness, and shows how hateful such a character is in God's eyes. He terminates his advice by uttering the warnings and predictions in the same strain as his predecessors.

Joseph—On Moderation.

He recounts his life, summing it up at first almost in the words of the Gospel (Matt. xxv.): "I was an hungered," etc., and then narrating the circumstances twice over at much length, with the addition of many legendary particulars. "See, then, my children," he continues, "how much may be effected by patience and prayer with fasting; for God loveth sobriety, and always helpeth the continent and self-controlling." He tells of a vision which he saw. There arose in Judah a virgin, clad in a linen robe, and from her came forth a lamb unspotted, and on his left there was, as it were, a lion. Against him all the beasts of the earth contended, but prevailed nothing; and the lamb trode them under foot, to the great joy of angels and men. "Do ye, my sons, observe the commandments of the Lord, and honour Judah and Levi, for from out of them shall arise the

---

[1] Ecclus. xlii. 24: "All things are double, one against another, and He hath made nothing imperfect."

Lamb of God, by grace saving all the nations and Israel."

BENJAMIN—CONCERNING A PURE MIND.

Benjamin tells that his mother Rachel was twelve years barren, and then, fasting and praying for twelve days, she conceived, and in due time bore him; and he was therefore called Benjamin, "son of days."[1] He gives much good advice concerning the direction of the thoughts, and simplicity of heart, and rectitude of conduct; in the course of his admonition he recounts this prophecy of Jacob: "In thee shall be fulfilled the prophecy of heaven touching the Lamb of God and the Saviour of the world; for He, the undefiled ($ἄμωμος$) shall be delivered up in behalf of sinners; and He, the sinless ($ἀναμάρτητος$) shall die for the impious, by the blood of the covenant, for the salvation of Gentiles and Israel, and shall destroy Beliar and his servants." There is much that is beautiful and edifying in this Testament. Here is a thought with which we are all familiar, though we scarcely expected to meet with it here: "As the sun, shining on what is filthy and noxious, is not defiled thereby, but rather purifies it and removes its ill savour; so the pure mind, mingling amid the pollutions of earth, dwelleth safely there and suffers no defilement."

[1] The name is usually explained as "Son of my right hand," *i.e.* of good fortune. The interpretation given in our text is that of the Samaritan copy, which has a different reading from the Masoretic. The expression would probably refer to his being born in Jacob's old age.

Such, in brief, are the contents of our book. We must glance at the writer or writers, and attempt to estimate the date of the production.

Of course, in this, as in all such literature, the author's personality is veiled and unknown. But we can form an estimate of his views, and see to what sect or party he belonged. And here we must at once protest against the free use made by some critics of the theory of interpolation.[1] These scientists form certain opinions concerning the age, author, objects, tendencies of a work; and when any paragraph or expression coincides not with their conception, they arbitrarily put it aside as a later addition inserted by some unscrupulous scribe or editor. If the criminated passage were evidently foisted into the original text without any connection with the context, if it were plainly the work of some clumsy glosser, if it differed from the style of the rest of the document and contained language or ideas not found elsewhere, the theory of interpolation becomes reasonable. But where, as in the present case, none of these suppositions can be verified, where the disputed paragraphs are in full keeping and tone with the rest of the work, and there is no substantial variation in MSS. or versions,

---

[1] If any one wishes to see this theory wantonly and largely developed, let him read *Die Testamente der XII. Patriarchen untersucht von L. F. Schnapp* (Halle 1884). This writer divides the greater part of the book between a Christian and a Jewish interpolator, relying entirely upon internal evidence for his conclusions. He regards as genuine only those parts of each Testament which contain biographical details and exhortations founded thereon; all predictions, visions, etc., he determines to be later interpolations.

the notion of unauthorised additions falls to the ground, and we may take the text as genuine without further disquieting ourselves about baseless criticism. At the same time it is, of course, possible, and, indeed, probable, that the work would exhibit traces of editing and revision, and that words or passages might have been inserted in the course of time by scribes or redactors. But these additions, if they do exist, would not affect the general tone of the book, and we found our view on this, and not upon isolated expressions. Now we gather from a careful perusal of the document that the writer was a Jewish Christian, of views not in all respects orthodox, addressing his own countrymen. To none other would the utterances of the patriarchs have been of any value or weight; to none other would the future destiny of Israel have been of any importance. And the object which he had in view was the conversion of his auditors to Christianity. He desires to show how the old Law led up to this consummation, and how the evil times upon which his contemporaries had fallen were a discipline to drive them to acknowledge the true Messiah. He holds that the New Testament was always hidden in the old covenant, and existed in germ in the patriarchal dispensation, so that Christianity is merely a continuation and development of the more ancient religion.

There were, as is well known, two parties in the primitive Church who held opposite views upon the subject of the duty of Christians with respect to the Jewish ceremonial law. While one would impose this routine on all Gentile converts as necessary to salvation, thus narrowing the merits of Christ's sacrifice and ignoring the new covenant, the other held that the Mosaic law was not of eternal obligation, and that Gentile converts must not be compelled to observe it. The former developed into Ebionites, the latter into Nazarenes. Of the heretical tendencies of the Ebionites there can be no question; not only on the question of circumcision did they separate from the orthodox as represented by St. Paul, but more especially in regard to the person and nature of Christ. The Nazarenes, on the other hand, accepting and recognising the Pauline view of the duty of Gentile converts, and seeking to be themselves altogether Christians while retaining their own nationality, had a very imperfect conception of the eternal generation of Christ, dating the hypostasis of the Divine nature in Him either from His birth or His baptism. To this sect our author seems to have belonged, for in his utterances we can trace the opinions which have been mentioned, erroneous tenets on the nature of Christ, generous appreciation of the great Apostle of the Gentiles, faithful adherence to the old ritual, and liberal views with regard to converts from heathendom. It has been also remarked that there is much in the ethics of the book which corresponds with the known tenets of the Nazarenes. Thus it advocates voluntary fasting, abstinence from flesh and wine, not only in order to avoid temptation, but also as an atonement for past excesses; it enjoins peaceableness, kindness to men and animals, benevolence, compassion, the avoidance of female seductions; it inveighs against covetousness, and sets a high value on poverty. All these points seem to suit the modified asceticism of the Nazarenes. It is asserted that no one author could have enunciated the views which are found in our book. No Jewish Christian, it is said, could ever have characterised the tribes of Levi and Judah as those which were to guide Israel, or exhorted his countrymen to submit to their authority; while it is certain that official Judaism, represented by those tribes, was most active in rejecting the gospel. To this it may be answered that the author is thinking of Levi and Judah in their ideal character, not as they had exhibited themselves during later events. Christ as Priest, Christ as King, takes His descent from the two; and it is the truth which this descent teaches that the writer wishes to enforce.

Concerning the date when the book was written, we have certain facts to guide us. Being quoted by Tertullian and Origen, it must have been extant in the second century A.D. To the same conclusion we are led by the writer's evident acquaintance with the Book of Enoch, a great part of which, as we have determined in our account of that production, was probably composed in the age of John Hyrcanus, about 110 B.C. In the Testaments we find this work continually alluded to under the titles of "the writing ($\gamma\rho\alpha\phi\acute{\eta}$) of Enoch;" "the book, books, or words of Enoch the Righteous," "the Scripture of the law of Enoch," and so forth; and there are many expressions borrowed, and facts employed, without special acknowledgment. It is true that most of these citations are not now found in the book as it has come into our hands; but that this work has been sadly mutilated, and originally contained much material no longer existing, is certain; and many of the passages which cannot be traced are probably rather appeals to the general tone and scope of the prophecy than actual quotations. But there are other criteria by which to judge of the age of our work. In it reference is made to the destruction of Jerusalem and the temple,[1] it was therefore written after A.D. 70. Also, according to the words of Benjamin (chap. xi.), the writings of the New Testament, especially the Acts and the Epistles of St. Paul, had been collected into a volume. At the same time, the Jewish priesthood is spoken of as if still existing, which could not have been the case after Hadrian's demolition of Jerusalem in punishment of the revolt of Bar-Cocheba, A.D. 135. We have therefore these limits between which our book could have been produced, A.D. 70–130; and we shall not be far wrong if we assign it to the end of the first or the earliest portion of the second Christian century.

We have now to notice some points of interest which are found in our book touching on history, Christology, and doctrinal, critical, and ethical questions. And first, let us look to the historical element. Here, as in the Book of Jubilees, and generally in Haggadistic literature, we meet with additions to, or amplifications of facts recorded in the Old Testament, some doubtless derived from tradition or from documents no longer extant, others which are owed to the inventive faculty of the writer. It is almost impossible in most cases to say where truth ends and fiction steps in; the probability is that generally there is some ground for the detail added,

[1] Levi xv.; Dan v.

and that the author is dealing with material ready to his hand. In his chronology, and in no few of his legends, he is indebted to the Book of Jubilees and the Book of Enoch; many of his statements have been repeated in the Targum, the Midrashim, and Josephus, being obtained by them from independent sources. This is a further argument for the authenticity of our history.

As additions to the Biblical record, we may note the following. The treacherous attack on the Shechemites at the hands of Simeon and Levi is justified by the violent conduct of these Canaanites in former time, when they persecuted Abraham, plundered his flocks, and even attempted to outrage Sarah;[1] and by a special communication from heaven, which directed vengeance to be taken upon them. During Jacob's sojourn at Hebron he waged successful war with the Canaanites, Judah taking the foremost place, and performing prodigies of valour, his acts being related at some length.[2] Likewise many particulars are added in connection with Judah's marriage with the Hamite Shuah, and the episode with his daughter-in-law Tamar. Esau, who at first had peaceable relations with his brother, after an interval of eighteen years came against him with a large force; but Jacob slew him; and his sons attacked his chief city, and reduced the Edomites to tribute. Joseph's greatest enemy among his brethren was Simeon, who quarrelled with Judah for sparing his life; and his envy was punished by the paralysis of his right hand,

---

[1] Levi v. and vi.
[2] Judah iii. There is a similar account in the Book of Jubilees xxxiv.

which was only healed on his repentance and prayers.¹ Zebulun tells us that he felt deeply for Joseph but feared his brothers too much to attempt his deliverance, though he refused to share in the price of their crime. The evil report which Joseph brought to his father concerning the sons of Bilhah and Zilpah referred to their killing the best of the flock and eating them.² The story of Joseph's sojourn in Egypt is related at considerable length, the account being apparently derived from two distinct documents, not worked together into one narrative. The youth concealed his identity, pretending to be a slave; but the Ishmaelites, who had bought him, were not content with this account of himself, and thinking that he was the son of some great personage, detained him in the house of their agent till they should determine what should be done with him. While he was thus placed, Potiphar's wife happened to see him, and induced her husband to interfere in his behalf, and in the end purchased him as a slave, Joseph all the time quietly submitting to be thus treated that he might not bring his brethren to shame. Potiphar, who is called $ἀρχιμάγειρος$, chief cook, entrusts his whole establishment to him, and greatly prospers. Then follows a detailed account of the seduction employed by his shameless mistress, and his chaste resistance to her words, caresses, and love potions. His wife Asenath, who brought him an enormous fortune as her dower, belonged to the same family as Potiphar.³

[1] Simeon ii.   [2] Gad i. ; Gen. xxxvii. 2.
[3] With the view of saving Joseph from the imputation that he intermarried with an alien race, the Targum, *Ps. Jon.* on Gen. xli. 45, makes Asenath the daughter of Dinah by Shechem. Sinker, p. 77.

It is especially noted that all the patriarchs were buried in the cave of Machpelah, the bodies of many of them being previously placed in coffins. The transmission of these bodies to Hebron was conducted with much secrecy, as the Egyptians kept careful watch over the corpse of Joseph, it having been predicted that the removal of his bones would be accompanied with signal plagues on the land and people. The opportunity for the undisturbed conveyance of the patriarch's remains to Canaan was afforded by the attention of the natives being occupied by certain warlike operations in which they were engaged.

Such are the chief additions to the Biblical narrative found in our book. Of the elaborate chronological details we cannot speak at length. These regard generally the dates of the births of the several patriarchs and the chief events in their lives; they are based almost wholly on the Book of Jubilees, and differ scarcely in any particulars from the statements in that work, though they give some few facts not found therein, *e.g.* the marriages and deaths of the patriarchs.

The writer's views on the nature and person of Christ are to be gathered rather from incidental statements than found definitely expressed in formal enunciations of dogma. In the absence of any authoritative creed, containing definitions and limitations and doctrinal pronouncements, an early writer, producing a treatise for popular use, was not constrained to put forward his opinions with logical precision, or to formulate a system of theology. Hence we find a certain haziness in our author's conception on this great subject, and it is somewhat difficult to arrive at his real sentiments. His ideas concerning the Messiah are, of course, essentially Jewish, and differ considerably from what we have learned to consider the orthodox Christian tenet. The straightforward simplicity of the Nicene doctrine is unknown to him, and he fluctuates between the notions of Christ as Divine and Christ as sanctified man, at one time regarding Him as God incarnate, at another seeming to speak of Him as human and nothing more. The passages which bear on the latter assumption are only three in number, and are these: in the Testament of Levi (chap. xvi.) we read, "the man who reneweth (ἄνδρα ἀνακαινοποιοῦντα) the law in the power of the Most High ye shall call Deceiver, and at last, as ye think, ye shall kill Him, not knowing His resurrection (ἀνάστημα), wickedly taking the innocent blood upon your heads. On account of Him your holy places shall be desolate." Judah, borrowing his language from Balaam's prophecy, proclaims (chap. xxiv.): "After these things a star shall arise to you from Jacob in peace, and a man (ἄνθρωπος) shall stand up from my seed, as a sun of righteousness, walking with the sons of men in meekness and righteousness, and no sin shall be found in Him." Naphtali warns his children of the fate that shall befall their descendants in punishment of their transgressions (chap. iv.): "The Lord shall scatter them over the face of all the earth, until the compassion of the Lord (σπλάγκνον Κυρίου) shall come, even a man (ἄνθρωπος) working righteousness, and showing mercy unto all those that are far off and those that are near." These passages regard purely the human nature of Christ, and taken by themselves might show that the writer did not believe in His Divinity. But other expressions modify this conclusion. Thus the passage above quoted from Judah proceeds: "The heavens shall be opened upon Him to pour forth the spirit and blessing of the holy Father; and He Himself shall pour forth upon you the spirit of grace. . . . This is the scion (βλαστός) of the Most High God, and this is the fountain unto life of all flesh." Levi (chap. xviii.) refers to the baptism of Messiah in these words: "The heavens shall be opened, and from the temple of glory shall come upon Him consecration (ἁγίασμα) with the voice of the Father (*al.* of the Spirit), as from Abraham, father of Isaac." This is explained[1] to mean that the relation of Christ to the Father is as close as that of a human son to his father. But the expression is obscure. We have, however, much more definite statements to produce. The pre-existence of the Messiah is fully allowed. Before He comes to perform His special work on earth He is called the Angel that intercedes for Israel, a mediator between God and man.[2] This is probably a term derived from the Old Testament idea of the Angel of Jehovah, or the Angel of the Presence, who adumbrated Christ. Benjamin (chap. ix.) speaks of Him as the "Only-begotten;" Levi (chap. iv.), as "Son of the Lord;" Simeon tells (chap. vi.) how "the Lord, the great God of Israel, shall appear upon the earth as man,[3] and shall save man (Adam) in Him." . . . "Then," he adds,

---

[1] By Dorner (i. 156), quoted by Sinker, p. 93.
[2] Dan chap. vi.; Lev. ii.-v.
[3] The words ὡς ἄνθρωπος occur in all the MSS. except the Oxford, which, as Mr. Sinker opines, has a tendency to omit words.

"I shall arise in gladness, and shall bless the Highest for His marvellous works, because God having taken a body, and eating with men, saved man;" and he proceeds (chap. vii.): "Do not lift up yourselves against Levi and Judah, for from them shall arise unto you the salvation of God. For the Lord shall raise up from Levi as it were a Priest, and from Judah as it were a King, God and Man. Thus shall He save all the nations and the race of Israel." In another place Levi appears to enunciate the heresy of Patripassianism, with which the Nazarenes were more or less infected. "Now, know ye that the Lord will take vengeance on the sons of men, because, when the rocks were rent, and the sun quenched, and the waters dried up, and fire cowered, and all creation was confounded . . . at the passion of the Most High, men unbelieving continued in their iniquities."[1] Judah (chap. xxii.) speaks thus: "The Lord shall bring upon them dissensions one with another, and there shall be in Israel continual wars, and among the Gentiles shall my kingdom be accomplished, until the salvation of Israel shall have come, until the appearing (ἕως παρουσίας) of the God of Righteousness to give rest in peace to Jacob and all the nations." From certain expressions in the Testament of Zebulun we should gather the writer's opinions to be that the man Christ was deified by union with the Godhead, a modified form of the Cerinthian heresy. We read (chap. ix.): "Ye shall see God in the form of man, whom the Lord shall choose; Jerusalem is

---

[1] Levi iv. This is one of the passages supposed to be an interpolation; but there is no sufficient ground for the supposition.

His name."[1] In many other places it is stated that God, the Lord, the Holy One of Israel, shall dwell among men, and be worshipped, and shall judge the nations.[2] Not to multiply examples to the same effect, we must infer that the author himself held somewhat indistinct views concerning the two natures of Christ and His relation to God, at one time identifying Him with God, at another plainly distinguishing Him from God. From two paragraphs which refer to Christ's baptism,[3] it would seem that it was not till that event that the man Christ became participant of the indwelling of God in the highest sense. That He was to be born of a virgin we have seen in our quotation from the Testament of Joseph, where the linen robe in which she is dressed implies a connection with the priesthood.[4] And His spotless character is gathered from the epithets which occur in the Testaments, *e.g.* guiltless, sinless, true, long-suffering, gentle, lowly. Schnapp, followed by Schürer and others, would regard all such passages as Christian interpolations foisted into a Jewish work; and, of course, such a theory would explain their appearance in the places where they are found. But the opinion which we have adopted

---

[1] This last expression is peculiar, and is varied in the MSS. Mr. Sinker's text is that of the Cambridge, with which the Roman agrees. The Patmos MS. has "in Jerusalem, for His name's sake;" the Oxford gives the same. The rendering of Grabe is: "Quoniam elegit Deus Hierusalem, nomen Deus ei." Probably the text is corrupt.

[2] Dan v.; Napthali viii.; Asher vii.; Benjamin x.

[3] Levi xviii.; Judah xxiv.

[4] Mr. Sinker appositely quotes the Apocryphal Gospels in illustration of the tendency to associate the priestly tribe with the royalty of Messiah through the Virgin Mary.

equally well accounts for such paragraphs; and the large extent of these Christian passages makes the opposite theory unlikely and difficult of acceptance. It may also be said that a later Christian would have had more definite views than those intimated herein.

The view taken of the office of Messiah is indicated by the continual reference to His origin from the tribes of Levi and Judah. He is Priest as well as King, and under the former aspect is supreme. But little is said of His death, and its connection with the Priesthood of Messiah is ignored; the teaching of the Epistle to the Hebrews has not been studied, and we are not told that Christ, by His own blood, hath entered once for all into the holy places, having obtained eternal redemption for men. But it is believed that sins are blotted out through the priesthood, though how this is exercised is not distinctly stated. As King, Messiah wars against evil, and crushes the power of Beliar; and this victory shall be finally accomplished when Israel has learned the lesson of faith. Of Christ's ascension and session in heaven some little is said; but of His return to judgment nothing definite can be found expressed. The author certainly holds that the just shall rise again, and be rewarded for all their sufferings on earth, and share in Messiah's kingdom; but he is very indistinct concerning the fate of the wicked, and has nothing to say of Messiah's part as Judge.

The indefiniteness of the writer appears conspicuously in the view which He takes of the Holy Spirit. Nowhere is He spoken of as God. He is called the Spirit of Sanctification, the Spirit of Understanding, and He is said to rest on Messiah; but no hint of His equality with the Father and the Son is given. Nor can we discover that our author believed in His distinct personality; but he seems to have regarded Him merely as an operation or manifestation of the Godhead.

For the criticism of the New Testament the book affords some assistance, as it contains quotations or allusions which show familiarity with most of our early Christian documents. References to the writings of St. John are not infrequent. Thus Dan (chap. xiv.) speaks of "the light of the world, which was given among you for the enlightenment of every man," which recalls chap. i. 9 and viii. 12; Benjamin (chap. iii.) and Joseph (chap. xix.) call the Saviour of the world "the Lamb of God."[1] Issachar (chap. vii.) has the phrase, "a sin unto death."[2] Levi (chap. xviii.) says that Messiah "shall give unto the saints to eat of the tree of life;" Dan (chap. v.) makes mention of "the new Jerusalem."[3] Traces of acquaintance with most of the other books of the New Testament may be found scattered throughout the work. Levi (chap. xviii.) tells of the Father's voice that came upon Christ in the water,[4] and of Him "who should redeem Israel."[5] We have allusions to the holy books, and the work and word of Paul,[6] which would imply that the Acts and Pauline Epistles were known to the writer. "The Spirit of God," says Benjamin (chap. ix.), "shall come upon the Gentiles, as fire poured forth."[7] Reuben

---

[1] John i. 29, 36. [2] 1 John v. 16, 17.
[3] Rev. ii. 7, xxi. 2. [4] Matt. iii. 16, 17.
[5] Luke xxiv. 21. [6] Benjamin chap. xi. [7] Acts ii. 3.

(chap. v.) admonishes, like St. Paul and St. Peter, "Flee fornication; and bid your women not to adorn their heads and faces."[1] Levi (chap. vi.) repeats St. Paul's difficult phrase in 1 Thess. ii. 16: "The wrath of God is come upon them to the uttermost," ἔφθασεν ἐπ' αὐτοὺς ... εἰς τέλος. "The God of peace," and "God in the form of man," are Pauline terms.[2] Levi (chap. x.) and Benjamin (chap. xi.) adopt this phrase, "the consummation of the ages," from Heb. ix. 26.[3] As bearing on the canonicity of disputed books, we may add that Reuben's (chap. v.) utterance, that the woman who is a deceiver "is reserved unto eternal punishment," seems to be a quotation from 2 Pet. ii. 4, 9 and Jude 6.

In De la Bigne's *Magna Bibliotheca*, where Grosseteste's Latin version is printed, the following verdict concerning our book is given: "Liber hic apocryphus est pseudepigraphus, fabulosus et indignus· plane qui legatur; multa enim continet partim erronea, partim vana et mendacia, nullo auctore aut fundamento subnixa, quæ facile lector et discernet et repudiabit." A careful student of the work would not nowadays assent to this conclusion. Far from being unworthy of perusal, it may justly claim the most attentive consideration, as the product of an important era too little understood, and embodying the views of a party which has left the scantiest literature. Whether it was composed at Pella, as Mr. Sinker supposes, we have no ground for deciding; but that it

[1] 1 Cor. vi. 18; 1 Pet. iii. 3.

[2] 2 Cor. xii. 11, Phil. ii. 7, compared with Dan chap. v. and Zebulun chap. ix.

[3] Συντέλεια τῶν αἰώνων. See a full collection of these coincidences in Mr. Sinker's Index II.

emanated from a Nazarene, at a time when dogma was still fluctuating and no authoritative decree had fixed the truth on doubtful questions, is obvious. We have here a glimpse of early Christian doctrine and ethics which is almost unique. The large-minded utterances of the Patriarchs are very notable. The author has accepted the Messiah as He really appeared, though His guise was far different from what was expected: and he aims at making his unbelieving countrymen see with his eyes, and recognise in the Jesus whom they slew the Messiah long promised and foretold, who should bring salvation, not to the Jews only, but to those who were far off, even unto the ends of the earth.

III.

LEGENDARY.

THE BOOK OF JUBILEES.

THE Book of Jubilees, or the Little Genesis, is mentioned by name continually in the writings of the early Fathers, and by a succession of authors reaching to Theodorus Metochita (A.D. 1332). Allusions to information contained therein, without actual naming of the origin of the statements, are very numerous, particularly in the Byzantine chroniclers, so that the work was well and widely known up to the middle of the fourteenth century; but from that time the original has been entirely lost. For four hundred years nothing but a few scattered fragments was known to exist. The age, however, which witnessed the rediscovery of "The Assumption of Moses" has been gratified by the reappearance of the Book of Jubilees. Dr. Krapff, an African missionary, found the book in Abyssinia, had it transcribed, and sent the manuscript to the University Library in Tübingen. The work was an Ethiopian version of the original, complete, indeed, in one sense, but full of errors, and not a trustworthy representation of the original. It was translated by Dillmann in Ewald's *Jahrbücher*, ii. and iii., with an appendix containing discussions on the main points of interest. With the aid of another MS., Dillmann published the Ethiopian text in 1859.[1] Some further fragments of two old Latin translations have been set forth by Ceriani and Rönsch,[2] and these with the Ethiopic text enable us to give a satisfactory account of this curious and long-lost work. Previously to the appearance of these publications, students who desired to know anything about the book had to refer to Fabricius' *Codex. Pseudep. V. T.*, wherein were collected such fragments as had been preserved by Jerome and other early writers. Some years later, A. Treuenfels[3] added a few other passages discovered by himself, comparing them with the Jewish Midrashim, the correspondence with which he was the first to proclaim. But these fragments gave a very inadequate impression of the contents of the *Parva Genesis*, and the announcement in 1844 of the existence

---

[1] Kufâlê, sive Liber Jubilæorum . . . nuper ex Abyssinia in Europam allatus. Æthiopice ad duorum librorum MSS. fidem primum ed. Dr. Aug. Dillmann (Kiliæ et Londini 1859).

[2] Ceriani, *Monumenta sacra et profana ex codd. præsertim Biblioth. Ambrosianæ*, Mediol. 1861, Tom. i. Fasc. i. Rönsch, *Das Buch der Jubiläen oder die kleine Genesis* (Leipz. 1874).

[3] "Die kleine Genesis," in *Literaturbl. d. Orients*, 1846, Nos. 1–6. Other works on the subject are these : A. Jellinek, *Bet ha-Midrasch*, Th. 1–3 (Leipz. 1853–1855). B. Beer, *Das Buch der Jubil. u. sein Verhältniss zu den Midraschim* (Leipz. 1856); and *Noch ein Wort über d. B. d. Jub.* (Leipz. 1857). Frankel in *Monatsschrift f. Gesch. des Judenthums*, 1856, 1857. Two treatises by Dillmann ; Krüger, "Die Chronol. im Buch der Jubil.," in *Zeitschr.* 1858. Rubin, *Das Buch der Jubil.* 1870. Ginsburg in Kitto's *Cyclopæd*. There is a translation by Schodde in *Bibliotheca sacra*, 1885.

of a complete copy was hailed with delight by the learned world.

Some difficulty had occurred in earlier investigations in fixing the identity of the book from which the citations were made, owing to the different appellations under which it was known, or by which reference was made to it. The oldest reference, that in Epiphanius,[1] calls it "Jubilees," or the "Book of Jubilees," a very fitting designation of a treatise which divided the history of which it treated into periods of Jubilees, *i.e.* of forty-nine years, the author, in his strong partiality for the number seven, departing from the Mosaic principle which counted the fiftieth as the year of release (Lev. xxv. 10). Epiphanius and many others also name it the "Little Genesis," Microgenesis, Leptogenesis, or τὰ λεπτὰ Γενέσεως—the minutiæ of Genesis[2]—appellations appropriate to it, not as being less in bulk than the scriptural record, but as giving particulars of name, date, and other "small matters" not found in the canonical book, or because it divides the history into small periods. Other references are current which probably, though not with certainty, appertain to this book. Thus Syncellus[3] more than once alludes to "what is called the Life of Adam," quoting from it passages which occur in the "Jubilees," so that it seems likely that the work which he names is merely a portion of the latter. The same is also true of the " Book of Adam's Daughters,"

---

[1] *Hæres.* xxxix.: ὡς ἐν τοῖς Ἰωβηλαίοις εὑρίσκεται, τῇ καὶ Λεπτῇ Γενέσει (al. λεπτογενέσει) καλουμένῃ.

[2] Hieron. *Ep.* 127, Ad Fabiol. Syncell. *Chronogr.* p. 3.

[3] *Chronogr.* pp. 7–9 : ὁ λεγόμενος βίος Ἀδάμ.

mentioned in a decree of Pope Gelasius.[1] The title "Apocalypse of Moses," Syncellus himself applies to "Little Genesis."[2] In the Ambrosian MS. our book is followed immediately by the "Assumption of Moses," as though this formed an appendix to the former; and in the catalogues of Pseudo-Athanasius and Nicephorus, the "Testament (Διαθήκη) of Moses" directly precedes the "Assumption;" so that it is not unlikely that the "Testament of Moses" is merely another name for the "Book of Jubilees." The Abyssinian Church names it the "Book of the Division of Days," from the first words of the inscription at the beginning.

The original language of the book is without doubt Hebrew or Aramaic. Many expressions in the version are unintelligible without reference to this text; Hebrew or Aramaic etymologies of proper names are given; and we have Jerome's express statement[3] that certain Hebrew

[1] Mansi, *Conc.* viii. 167, where, according to Rönsch, p. 478, the correct reading is: "Liber de filiabus Adæ, hoc est Leptogenesis." This, at any rate, proves that the book was known in the West, which, indeed, the fact of the existence of a Latin version would also show.

[2] P. 4: ἦν καὶ Μωυσέως εἶναί φασί τινες ἀποκάλυψιν. So, p. 49, a little before, Syncellus refers the clause in Gal. vi. 15: "Neither circumcision availeth anything," etc., to the "Revelation of Moses." Tischendorf in his critical note writes: "Item Syncell. teste Gb., sed ignoro locum." The clause in question is not found in our present text of "Jubilees;" but as this is confessedly very imperfect, the omission proves nothing.

[3] *Ep.* 127, Ad Fabiol.: "Hoc verbum [רָסַע, Num. xxxiii. 21], quantum memoria suggerit, nusquam alibi in Scripturis sanctis apud Hebræos invenisse me novi absque libro apocrypho qui a Græcis Μικρογένεσις appellatur. Ibi in ædificatione turris pro stadio ponitur, in quo exercentur pugiles et athletæ et cursorum velocitas comprobatur." The passage referred to is lost in the Ethiopic version.

words on which he is commenting are found in what he calls "Microgenesis." The wives of the Sethites are called by names which are expressive of beauty or virtue in Hebrew. That Seth married Azurah, *restrain;* Jared, Beracha, *blessing;* Enoch, Adni, *pleasure;* while Cain married his sister Avan, *vice*. There are also numerous passages wherein our book agrees with the Hebrew in opposition to the Septuagint,[1] and some where it follows an independent Hebrew original. The present Ethiopic version, however, was made from a Greek and not a Hebrew original. This fact, which the history of other Abyssinian literature made antecedently probable, is confirmed by the introduction of Greek words into the text, *e.g.* δρῦς, βάλανος, λίψ, φάραγξ, etc. Thus, too, we have the Septuagintal forms, Mambrim for Mamre, Geraron for Gerar, Kiriath Arbok for Kirjath-Arba, Aunan for

---

Jerome again appeals to our book in the same Epistle, *Mansio*, 24: "Hoc eodem vocabulo [תֶּרַח, Num. xxxiii. 27] et iisdem literis scriptum invenio patrem Abraham, qui in supradicto apocrypho Geneseos volumine abactis corvis, qui hominum frumenta vastabant, abactoris vel depulsoris sortitus est nomen."

[1] *E.g.* Gen. xlv. 22: "Three hundred pieces *of silver;*" Sept. "gold." iii. 17: "Cursed is the ground *for thy sake;*" Sept. "in thy works." xv. 11: "And when the fowls came down upon the carcases, Abram *drove them away;*" Sept. "sat among them." xxxvii. 29: "Let thy *mother's* sons bow down to thee;" Sept. "thy father's." On the other hand, some passages agree with the Greek version and not with the Hebrew. Thus Jubil. chap. xxiv.: "And the servants of Isaac digged yet another well and found no water; and they went and told Isaac that they had found no water." The Hebrew of Gen. xxvi. 32 is: "We have found water;" but the LXX. give οὐχ εὕρομεν ὕδωρ. The introduction of Cainan as son of Arphaxad (chap. viii.) is supported by the Sept. but not by the Hebrew, and is further warranted to be original by the comparison of the number of created works, viz. twenty-two, with the number of the patriarchs from

Aner (Gen. xiv. 24), Heliopolis for On, Gesem for Goshen. On the other hand, if the old Latin may be supposed to have been translated directly from the Hebrew,[1] containing as it does many grammatical forms or phrases peculiar to that language, which would hardly have escaped alteration in passing through Greek into Latin, yet the translator seems to have been well acquainted with the work of the Seventy, and to have referred to this version in rendering his original.

As to the date of the composition, nothing can with certainty be determined. The author was well acquainted with and refers to some sections of the Book of Enoch, and has adopted many of its glosses on Old Testament history.[2] Thus, as Ewald and Schürer note, it is said of Enoch that "he wrote in a book the signs of heaven in the order of their months, in order that the children of

Adam to Jacob, who amount to twenty-two only by including this Cainan. See Frankel, v. p. 345. And some few differ from both. Thus Gen. xiii. 14 (Heb. and Sept.): "North, south, east, west;" Jubil. "West, south, east, north" (according to the Latin version). Gen. xxviii. 5: "The mother of Jacob and Esau;" Jubil. "mother of Jacob." After Gen. xxx. 28, Laban says: "Remain with me for wages, and feed my flocks again, and take thy wages,"—which has no exact counterpart in Heb. or Sept. For Gen. xxxiii. 18, where Heb. and Sept. coincide, Jubil. gives: "And Jacob moved further and dwelt towards the north in Magd Ladra Ephrathah." In the honour paid to Joseph, Gen. xli. 43, it is proclaimed before him, "El el Waabrir," in the Latin, "Elel et Haboid," or "El el et abior." From these variations it is natural to conclude that the writer used a text differing materially from the Masoretic recension.

[1] For the grounds for this statement see Rönsch, § 15, where the opinions on both sides are presented, the writer himself concluding that the Latin translator had before him the Greek rather than the Hebrew text.

[2] See Jubil. chap. iv.; *Jahrb.* ii. pp. 240, 241.

men might know the seasons of the year, according to the order of the various months. . . . He saw in his dream the past and the future, what was going to happen to the sons of the children of men in their generations one after another down to the day of judgment. All this he saw and knew, and wrote it down as a testimony, and left it on the earth as a testimony for all the sons of the children of men, and for their generations." This is quite a correct account of the contents of part of the Book of Enoch as it has come down to us. On the other hand, he himself has been known to, and probably quoted by, the writer of the "Testaments of the Twelve Patriarchs." There are many verbal parallelisms or plagiarisms which have been noted by Rönsch and others; there are also some details which may be derived from the same source. The account of Reuben's crime agrees with the narrative in the Jubilees. Other matters are, Levi's dream concerning the priesthood, and the favour which the Lord should shower upon him; the names of the wives of Levi and Judah; the war against the Canaanite kings; Zebulon's prediction of Israel's apostasy; Joseph's temptations, which are plainly an imitation of Abraham's. In these and many other passages the Testaments reproduce the facts of the Jubilees. In the chronology also there is remarkable similarity. Now, if this connection is established, as Rönsch and others [1] have with tolerable certainty demonstrated, we have at once a limitation of the period during which Leptogenesis was composed, and may assign it to

[1] Rönsch, § 11; and Dillmann, *Jahrb.* iii. p. 91 ff.; Sinker, *Test. of the Twelve Patriarchs*, pp. 41 ff.

some date between B.C. 100 and A.D. 100. But further limitation is possible. The author appears to have used the Second Book of Esdras, the genuine portions of which are attributed to the age immediately preceding the Christian era. Whether the writers of the New Testament were conversant with the Book of Jubilees is a question which we cannot here discuss. Certainly there are many points in the Angelology and Demonology of both which afford a striking similarity, and many expressions which are analogous or identical;[1] but we will found no argument upon this. Some have traced an intentionally antichristian spirit in the work, and have thence inferred that it was produced some few years after the death of our Lord. We must at any rate date it before the destruction of Jerusalem, A.D. 70. The seer speaks (chap. i.) of the Lord dwelling for ever in Zion, of the temple lasting to all time, and its holiness enduring to all eternity. Like Enoch (chap. lvi.), he makes Jerusalem the centre of the earth and the seat of sovereignty. Such expressions could not have been used by one who had witnessed the overthrow of the sacred city at the hands of the Romans. The great stress laid on the duty of sacrifice and of making the legal offerings points to the same conclusion. The writer must have had in his view a regular ritual, and a temple wherein sacrifices were then offered, which, as he ex-

[1] Thus: Abraham is inscribed in the heavenly tables as "a friend of the Lord," chap. xix. Cf. Jas. ii. 23. Noah, chap. vii., is said to have taught his sons and grandsons all God's commandments and the way of righteousness. Cf. 2 Pet. ii. 5 ; and the fate of the evil angels in ver. 4 ; and the giving of the Law through the medium of angels, Acts vii. 53 ; Gal. iii. 19 ; Heb. ii. 2.

pressly says (chap. xxxii.), were to continue to the end of the world. We may therefore from the above considerations conclude that the book was composed about the middle of the first Christian century.

That Palestine was the abode of the author may be justly inferred from the language in which the work was originally written. The few striking cases, where apparently the wording of the Septuagint has been adopted, must be attributed to the translator, as the well-known animosity against the Greek version exhibited by the Palestinian Jews precludes the possibility of the author himself employing it in writing his history. The angel of the vision orders Abram to transcribe the Hebrew books, and to teach that language to his descendants (chap. xii.)—an injunction which, understood as the author intended, could be carried out in no foreign land, but only in Palestine, the home of "Adam's primitive language." Joseph speaks Hebrew when he makes himself known to his brethren. The stress laid upon complete separation from the heathen, and the necessity of holding aloof from all communication with exterior peoples, would have been absurd if addressed to any but dwellers in the promised land; and although attempts have been made to show that the writer was a priest of the temple of Leontopolis, in Egypt, the evidence for this theory is feeble, and the argument is based on assumptions which are unproved. There are indeed certain intimations that the author followed sometimes a different tradition from that which obtained among the Jews of Palestine, as where he enjoins that the first-fruits of a tree in its fourth year should be brought to the altar, and that the remainder should be eaten by the ministers of the Lord before the altar (chap. vii.); whereas, according to the Palestinian Halacha, the fruit belonged to the owner of the tree absolutely, who was bound to consume it in Jerusalem.[1] And hence arises one of the arguments for the theory that the work was composed in Egypt; but we have no proof that any of the traditions adopted by the author were especially of Egyptian origin; nor is it probable that a Hebrew treatise would emanate from that country. The Jews in Egypt, if we may believe the translator of Ecclesiasticus, had not maintained the knowledge of their ancient tongue; and the writings of Philo, the Book of Wisdom, and other works of that era, lead to the same conclusion.

The author is certainly a Jew. The careful description of the Sabbath and the festivals, with their ceremonies and rabbinical observances, and the heavenly authority attributed to them, could have emanated from none but a Hebrew of the Hebrews. To the same conclusion points the elevated position ascribed to the nation of Israel. There is no Christian sentiment or opinion in the book, not even a reference to a personal Messiah.[2]

---

[1] See Frankel, *Monatsschr.* v. 384 ff.; Beer, *Das Buch. d. Jubil.* and *Noch ein Wort.*

[2] Frankel (*Monatsschr.* v. 314) has detected a Christian influence in the wording of some passages; but the examples given are very far from being decisive. Thus in blessing Judah, Isaac says: "Be thou lord, thou and one of thy sons, over the sons of Jacob," where nothing more than the supremacy of Judah is necessarily implied. "I will send them witnesses," says the Lord to Moses (chap. i.), "and my witnesses they will slay." Here, it is said, is plainly introduced the Christian word μάρτυρες, where a Jew would have written "pro-

The only passage that can be supposed to have a Messianic meaning is one referring to Abraham's seed (chap. xvi.): "From him would come the plant of righteousness for the generation of eternity; from him should also come the holy seed like him who had made all things" (Schodde). But this is too vague to form the basis of any notion of Christian feeling in our book. Equally free is it from Alexandrian philosophy. The author never allegorises. He expands, explains, particularises the scriptural accounts, but does not see in them types or figures of moral truths, and founds on them no philosophical speculations. He seems to stand between the apocryphal writers of the Old Testament and the composers of those pseudepigraphic books which were produced in early Christian times, as the Testaments of the Twelve Patriarchs and the Ascension of Isaiah. The teaching concerning angels and demons differs considerably from that which obtains, *e.g.*, in the Book of Enoch, and appears to be less developed and complete. From the reverence shown to the number seven and the marked importance attributed to the feast of the Sabbath, some have assigned the writer to the sect of Essenes;[1] but the grounds of this opinion are of little weight, more especially as there is no mention of the washings and purifications which were an essential feature of this sect. Nor can the writer be a Samaritan, for, in speaking of

phets," as 2 Chron. xxxvi. 15, 16. But such expressions may fairly be laid to the account of the Ethiopian translator. Rönsch has endeavoured to show that the author levied some of his statements directly against Christian practices and doctrines: his arguments are to my mind inconclusive.

[1] See Jellinek, *Bet ha-Midrasch*.

the four places favoured by God in all the earth, he names Eden, Sinai, Zion, and the mountain of the east, but not Gerizim. That he was not a Sadducee is proved by his belief in angels and the immortality of the soul. We must be satisfied with conjecturing that he was a Pharisee of the dominant type, a man of learning, well read in Scripture, well acquainted with myth and legend, and belonging probably to the body of scribes. Many apocalyptic writers have, with more or less fulness, narrated the history of the Jewish nation from the earliest times unto their own; but the method pursued by our author is, as far as we know, peculiar to himself, and can have been invented only by one who was not merely conversant with the sacred text and the traditions connected with it, oral or written, but was capable of taking a comprehensive view of a great subject, and had the desire of expressing some personal views of his own, and of effecting important reforms in the observances of his co-religionists.

The form of the book is peculiar. Professing to give a history of the world from the creation to the settlement in Canaan, it breaks up this period into divisions of Jubilees, and arranges all the facts narrated in the scriptural accounts into these segments of time. In order to confer on his new matter the same authority which Scripture possessed, the writer introduces Moses as receiving this revelation of past and future from an angel of the Presence, while he tarried on Mount Sinai in the first year of the Exodus. This system of chronology is supposed to be a direct Apocalypse; it had not its origin in the days of Moses, but was known long before to the patriarchs, partly by tradition, partly by direct communication from God, and was a portion of the original design of God which He purposed from the creation. So the jubilee-reckoning is a heavenly system: all the history of God's people falls into this form, and Moses could not have known it had it not been revealed to him by the Lord. Thus the author presents his work stamped with the highest sanction, and at once disarms prejudice and wins assent by assuming Divine authority for his statements. "Moses was in the mount forty days and forty nights, and the Lord taught him of the past and the future; He declared unto him the division of the days and the law and the testimony, and bade him write it in a book, that his posterity might know it and be warned against breaking the commandments of the Lord. And the Angel of the Presence, who went before the camp of Israel, wrote out the revelation for Moses, and took the heavenly tables which contained the account of jubilees and weeks and days and seasons, and told him all that follows" (chap. i.). Thence to the end of the book we have history poured into this mould, the earlier part being made consistent by transferring to patriarchal times feasts and observances of later date. The events are treated with much freedom, and illustrated by amplification and tradition, so that the whole deserves the appellation which has been affixed to it, "a Haggadistic Commentary on the Book of Genesis."[1]

We proceed to give some specimens of the treatment of Biblical stories herein, premising that many of the additions and explanations may be found in other

[1] Dr. Bissel in Lange's *Comment. on the Apocrypha*, p. 670.

apocryphal works as well as in the Talmud and Midrashim, while others are peculiar to the author, and have no existence in other treatises. We will for a moment omit chronological matters, with which our book is greatly concerned, and confine our attention to other points. Some have hoped to find herein grounds for revision of the Hebrew text of the Pentateuch; and certainly there are passages which seem to point to readings that differ from the received wording. But in the absence of the original text such indications are scarcely reliable, and nothing of importance has been elicited from them. And first, with regard to religious observances; with the view of giving indisputable authority to Mosaic ordinances, the writer refers them to primitive times far removed from the Sinaitic incidents. The feast of Pentecost dates from the covenants made by God with Noah and Abraham; the feast of Tabernacles was first celebrated by Abraham at Beersheba, and further solemnised by Jacob after his vision at Bethel. The mourning on the Day of Atonement commemorated the loss of Joseph. Other matters are manipulated in a similar manner. Many of the glosses on the inspired statements are made with a view of obviating real or supposed difficulties. Thus concerning the speech of the serpent, it is explained that in Paradise before the fall all animals spoke, but lost their power in consequence of Adam's sin (chap. iii.). Cain and Seth took their sisters as wives; and the names of the wives of all the chief patriarchs are carefully given as if from traditional genealogies. Adam's death at seventy years short of a thousand is a literal fulfilment of the curse, Gen. ii. 17, because he did die in "the day" in which he ate the forbidden fruit, one day being with the Lord as a thousand years (chap. iv.).[1] The angels brought the animals to the ark (chap. v.). Canaan, contrary to the advice of his father and his brethren, persisted in colonising the land of Libanus from Hamath to the river of Egypt; and when Japhet moved westward, his son Madai dwelt in the Median land—statements made to account for the fact that descendants of Ham and Japhet were found in the Semitic domain (chap. x.). It was Satan who induced God to order Abraham to sacrifice his son. Rebecca loved Jacob, because she knew that Abraham had been warned that that son of Isaac should be specially favoured by God (ch. xvi., xix.); and it was in the time of a great famine that Esau sold his birthright (chap. xxiv.). Reuben escaped the punishment due to his crime, because the law had not at that time been fully revealed (chap. xxxiii.). Er was slain because he would not receive the wife offered him by his father, but preferred to take one from the Canaanitish relations of his mother (chap. xli.). Judah's ignorance at the time and subsequent repentance obtained for him forgiveness of his sin with his daughter-in-law Tamar. Moses lay for seven days in the ark, during which time his mother came and suckled him by night, and his sister watched him by day to defend him from the birds (chap. xlvii.). It was not God, but the arch-enemy, Mastemah, who hardened the hearts of the Egyptians.

---

[1] The same explanation is given by Just. Mart. *Dial. c. Tryph.* c. 81, cited by Dillm. and Rönsch, who have noted the particulars mentioned above.

Sometimes remarks are introduced which have reference to earlier or later passages, and are intended to give a completion to the bare fact mentioned in the sacred text.[1] Of this nature is the appearance of the angels to Abraham and Sarah (chap. xvi.), in fulfilment of the promise in Gen. xviii. 14; Jacob's tithing of his goods in Bethel (chap. xxxii.), according to his vow (Gen. xxviii. 22); his purposing to build a sanctuary there, from which he was dissuaded by the angel in his dream; Jacob's war with seven Amorite kings (chap. xxxiv.), when he obtained the portion which he gave to Joseph (Gen. xlviii. 22).[2] The difficulties connected with the names and number of the members of Jacob's family that came into Egypt are not materially lightened by the statements of our book, which, omitting the two sons of Pharez and of Beriah (Gen. xlvi. 12, 17), adds in their place four sons of Dan and one of Naphtali, all of whom died prematurely in Egypt, and makes Dinah to have met her death in the land of Canaan before the removal (chap. xliv.).

As additions to the inspired account may be mentioned such particulars as these: Adam took five days to name all the animals which came unto him, and having seen them all, found none like himself, which could be a helpmate for him (chap. iii.); as soon as Eve had eaten of the fruit, she was ashamed, and made herself a garment of fig leaves; Adam was seven years in the garden of Eden,

---

[1] I avail myself here of the references in Rönsch, p. 495, and *Jahrb.* iii. p. 79.

[2] This war is mentioned in the Test. of the Twelve Patr. (Test. Jud.). A different account is given in Josh. xxiv. 32.

where he guarded the ground from birds and beasts, collected and stored the fruits, "dressed and kept it;" in the days of Jared the angels came down to earth to teach men righteousness (chap. iv.); Adam was the first who was buried in the earth; Cain met with his death by the fall of his house, a just retribution, that he who had slain his brother with a stone should himself be killed by a stone; the three sons of Noah built three towns on Mount Lubar, the part of Ararat on which the ark grounded, and where Noah was afterwards buried (chap. vii.). To these may be added the prolix account of Noah's distribution of the earth among his sons, and the curse laid on either who sought to take any portion which had not fallen to his share (chap. ix.); the statement about the position of the Tower of Babel, that it stood between the territory of Assyria and Babylon in the land of Shinar, and that the asphalt used in its construction was brought from the sea and the springs in Shinar; the explanation of the selection of Levi for the priesthood by the principle of taking the tithe for God's use, Jacob counting upwards from Benjamin and thus reckoning Levi as the tenth; Jacob's wrath at the deception practised on him in the matter of Leah and his angry speech to Laban, "Take thy daughter and let me be gone, for thou hast dealt ill with me;" Joseph's observation of his brethren's return to better feeling before he made himself known to them; the war between the kings of Canaan and Egypt, which was the reason of Joseph's interment in the Holy Land being postponed till the Exodus. We have also an intercalation between vers. 1 and 2 of Gen. xlvi., showing how Jacob, fearing to go down into Egypt, waited patiently for a vision, and on the seventh day of the third month celebrated the feast of harvest; and a long addition between vers. 27 and 28 of Gen. xxxv., containing Rebecca's advice to Jacob, and her exacting an oath from Esau not to injure his brother, and many other particulars, including Leah's death and burial. Here may be mentioned Jacob's war with the Amorite kings, which is also recorded in the Testaments of the Twelve Patriarchs (Testam. Jud.). The identification of some of the names of the cities of these kings is very difficult. The first is Thapha (Tapho, *Lat.*), which is probably Tappuah (Josh. xii. 17); the second, Aresa (Arco, *Lat.*); the third, Saragan, cannot be identified; the fourth, Selo (Silo, *Lat.*), is doubtless Shiloh; and the fifth, Gaiz (Gaas, *Lat.*), is the Gaash of Judg. ii. 9. The Amorites combined against Jacob to rob him of his cattle and to destroy him and his family; and the patriarch, with his three sons, Levi, Judah, and Joseph, went out against them, slew the five kings, and made the people tributary. So again the account of Enoch is much enlarged, and gives evident proof of reference to the Book of Enoch, so called. "He was the first of men who taught learning and wisdom; he wrote in a book the signs of heaven according to the order of the months; he bare testimony to the generations of men, showed them the weeks of the jubilees, and the days of the years, and the sabbatical year. In his visions he saw the past and the future, how it should happen to the sons of men until the day of judgment, and wrote it all in a book. After the birth of Methuselah he was for six years with the angels, who instructed him in heavenly and earthly lore, which he transcribed at their dictation. He bore testimony against the angels who had sinned with the daughters of men. And for his reward he was taken away from among the sons of men, and carried by angels into the garden of Eden, where he learned the judgment and the eternal punishment of sinners, and wrote it all in a book." This is indeed a fairly complete account of the contents of the Book of Enoch as known to us. Sometimes the speeches of the actors in the Biblical drama are altered and lengthened. Thus Gen. xliv. 9 becomes: "he shall die, and we with our asses will become servants of thy lord;" ver. 10: "Not so; the man with whom I find it I will take as servant; but ye, go home in peace;" ver. 15 (in order to eliminate the idea of divination): "Know ye not that such a man as I, who drink from this cup, dearly loves his cup?" and ver. 20, instead of "his brother is dead," "one is gone and was lost, so that we have never found him again."

Under the same category come the names of the wives of the patriarchs from Adam to Terah, and those of the sons of Jacob (whence these details are derived is wholly unknown); the number of Adam's sons, who seem to have been twelve in all; the four sacred spots in the earth, Eden, the mountain of the East (probably Lubar),[1] Sinai, and Zion; the inscription found by Canaan, son of Arphaxad, containing astronomical lore taught to the forefathers by the angels (chap. viii.);[2] the

---

[1] See the identity of this mountain discussed by Rönsch, pp. 504 ff. If this mountain be the peak of Ararat, then the four holy places correspond respectively to Adam, Noah, Moses, and David.

[2] Comp. Joseph. *Antiq.* i. 2. 3.

division of the earth by lot among the sons of Noah; the mention of the forty-three years consumed in the building of the Tower, with the avowed intention of thereby ascending to heaven (chap. x.); the beginning of war and the practice of slavery among the sons of Noah; the introduction of idolatry by Ur, who built a town which he called after his father Kesed (chap. xi.);[1] Jacob's yearly presents to his father and mother after his return from Mesopotamia; the assertion that Zebulon and Dinah were twins, that Zilpah and Bilhah were sisters (chap. xxviii.); the dream of Levi about his future priesthood (chap. xxxii.); the death of Bilhah and Dinah for grief at the loss of Joseph (chap. xxxiv.); the war which, at the instigation of his sons, Esau makes with Jacob after Isaac's death, and wherein he himself falls by his brother's hand, and his forces are defeated and slain (chaps. xxxvii., xxxviii.); the failure in the annual rise of the Nile, which was the cause of the famine in Egypt; the hostilities between the Egyptians and the Canaanites, during which the remains of the other sons of Jacob, except Joseph, were taken into Canaan and buried in the cave of Machpelah on Mount Hebron;[2] the lingering of some of the Jews in Canaan after this business of sepulture, and among them, Amram, who

---

[1] Here doubtless is an attempt at accounting for the name "Ur of the Chaldees," Gen. xi. 28.

[2] In Acts vii. 16, St. Stephen says the patriarchs were buried at Sychem, and Jerome affirms (*Ep.* 86) that their sepulchres were shown there in his day. Josephus, *Antiq.* ii. 8. 2, agrees with our book; but in *Bell. Jud.* iv. 8. 7 introduces the same story with λέγουσι. Perhaps some jealous feeling against Samaria may have led to the alteration of the locality in popular tradition.

returned to Egypt shortly before Moses' birth (chaps. xlvi., xlvii.); the name of Pharaoh's daughter, Tharmuth (*Lat.* Termot); the order for the drowning of the Israelites' children executed for seven months only; Moses' instruction for twenty-one years by his father Amram, and his residence at Pharaoh's court for the same period; the binding of the evil spirit from the fourteenth to the eighteenth day, to give the Israelites time to escape from Egypt (chap. xlviii.).

We have mentioned the introduction of the names of persons who are not specially designated in Scripture. Names are also affixed to places, rivers, etc., which are elsewhere not defined, or are called differently. Thus Shem's possession extends from the mountain Rafu (Rhiphaei M.), where the river Tona (Tanais) flows, to the sea Miot (Pal. Mæotis) and Karaso (Chersonese). Adam's second place of abode is the land Eldad. Ham claims territory up to the fiery mountains, and westerly unto the sea Atil (Atlantic) and "the end at Gadith" (Gades). To Japhet appertains the district of Lag (Liguria), the mountain of Kilt (Kelts), the country to the west of Para (?), opposite to Apherag (Africa), and to his son Ijoajon (Javar) the land Adlud (Italy) and the neighbouring islands. Then Jacob after his return dwells at Akrabit; Rachel bears her son Benjamin in Kebrathan (Gen. xxxv. 16, Sept.). The Amorites build two towns, Robel and Thamuathares; the king of Canaan pursues the Egyptians up to the walls of Fromon (Heroopolis).

The legendary lore connected with Abraham is a study in itself. Many of the following Sagas are found in the Targum and elsewhere; but the labour of identifying them or tracing them to their sources is, for Bible students, more curious than profitable. The child Abram was, from very early years, filled with loathing for the vices of those among whom he lived. When only fourteen, he separated himself from his father, refusing to worship his idols, and praying to the great Creator to save him from being led astray by the evil practices of his countrymen. At his command the ravens refrained from devouring the seed that was sown in the fields; more than this, he invented a kind of drill, which was attached to the plough, and covered up the seeds as they were sown. As he grew older, he spoke seriously to his father about the folly and wickedness of worshipping idols; and Terah assented to his words, but dared not openly avow his sentiments for fear of his relations, who would slay without scruple all who opposed the prevailing religion. But when he was sixty years old, Abram could endure it no longer, and set fire to the temple by night; and Haran, his brother, perished [1] in the attempt to save the idols. Upon this, Terah and his family removed to Charran,[2] where they remained fourteen years. Here Abram learns the futility of astrology, shows entire dependence upon God, prays for deliverance from evil spirits who lead men's hearts astray, and is told by an angel not to return to Ur, but to leave his father's house, and to travel to Canaan. During his life he was subject to ten great trials or temptations:[3]—1. The departure

---

[1] Gen. xi. 28.
[2] This is the first call, Acts vii. 2–4; Gen. xi. 31.
[3] These are variously given in rabbinical tradition. See Rönsch, pp. 382 ff. Only the tenth is actually numbered in "Jubilees."

from his native land. 2. The famine which occasioned his retreat to Egypt. 3. The abduction of his wife. 4. The war with the kings. 5. The painful rite of circumcision. 6. The dismissal of Ishmael. 7. The expulsion of Hagar. 8. The sterility of Sarah. 9. The offering of Isaac. 10. The death and burial of Sarah. It is said that while the descendants of Noah down to Abraham's time violated the command not to eat blood, Abraham strictly observed it, and taught it to his posterity.

Variations from the received ritual observed in the celebration of festivals sometimes occur in our book. The beginnings of the first, fourth, seventh, and tenth months are to be observed as feasts, as they had already been observed by Noah. In the case of the feast of Tabernacles, no mention is made of the custom of drawing water from the pool of Siloam, and pouring it out solemnly at the altar, to which our Lord is supposed to allude in John vii. 37, 38. The omission may possibly be intended to befriend the Sadducees, who made the practice a subject of contention with the Pharisees, urging that it was never formally ordained by Moses, and therefore ought not to be observed.[1] Not, as already remarked, that the author was a Sadducee, but he may have wished to write in a conciliatory spirit, and not unnecessarily to obtrude points of difference. Other omissions are the injunction of fasting on the Day of Atonement, the exclusion of the uncircumcised from the Passover, and the appointment of Pentecost about the middle of the third month without specially naming the day. The time for the observance of the Passover is thus ordained: "The children of Israel

[1] See the authorities, *ap.* Rönsch, p. 514.

shall keep the Passover on its appointed day, the fourteenth day of the first month, between evenings, in the third part of the day unto the third part of the night; for two parts of the day are given to the light, and the third to night. This is that which the Lord hath commanded, that thou shouldst do it between evenings. And it shall not be done (sacrificed) in the morning, at any hour of the light, but in the confines of the evening. And ye shall eat it in the evening unto the third part of the night, and what remains after the third part of the night shall be burned with fire." The author divides the day and the night into three parts each; his "evening" consists of the third part of the day and the first two parts of night, his "morning" of the last part of the night and the first two parts of the day. The whole ceremony connected with the lamb must take place within the limits of the "evening" thus defined; it must be killed in the last third of the day, and eaten within the first two parts of the night, or, as he puts it, "unto the third part of the night," *i.e.* exclusive.[1] This interpretation of the phrase, "between the two evenings," Ex. xii. 6, and the other directions, express the practice which obtained in the writer's time, and offer a possible solution of what has always been a subject of dispute.

Explanations of the meaning of names are sometimes given.[2] Thus Eden is interpreted *pleasure*, which reminds one of the LXX. παράδεισος τῆς τρυφῆς, *Paradisus voluptatis*, Vulg. Sala (son of Cainan) is *dismissal*;

---

[1] Krüger, *Die Chronol. im B. d. Jub.* p. 298.
[2] These examples are collected by Rönsch, pp. 496 ff., and Frankel, *Monatsschr.* v. pp. 380 ff.

modern authorities make it to signify *extension*. Phalek is *division*, "for in his days the sons of Noah began to divide the earth." Ragev (= Reu or Ragau) is so named "because the sons of men have become *evil*" (chap. x.). Seruch refers to his *turning away* in order to commit wickedness (chap. xi.). Ur Kasdim takes its appellation from its founder Ur, and his father Kesed (chap. xi.). Tharah (Terah), son of Nakhor (Nahor), was so called by his father "because the birds stole and devoured the seeds sown in the fields."

Corrections of passages in the inspired narrative misunderstood, or liable to be misinterpreted, are offered, and supposed omissions or gaps are supplied from other sources. Some of these intercalations have been given above. The following are a few further examples. On the day that Adam fell, the mouths of all animals were closed, and they spoke no more as heretofore; our first parents were clothed in order to show their superiority to the beasts of the earth, and the directions concerning apparel were given to the Israelites to differentiate them from the heathen; the gradual deterioration of men was induced by the efforts of evil demons, who, until checked by God's interference, exercised terrible power upon earth; Noah's sons were saved, not for their own, but for their father's sake; the blessing of Shem (Gen. ix. 26, 27) was, "Blessed be the Lord God of Shem, and may the Lord dwell in his habitations;" it was at a religious festival that Noah drank wine; Terah abode in Charran when Abram left his home, but prayed his son to come and fetch him when he was settled in his new abode; Hagar died before Sarah, and it was after the death of both that Abraham married Keturah; before his death Abraham summoned Ishmael and his twelve sons, Isaac and his two sons, and the six sons of Keturah with their children, and gave them a solemn charge to cultivate purity and righteousness, and to live at peace with each other; Judah and Levi remained at home with their father (while the other sons were sent forth to tend the herds), and received special blessings and prerogatives from Isaac; for his action against the Shechemites, Levi was highly honoured, and his posterity was elected to the everlasting priesthood; Joseph withstood the solicitations of Potiphar's wife for a full year, being then seventeen years old; he was beloved by all the courtiers, because he was perfectly upright and fair, took no bribes, and behaved with affability to all; Jacob his father gave him two portions in the land of Canaan, and thenceforward Joseph lived in peace, and nothing evil happened to him till the day of his death.

In the chronology of our book many points are noteworthy. We have the formal announcement: "These are the words of the division of the days, according to the law and the testimony, according to the events of the years in sabbatical years and in jubilees." The Flood occurs A.M. 1353; and from the Creation to the Exodus, the period comprised in the work, the author reckons forty-nine jubilees, one year-week, and two years, *i.e.* 2410 years, and makes the passage of the Jordan to occur A.M. 2450. This date is composed exactly of fifty jubilees of forty-nine years each, and allows a new jubilee period to commence with the entrance into the promised land. Then his year consists of fifty-two weeks, *i.e.*

364 days. "The sun," he says, "was made for a great sign upon the earth to regulate days, and sabbaths, and years, and jubilees, and all seasons" (chap. ii.); "but the moon confuses and mars the order, and comes every year ten days in advance" (chap. vi.); and the only way of preventing confusion and error in the whole system of feasts, is to make the year number 364 days. Taking for granted that a new jubilee began at the entrance of the Israelites into Canaan, he had to arrange his chronology accordingly, and he therefore reckons, as we have said, fifty jubilees of forty-nine years each to the close of the wanderings in the desert. In very many particulars he agrees entirely with the Masoretic texts of Genesis and Exodus, but he takes liberties or follows a different reading in other passages. To give a few examples:—Jared was sixty-two years old when he begat Enoch, the present Hebrew text giving his age as one hundred and sixty-two; Methuselah's son Lamech was born when his father was sixty-seven (187, Heb.); Lamech was fifty-three (182, Heb.) when he begat Noah. These details are supported partly by the Septuagint, partly by the Samaritan Pentateuch. But in enumerating the post-diluvian patriarchs, the author is greatly at variance with existing authorities. Arphaxad begets Cainan seventy-four years after the Flood;[1] Cainan begets Salah in his fifty-seventh year; Salah begets Eber in his sixty-seventh; Eber, Peleg in

[1] The introduction of Cainan between Arphaxad and Salah is authorised by the LXX., but the chronology is different. Those who desire to enter further into the chronology of the Jubilees will find help in Dillmann, and in *Zeitschrift der Deutsch. morgenl. Gesellschaft*, 1858, pp. 279 ff., only rejecting the writer's unwarrantable conclusion that the book was written some three hundred years B.C.

his sixty-eighth; Peleg, Reu in his sixty-first; Serug, Nahor in the 116th year after the birth of Reu; Nahor, Terah in his sixty-second year. All these numbers differ from those in the Hebrew and the Septuagint. On the question of the "four hundred and thirty years," in Ex. xii. 40, the Jubilee Book would seem to agree with the LXX. in reading "in the land of Egypt and in the land of Canaan;" for the date of Isaac's birth is fixed A.M. 1980, *i.e.* 430 years before the Exodus, and thus the reckoning includes the sojourn in Canaan; but it dates the arrival of Jacob in Egypt at A.M. 2172, thus making the residence of the Israelites in that country last for two hundred and thirty-eight years. The arrangement of the years of Moses' life is not altogether in accordance with Scripture. He is born A.M. 2330, is introduced at the king's court at the age of twenty-one, kills the Egyptian and flees when he is forty-two, and remains in Midian for thirty-six years. Joseph's birth is set A.M. 2134, he is sold when seventeen years old, was a slave for ten and in prison for three years, and held supremacy in Egypt for eighty years, dying at the age of 110, "in the second year of the sixth week (year-week) of the forty-sixth jubilee," A.D. 2242. This would make him only 108 years old at his death. There are very many other passages where the dates given do not harmonise with preceding or succeeding statements. Some of these miscalculations are doubtless ascribable to clerical errors in MSS., some are corrected in the old Latin versions, but a great number of deviations remain which can only be explained by carelessness in the translator, or lapse of memory in the writer. Abraham is born A.M. 1876; he dies at the age of 175, "in the first week of the forty-fourth jubilee, in the second year," *i.e.* A.M. 2109, which is quite wrong, and would make him 233 years old at his death. And if, as Dillmann proposes, we read "the forty-third jubilee," we shall set his decease in A.M. 2060, which is still nearly ten years wrong according to the jubilee date of his birth. Such manifest mistakes we should be inclined to attribute to the scribe or the translator, rather than to the author himself. His plan, indeed, required great skill and precision. Starting from the principle that the period from the creation to the entrance into Canaan consisted of fifty jubilees of forty-nine years each, and being dominated by the idea of the sacredness and preponderance of the number seven, he had to fit events into their proper place in this septenary system. And certainly, if we consider the use of numbers in Holy Scripture and the mystery which attaches to them, we cannot but allow the importance of the number seven. In his zeal, however, for the use of this number, our author sometimes introduces it where Scripture is silent, sometimes for this purpose even alters the wording of his text. Thus he affirms that God opened seven sluices in heaven to produce the Flood, and that Benjamin's mess was seven times as great as his brethren's. But other considerations lead us to think that there is a significance in the scriptural employment of this number which is not to be disregarded. Its continual recurrence in the Revelation of St. John confirms this view. It is the number of forgiveness, of covenant, of holiness, perfection, and rest. The idea of rest, of course, meets us at the close of the work of creation; but there are many other instances of a similar use. Enoch, the seventh from Adam, never tasted death, but was translated and entered into his rest; six times seven stations brought the Israelites to the promised land; on the seventh day the walls of Jericho fell down, and the people took possession of the city, after they had marched round it seven times with seven priests blowing seven trumpets. I need here hardly mention the sabbatical year and the year of jubilee, by the former of which the soil obtained a period of rest after being cropped for six successive years, and by the latter the state, the body politic, had its rest and sanctification, for then estates returned to their original possessors, and slaves were manumitted. All the feasts were more or less connected with the sabbatical system. The Passover and the feast of Tabernacles lasted each of them seven days; seven weeks after the Passover came Pentecost; the great Day of Atonement occurred in the seventh month of the year, itself a sacred month; the days of holy convocation were seven. Further, the blood of propitiation was sprinkled seven times before the mercy-seat; seven were the pieces of furniture pertaining to the tabernacle; seven were the branches of the sacred candlestick.[1]

With such grounds for giving considerable importance to the number seven, our author with great skill reduced his historical facts to these dimensions; and it is not unlikely that many errors have crept into the present

[1] Some of the above remarks concerning the number seven are quoted from an article contributed by me some years ago to a now forgotten Review.

text from the scribes' or translators' neglect of this principle, and that many difficulties might be removed by the restoration of the septenary reckoning where it seems to be neglected. Where the chief dates, the epochs assigned to leading events, are not divisible by seven, we may reasonably conclude that there is some error in our versions which did not exist in the original, or that some passages have perished which would have introduced consistency in statements now incomplete or contradictory. The intended precision in the text, which to some events assigns not only the year, but even the month and the day, is attained by a comparison of the various dates afforded by the Hebrew, by arbitrary alterations, by rabbinical glosses, and by the introduction of later holy days and seasons into these earlier times. Many of the dates thus obtained are interesting. Thus the Fall takes place on the seventeenth day of the second month in the year 8; Abel offers his sacrifice in his twenty-second year at the full moon of the seventh month = the feast of Tabernacles, A.M. 99; Noah is born A.M. 709, and dies at the age of 950, A.M. 1659, having observed the feast of Weeks for 350 years, and being contemporary with Adam for more than 200 years. The sons of Noah were born thus:—Shem in 1207, Ham in 1209, and Japhet in 1212, and the Flood began in 1308; Noah divides the earth among his three sons in 1569; the tower of Babel was begun in the fourth week of the thirty-fourth jubilee = 1645 A.M., and the construction was stopped forty-three years afterwards. Abram leaves Egypt in 1961, when Tanis was built, and receives the covenant of circumcision on the feast of

First-fruits in 1979; Isaac is born on the same festival in the following year; he marries Rebecca in the same year that his father married Keturah; Abraham before he dies (A.M. 2060), blesses and instructs Jacob. Jacob is sixty-eight years old when he is sent away to Mesopotamia, A.M. 2114. Isaac dies (A.M. 2162) in the same year that Joseph, being then of the age of thirty, is raised to be next to King Pharaoh. The birth of Pharez and Zarah coincides with the end of the seven years of plenty in Egypt.

In the above chronological arrangements there are many inconsistencies and inaccuracies which are easy to point out; but the labour is hardly profitable, as the dates have been quoted merely to give a notion of the treatment employed which satisfied the author's requirements, and not with any idea of effecting an improvement in the received chronology, faulty and deceptive as it undoubtedly is. The subject has been taken in hand by Krüger (in *Zeitschrift der Deutsch. morgenl. Gesellschaft*, 1858), who has examined most of the chronological statements in the book, showing their various inconsistencies and correcting errors where possible.

There are passages relating to events then future, sometimes not told in prophetic character. Thus it is said (chap. xxxviii.): "There were kings who reigned over Edom, before that a king reigned over the children of Israel, even unto this day. There was a king in Edom, Balak son of Beor, the name of whose city was Dinaba." But commonly many matters of later history are assigned to early times, especially those that are concerned with ceremonial and ritual observances. Thus the Sabbath was observed by the angels in heaven [1] before it was appointed for men at the end of the creation. The law about the purification of women after childbirth (Lev. xii.) is traced to the fact that Adam was made in the first week and Eve in the second; hence the enactment, "seven days for a man-child and two weeks for a maid-child." And the further law concerning the time of separation after parturition is grounded on the introduction of Adam into Eden forty days after his creation, and of Eve eighty days after her formation. This law is still observed in the Abyssinian Church. At sunrise on the day that Adam was banished from the garden, he offers incense composed of the four ingredients specified in Ex. xxx. 34; Cain's fate was an example of the law of retaliation afterwards re-enacted, Lev. xxiv. 18 ff.; the use of the jubilee periods was taught by Enoch to his contemporaries; Noah does all in accordance with the Mosaic Law, offering sacrifice of the appointed animals, and first-fruits and drink-offerings. The law of tithes is established from the time of Abraham, who also celebrated the feast of First-fruits and of Tabernacles, and made it an ordinance for ever according to Lev. xxiii. 34 ff. Abraham anticipates the special instructions concerning laying salt on the sacrifice, using certain wood for the fires,[2] purifications, and

---

[1] This notion is found also in the Assumption of Moses, chap. i. 17.

[2] There are some fourteen trees mentioned whose wood may be used in the sacrificial fire (chap. xvi.). Many of these cannot be identified. A wood offering is spoken of Neh. x. 34, xiii. 31. Abraham's incense consists of the seven substances mentioned in Ecclus. xxiv. 15.

washings. The prohibition against intermarrying with the Canaanites was originally uttered by the same patriarch; and the rule concerning the betrothing of the elder daughter before the younger was transcribed in the heavenly tables, which also enacted the punishment of death for Israelites guilty of mixed marriages or harlotry. The Day of Atonement on the tenth day of the seventh month (Lev. xxiii.) was established by Jacob in memory of the loss of Joseph. Joseph resisted the temptation of Potiphar's wife because he knew of the eternal law against adultery which had been delivered to Abraham and transmitted by him to his children; and Judah's sin with his daughter-in-law Tamar led to the statute against such incestuous unions, and the punishment of them by fire. It was at the feast of Tabernacles that Levi was consecrated to be priest by his father in Bethel, when "he clothed him in sacerdotal robes, and filled his hands," offering very ample sacrifices, and assigning to him from that day forward not only the first-fruits, but also the second tithe which was now introduced. We may add that, according to our book, there was much esoteric teaching which was not openly divulged to the people, but was communicated to the patriarchs in secret writings and by them transmitted to posterity.

Having given the above sketch of the contents of our book, we may now briefly examine the author's teaching upon certain points of doctrine, and then we shall be better able to come to some conclusion concerning the aim and tendency of the document.

The teaching concerning angels and demons is in many respects such as is found elsewhere. The former are often called Watchers, as in other apocalyptic works. The Angel of the Presence and his companions convey God's will to men, instruct them in all useful knowledge of things in heaven and in earth, and execute God's wrath against sinners. The serpent is not identified with Satan in the account of the Fall. The great flow of iniquity overspreading the earth is traced to the intercourse of angels with the daughters of men, which introduced a race of beings gigantic in stature as in wickedness. And when God determined to destroy men with the Flood, he punished the sinning angels by confining them in the depths of the earth till the great day of judgment. But a race of evil demons sprang from them,[1] who vexed and deceived and tortured the sons of Noah so grievously that they came to their father and asked his intercession to free them from their malice. And Noah prayed to God to check their power and withhold them from having dominion over the righteous seed. And the Lord commanded His angels to take and bind them and cast them into the place of torment. But Mastema,[2] the chief of the demons, requested that some might be left to execute his will in the earth; and God permitted one-tenth of them to remain, reserving the rest for the place of judgment. And to counteract the

---

[1] The same idea is found in the Book of Enoch xv. 8–10.

[2] Mastema is often mentioned in Lepto-Genesis, generally with the epithet "supreme," "highest." The Hebrew word Mastemah is found in Hos. ix. 7, 8, in the sense of "hatred," where the LXX. translate μανία and Aquila ἐγκότησις. The word in the Ethiopian is written Mastema, in the Latin Mastima, and in later Greek Mastiphat. In the apocryphal *Act. Apost.* (ed. Tischend., Lips. p. 98) the form is Mansemat.

diseases which the demons had introduced among mankind, one of the good angels taught Noah the use of medicines and the virtues of herbs, all which lore he wrote in a book and imparted to his son Shem before his death. There is some appearance of a classification of angels in Lepto-Genesis. The highest is the Angel of the Presence, who leads the Israelites in the pillar of fire and cloud; the second are the archangels, or the angels of blessing; the third are the angels of the elements, who direct the powers of nature. These were all created on the first day with the heaven and earth (chap. ii.); and their agency is introduced on every occasion. Nothing happens or is done without their co-operation. They bring men's sins before God. Adam was indebted to them for learning his work in Eden, Enoch for his knowledge of all things in heaven and earth. It was they who bound the fallen angels, taught Noah the use of feast days, presided at the division of the earth among his sons, came to inspect the Tower of Babel. Abram was called by an angel to the Land of Promise, and instructed in the Hebrew tongue; by an angel was his hand arrested at the sacrifice of Isaac. Angels unfold the future to Abram and to Jacob, save Moses at the inn from the demon who thought to slay him, bring to naught the devices of the Egyptian magicians.

Concerning the immortality of the soul, though it is an article of the author's creed, very little is said, nothing concerning the resurrection of the body. Speaking of the prosperity of Israel in the latter days, the writer observes (chap. xxiv.): "They shall see the punishment of their enemies, and their bones shall rest in the earth, but their spirit shall have much peace, and they shall know that the Lord is He who keeps justice and shows mercy on hundreds and thousands and on all who love Him." If, as is probable, the author wished his work to be acceptable to all his countrymen without regard to sects and parties, the omission of a tenet repudiated by the powerful sect of the Sadducees may be accounted for.

The idea of a personal Messiah is nowhere recognised. Moses is told to write the account of his revelation for the use of posterity, " till the Lord should descend and dwell with them for ever and ever, and His sanctuary should be raised in their midst, and He Himself should be seen by them, that all might know that He is the God of Israel" (chap. i.). So in the Assumption of Moses the seer looks forward to no earthly monarch or heaven-sent delegate who should fill the throne of David and lead the people to victory, but he expects the manifestation of Jehovah Himself, as in the wilderness of old, guiding and ruling with some evident token of His presence. In Lepto-Genesis, Zion is to be the seat of this Epiphany; for "in the new creation Zion shall be sanctified, and through it shall all the world be purified from guilt and uncleanness for ever and ever" (chap. iv.). And as for Israel, it is written and firmly established, that if they turn to the Lord in righteousness, He will remove their guilt and forgive their sin, "and compassion shall be shown to all who turn from all their misdeeds once a a year" (chap. v.), *i.e.* on the Day of Atonement. In another place (chap. xv.) the author says, that God has appointed no one to reign over Israel, neither Spirit nor angel, but that He Himself is their only Lord and Sovereign. Other nations have their appointed guardian angels, and depend less directly upon God for government, but Israel is guided and protected by the immediate interference of the Lord.[1] He is the first-born, chosen out of all the peoples, selected to be the depositary of the law, and bound to mark his superiority to the rest of the world by the observance of the Sabbath and the rite of circumcision. In his family is the race of priests who intercede with God for all flesh and do Him acceptable service. The writer is copious in enunciating the pre-eminence of his people, and looks forward to a time when, as a reward for their repentance and renewed adherence to God, they should triumph over their enemies and reign supreme in the earth. What is to become of the rest of the world is nowhere definitely expressed, as in pursuance of his plan the seer was not bound to extend his gaze beyond the occupation of the Promised Land and the results consequent thereon; and if he looks forward to a time when Israel shall revolt from God and disobey His law, he is really recalling the warnings given in Deuteronomy with only faint allusion to the events of later times or the prospects of a dim futurity. At the same time the narrow insularity of the writer and his contempt for, and hatred of other nations are continually appearing in his pages, so that what Tacitus (*Hist.* v. 5) says of the feeling of the Jews may certainly be predicated of our author: "Adversus omnes alios hostile odium." Ammon and Moab, the Edomites and Amorites, are exhibited as

[1] Comp. Deut. xxxii. 8, 9, 12, Sept., and Ecclus. xvii. 17.

the enemies of God's people, the object of Heaven's curse, and doomed to destruction. The feud with the Canaanites dates from very early times. They were to be exterminated, not merely for their enormous wickedness which cried aloud for chastisement, but chiefly because Canaan the son of Ham seized on the region from Lebanon to the brook of Egypt which appertained to the inheritance of Shem, thus dispossessing the righteous seed. While Israel was under God's immediate rule and guidance, other nations were governed not merely by guardian angels, but by demons who alienated them from the Lord. And the reward of Israel's repentance is to be found in the utter subjection of enemies and the heavy punishment inflicted on subject peoples.

Inflated with the notion of the superiority of Israel, the author can ill admit errors in the conduct of the chief fathers of the race, and takes pains to palliate the faults which are attributed to them in the canonical accounts, or to pass them over in silence. They are in his view paragons of virtue and piety, scrupulous observers of the ritual and ceremonial law before it was publicly enacted. Such excellent personages could not greatly err. Thus Abram's deceit in the matter of Sarai at the court of Pharaoh is left unrecorded, while various particulars of his early piety, learning, and devotion, not mentioned in Genesis, are painted in glowing colours. In Isaac's question to Jacob the omission of the name Esau—"Art thou my very son?" and his answer, "I am thy son"—clears Jacob from a verbal falsehood; just as the alteration in Gen. xliv. 15, mentioned above, is intended to secure Joseph from the charge of practising divination.

Isaac repents of his partiality for Esau and learns to regard Jacob as his true son and heir; so Jacob in late life loves and honours Leah, having freely forgiven the treacherous part which she once had played. His piety is exhibited in every circumstance of his life; when he flees from Laban, he prays and worships the God of his fathers before he sets forth; he affords a pattern of filial devotion by his obedience to his parents, and the care he takes in ministering regularly to their wants. Not to weary the reader with particulars, one can say shortly that the book is filled with the glorification of the patriarchs, who were represented as adorned with every virtue, and as genuine Israelites, observers of the Mosaic Law, moral and ceremonial.

A few words may now be added concerning the object and intention of this treatise. The aim of the writer is not difficult to define. In the first place, he evidently desired to explain difficulties which had met him in reflecting on the statements of Scripture. Some things had been misunderstood; he would interpret them aright. Some things were obscure; he would make them clear. Some omissions occurred; he would supply the missing links. Some points were only hinted at or too briefly stated; he would develop these intimations into complete and well-rounded statements. Especially seemed the glosser's hand to be needed in arranging the chronology of the patriarchal times. In this matter, however, as we have shown above, he has not been uniformly successful, his arithmetic being sometimes faulty and landing him in impossible results. As he claims credit for his statements on the ground of a heavenly revelation, we should be inclined to attribute these errors to copyists; but unfortunately they are of such frequent occurrence, and many of them are so interwoven with the narrative, that they must be assigned to the author's carelessness or his inability to keep in hand all the links of his long history.

Another object was in the writer's mind. Around the sacred record of Genesis and Exodus had arisen a rank growth of legends, additions, and traditionary statements; some features of Biblical characters were exaggerated, the merest hints were expanded into detailed narratives, and sagas took the place of the simple authentic accounts. In the Alexandrian school persons and events were idealised into abstractions, and became merely metaphors and pictures of vices and virtues. The Book of Jubilees recalls men from these speculations to plain historical, or quasi-historical, facts. It makes the heroes of the Bible living characters. Discarding much legendary matter, it claims for the narrative, with its many additions to the sacred text, a supreme importance, and tells the tale of the patriarchs in an authoritative style which enforces acceptance, and with such amplification as requires no further increment. It recounts early history in the spirit of the writer's own day. We here are shown what a pious Jew felt and believed at the commencement of the Christian era. His opinions on momentous topics, such as Satan, the immortality of the soul, future judgment, are intimated or distinctly set forth. The writing aims to be a popular work, such an one as would seize upon the mind of the less instructed, whether Jews or proselytes, and hold them to their faith by fear as well as reverence. Hence come the exaggerated penalties for certain common offences, and the claim of primitive revelation for many peculiarly Jewish observances. Compared with the heavenly origin and hoar antiquity of Jewish customs, morals, and ritual, all other religions were inferior and of no account; and the Hebrew must be known among all nations by his strict adherence to the precepts of his forefathers. Having this object in view, the writer takes special pains to enforce certain portions of the Mosaic Law, both by glorifying its origin and by denouncing vengeance on its infringement. Notably is this the case with the law of sacrifice and offering. He is most particular in showing the customs of the earliest patriarchs in this matter, how that they never failed to make offerings on every suitable occasion, how that Abraham delivered to Isaac most stringent commands concerning sacrifice, and how highly honoured was Levi as the father of the priestly family. In other cases the inculcation of a command goes far beyond Scripture in strictness. The man who eats blood shall be utterly destroyed, he and his seed for ever, as long as the earth exists (chap. vi.). The father who gives his daughter, or he who gives his sister, in marriage to a heathen shall be stoned to death, and the wife shall be burned with fire (chap. xxx.). The Sabbath is broken even by speaking of taking a journey, or of buying and selling, by lighting a fire, by drawing water, etc.,[1] and the offender is to be put to death. A second tithe is due to the Lord, and must be paid for ever by all true

---

[1] Among Sabbath-breakers is reckoned, according to Dillmann's version, "der bei seinem Weibe schläft," a deduction from Ex. xix. 15.

Israelites. Only certain named (chap. xxi.) woods are to be used for the fire of the burnt-offering. The feast of Tabernacles is to be celebrated with garlands on the head, and with a procession round the altar seven times on every day of the festival. There is a multitude of other strict and irksome enactments, which, as they were in force in the time of our Lord, justified His saying of the scribes and Pharisees (Matt. xxiii. 4): " They bind heavy burdens, and grievous to be borne, and lay them on men's shoulders." One sees in the Jubilees the spirit and temper which met our blessed Lord in His earthly teaching, the way in which a strong and dominant party used the Old Testament to support their objects. Close observance of the law, minutiæ of ceremony, strictness of ritual, were enjoined by our author with the view of differentiating his own people from all other nations, and raising them to the highest eminence as specially favoured by God, and bound to uphold their just prerogatives. They were subject to many perilous attractions at this time. Greece with its science and culture, Rome with its might and supremacy, alike drew away adherents from Hebraism. Many had become ashamed of their religion and their very nationality. Herod's party was Jewish only in name. It may be that the teaching, miracles, and example of Christ had also begun to move men's minds. All these dangers required some counteracting energy to resist their influence. Our author offers his book as a panacea. The law, which he endeavours to enforce, was of no human origin, and of no ephemeral existence; it was eternal, always written in the heavenly tablets, and intended to last and to be executed for ever and ever. Evidently he desires to reanimate the spirit of Judaism, which he saw to be endangered by contact with its surroundings; and, taking no prominent side in the contest of parties, he wishes to combine all true Israelites together in resistance to the worldly or heathen influences around them, which were undermining the faith of the people, and introducing laxity and innovation, to unite under one banner the divided elements of the holy nation, "till the sanctuary of the Lord should be raised on the hill of Zion, and the portion of Israel should be holiness, and peace, and blessing, from henceforth and for ever" (chap. i.).

THE ASCENSION OF ISAIAH.

PASSING through Drury Lane in the year of grace 1819, and examining the bookstalls which then rendered that locality a happy hunting-ground for bibliomaniacs, Richard Laurence, Archbishop of Cashel, at the counter of one J. Smith, lighted upon an Ethiopic version of the Prophecy of Isaiah, to which was appended a further treatise, called the "Ascension of Isaiah." The bookseller, not recognising the value of the work, sold it for a trifle; but the Archbishop, who was tolerably well acquainted with the language in which it was written, at once perceived that he had become the possessor of a long-lost book, and one which was a precious contribution to the study of Jewish-Christian thought in the first period of Christianity. Nor was it long before he made the literary world cognisant of his discovery, publishing the Ethiopic text with an English and a Latin version, critical notes, and observations on the date, contents, and bearing of the tractate.[1] Of this pseudepigraphical work, considered to belong to the earliest Christian centuries, I propose to give some account.

The history of the text is soon told. The MS. on which Archbishop Laurence based his edition is now in the Bodleian Library, and was for a time deemed to be the only authority extant or available. It had previously passed through perilous experience. Written originally for the use of a monk, Aaron, who was about to travel in the Holy Land, it had been brought back from Jerusalem by Th. Petræus, who, in his edition of the Prophecy of Jonah translated from the Ethiopic into Latin (A.D. 1660), mentions that he had examined it. How it arrived at the bookstall in Drury Lane is unknown. At the time it appeared no other copy was known to exist.

But since that date supplementary aids for determining the text have come to light, and scholars on the Continent have exercised their ingenuity in correcting erroneous readings and renderings, and in elucidating and illustrating the work. In 1828, Angelus Mai published two fragments of an ancient Latin version of portions of the work, containing chaps. ii. 14 to iii. 13, and vii. 1-19, without being aware of what work they

---

[1] "Ascensio Isaiæ vatis, opusculum pseudepigraphum, multis abhinc seculis, ut videtur, deperditum, nunc autem apud Æthiopas compertum, et cum versione Latina Anglicaque publici juris factum a Ricardo Laurence." Oxoniae 1819.

formed a portion. Their right position was discovered by Niebuhr, and fully discussed by Nitzsch in *Stud. und Krit.* 1830. Another section (chaps. vi.–xi.), containing what is called the "Vision of Isaiah," was known to have been printed at Venice in 1522, and was quoted by Sixtus Senensis in his *Bibl. Sancta* (lib. ii. p. 59) under the title of "Anabasis" or "Anabatikon," but no copy was forthcoming, till one was found in 1832 in the library at Munich, and edited with preface and notes by J. C. L. Gieseler. The Abyssinian war in 1868, as it was magnificently named, if it conferred no glory on its promoters and executors, brought into our possession some literary treasures which have proved of great interest. Among the plunder thus obtained at Magdala were two Ethiopic MSS. of the "Ascension," which are now deposited in the British Museum. They are of no great antiquity, being attributed to the fifteenth and eighteenth centuries respectively; but they have been employed with good effect by Dillmann in preparing his useful edition of the work.[1] By collating these MSS. with Laurence's text, he has been enabled to correct the

---

[1] "Ascensio Isaiæ Æthiopice et Latine cum Prolegomenis, Adnotationibus criticis et exegeticis, additis versionum Latinarum reliquiis, edita ab Augusto Dillmann." Lipsiæ 1877. Of this excellent little work I have made much use, and hereby thankfully acknowledge my obligations to the author. A translation of the Ascension is given in the *Lutheran Quarterly* of October 1878, vol. viii. pp. 513 ff.; but this I have been unable to consult, as it is not to be found either in the British Museum or in the Cambridge University Library. Many learned Germans, *e.g.* Grimm, Gieseler, Nitzsch, Ewald, Gfrörer, Movers, have treated of the work with completeness, not to say prolixity. It is also handled by Gesenius in his *Commentary on Isaiah*, vol. i. p. 45 ff. (1821).

latter in numerous places, to fill up *lacunæ*, and to prove the existence of many interpolations and corruptions. In the year following this publication another discovery was made. The National Library at Paris was found to possess a Greek MS. with the title: "The Prophecy, Revelation, and Martyrdom of the holy and glorious and greatest of the prophets, Isaiah the Prophet," and it was concluded that at length the original and long-lost text had been discovered. Further examination proved that this expectation was by no means realised. The document in question was a beautiful parchment of the twelfth century, containing a collection of Legends of the Saints commemorated in the Calendar between the first day of March and the last of May. In the Eastern Church Isaiah is commemorated, May 9, in company with the martyr Christopher, and as appointed for that day the MS. inserts the Legends of these two worthies. The Latin Church observes another day in memory of the prophet; but neither in the Roman Breviary nor in the Greek Menaion is there any trace of this particular form of the myth. Disappointment met the sanguine examiners of this manuscript. It was found to contain only a portion of the work, and that in a different order from that of the Ethiopic text, and with the omission of an important and lengthy passage. It is to be regarded merely as an extract from the original as contained in chaps. vi.–xi. and ii.–v., with many glosses and additions. The omitted part is that which, from internal evidence, is supposed to be of Christian origin, and was doubtless absent from the copy whence the Greek MS. was taken; otherwise, as it contains matter most suitable for a legendary, it would have found a place there. In this document, to the legend concerning Isaiah's death is appended a myth concerning his burial and the origin of the Pool of Siloam, which came into existence in answer to his prayers. The legend here takes the same form as that which is found in the *Chronicon Paschale* of the Byzantine Histories. There is no doubt that it is not a correct copy of the original Greek work, but is a compilation from it, containing doubtless many genuine passages, retaining much of the actual wording, but with the whole story abbreviated, epitomised, and refashioned. The fragment is printed with prefatory remarks by Dr. Oscar von Gebhardt in Hilgenfeld's *Zeitschrift* for 1878, pp. 330 ff. Since this publication I am not aware that any further aid for the settling of the text has appeared.

Postponing for a time the consideration of the internal evidence for the date of the work, which will be more satisfactorily treated after we have glanced at the contents, we may proceed to examine its external claims to be regarded as contemporaneous with primitive Christian times. In suchlike investigations, where the original is no longer extant, we are reduced to searching for citations and references in early writers, whether acknowledged or recognisable. Speaking of the trials of God's servants in old time, the author of the Epistle to the Hebrews mentions (chap. xi. 37) that some of them "were sawn asunder." Now to the other trials, or forms of death noticed in the passage, we can find parallels in the histories of the worthies of the Old Testament, or in the Books of Maccabees; but there is no instance of a primitive saint meeting his death by the saw. It is true that David is said to have put the Ammonites under saws; but these were not martyrs, but enemies of Israel, and it is quite possible that the expression means no more than that they were put to the servile work of sawing timber. It is true also that, according to the Greek version of Amos, the Damascenes sawed asunder the Gileadite women;[1] but the writer in the Epistle is not speaking of such wholesale cruelty practised on a large district, but of the tortures and murders of individuals. The only saint who is supposed to have experienced death in this manner is Isaiah; and the tradition which asserts that he was sawn asunder with a wooden saw is found embodied in the book which we are considering, where we are told that Manasseh, incensed at Isaiah's warnings, had him thus slain, and with his fawning false prophets around him stood by deriding the holy man's sufferings.[2] Of course, the reference in the Epistle may belong to some other person than Isaiah, though we know of none to whom it would apply; or the writer may have derived the tradition from a different source than the "Ascension;" and therefore no argument for the date of the work can be grounded on this allusion; but there seems to have been a curious consensus of commentators in regarding the expression as appertaining to the peculiar end of Isaiah as detailed in the Jewish story, which also seems to have been known to Josephus, as he speaks of Manasseh not

[1] See 2 Sam. xii. 31; Amos i. 3.
[2] The spot where this event took place is still pointed out traditionally. It is marked by an ancient mulberry tree standing at the side of the Red, or Lower, Pool, a reservoir formed by the overflow from Siloam.

sparing even the prophets of the Lord (*Antiq.* x. 3. 1). But there are early references to the book itself under different names. Justin Martyr, indeed, who, in his *Dialogue with Trypho the Jew* (chap. cxx.), alludes to the death of Isaiah, does not mention our book by name, but he refers unmistakably to the tradition therein embodied. He is showing from the Old Testament the mission and character of Christ, and he tells his antagonist that, had the Jews understood the full import of such passages, they would have removed them from the text, as they have removed "those relating to the death of Isaiah, whom," he says, "ye sawed in pieces with a wooden saw." It is not clear what part of Scripture Justin supposes to have been thus violently handled, but his reference to the mode of the prophet's death recalls the wording of the "Ascensio." There can, however, be no mistake about Tertullian's acquaintance with the work, and with that part of it which is evidently of Jewish origin. In his treatise *On Patience* (chap. xiv.), he writes, "Exhibiting such powers of patience, Isaiah is cut asunder, and holds not his peace concerning the Lord." Evidently he has in view that passage of the Ascension given below, where it is said that Isaiah continued to converse with the Holy Spirit till he was sawn asunder. In the so-called *Apostolical Constitutions* (vi. 16), the work is mentioned among certain ancient productions and termed ἀπόκρυφον Ἡσαΐου. The same name is given to it by Origen, who more than once appeals to it as his authority for the martyrdom, and derives other observations therefrom. In his *Epistle to Africanus* (chap. ix.), after remarking that the Jews were accustomed to remove from popular cognisance all things supposed to be derogatory to elders and judges, while preserving many of such facts in secret books, he instances the story of Isaiah, which, he says, is confirmed by the testimony of the Epistle to the Hebrews, thus making the document that contains the legend of more ancient date than the Epistle. And he continues: " It is clear that tradition reports that Isaiah was sawn asunder ; and so it is stated in a certain apocryphal writing (ἔν τινι ἀποκρύφῳ), which was perhaps purposely corrupted by the Jews who introduced incongruous readings in order to throw discredit on the whole narrative." So again, in the Commentary on St. Matthew (xiii. 57, xxiii. 37), he writes: " Now, if any refuse to receive this story because it is recorded in the Apocryphon of Isaiah (ἐν τῷ ἀροκρύφῳ ʽΗσαΐᾳ), let him believe what is written in the Epistle to the Hebrews, even as the account of the death of Zechariah, slain between the temple and the altar, is to be believed on the testimony of the Saviour, though the tale was not drawn from the common and published books, but, as I suppose, from some apocryphal writing." His acquaintance with our book is still further expressed in one of his Homilies on Isaiah (tom. iii. p. 108), where the resemblance to a passage quoted below is perfectly obvious. " They say that Isaiah was cut asunder by the people, as one who depraved the law and spoke beyond what Scripture authorised. For Scripture says, No one shall see my face and live; but he says, I saw the Lord of Hosts. Moses, they say, saw Him not, and thou didst see Him! And for this cause they cut him asunder and condemned him as impious." Quoted from memory, as this doubtless was, it is sufficiently close to the original to show whence it was derived. St. Ambrose (in Ps. cxviii. tom. i. p. 1124) refers to Satan's attempt to make Isaiah save his life by apostasy, narrated in chap. v. of the Ascension. "It is recorded by many that a certain prophet, being in prison, and in danger of immediate execution, was thus addressed by the devil: Say that the Lord hath not spoken by thee in all that thou hast uttered, and I will turn all men's hearts and affections to thee, so that they who now are wroth at thy offence shall be the first to pardon thee." The author of the *Opus imperfectum* on St. Matthew, inserted among the works of St. Chrysostom, which is assigned to the fifth century, gives some details which must have been derived from what is now the first and second chapters of our book. He is commenting on the name Manasseh in the genealogy of our Lord, and he asserts, resting on the etymology of the word, "one who forgets," that he was proleptically so called, because he would *forget* all the holy conversation of his father and all the benefits which he had received, and at the instigation of the devil would do everything to provoke the anger of the Lord. This, as we shall see below, is in exact agreement with the beginning of the martyrdom in our book. But there is more than this. The passage that follows is evidently borrowed from the *proëmium* of the Apocryphon, as a comparison with the words in brackets will show: "Now when Hezekiah was sick at a certain time, and Isaiah the prophet came to visit him, he called for his son Manasseh, and began to admonish him that he ought to fear God, and told him how to reign, and many other things. (It came to pass in the twenty-sixth year of the reign of Hezekiah, king of Judah, that he sent for his only son Manasseh, and called him before Isaiah, the son of Amos, the prophet, and before Josab, the son of Isaiah, that he might deliver unto him the words of truth in which he had himself been instructed . . . and the truths relating to the faith of the Beloved which had been communicated to him in the year of his reign when he was visited with sickness.) And Isaiah said unto him: These words of mine do not descend into thy son's heart, and therefore I myself must needs die by his hand. (And Isaiah spake unto King Hezekiah in the presence of Manasseh, and said: As God liveth, Manasseh thy son will surely disregard all these precepts and words, and by the deed of his hands, with great torment of body, shall I depart this life.) When Hezekiah heard this, he wished to kill his son, saying: It is better for me to die childless than to leave a son who will provoke the wrath of God, and persecute His saints. (When Hezekiah heard this he wept abundantly, rent his garments, put dust upon his head, and fell upon his face. . . . And Hezekiah secretly intended to kill his son Manasseh.) But the prophet Isaiah restrained him with difficulty, saying: May God frustrate this thy purpose; for he saw the piety of Hezekiah, that he loved God better than his son. (But Isaiah said: In these things I cannot indulge thee . . . the beloved hath frustrated thy purpose, and the thought of thy heart shall not be fulfilled.") Epiphanius [1] attests that certain heretics of

[1] Epiphan. *Hæres.* lxvii. 3 (p. 712); xl. *De Archonticis* (p. 292).

the third century made use of our work, which he calls τὸ ἀναβατικὸν (Ascensio) Ἡσαΐου, to support their opinions. Thus one Hieracas, an Egyptian heresiarch, grounded his position that Melchisedek (of whom it is said, Heb. vii. 3, that he was like the Son of God, and abideth a priest continually) was the Holy Spirit, upon certain passages in chaps. ix. and xi. of the Ascension. "The angel showed me of all things before me, and said: Who is this on the right hand of God? And I answered: Thou knowest, O Lord. And he said: This is the Beloved. (I beheld one standing whose glory surpassed all things. . . . This is the Lord of all the glory which thou hast beheld.) And who is the other like unto Him coming on the left hand? And I answered: Thou knowest. This is the Holy Spirit that speaketh in thee and in the prophets. And He was like to the Beloved. (While I was conversing, I perceived another glorious being, who was like to Him in appearance. . . . The second which I saw was on the left hand of my Lord. And I asked: Who is this? And he replied: Worship Him, for this is the angel of the Holy Spirit who speaketh in thee and other saints. . . . I perceived that He sat down on the right hand of that great glory. I perceived likewise that the angel of the Holy Spirit sat down on the left hand.") Epiphanius says of the Archontici (a sect who held that the world was created by angels, and that there were seven heavens, each presided over by an archon or ruler) that they derive their tenets from the Ἀναβατικὸν Ἡσαΐου, and other apocryphal works. The statement on which they relied is found in the seventh and following chapters of the

Ascension, where Isaiah's passage through the seven heavens, with their presiding angels, is described. The work was also known to St. Jerome, who refers to it in his commentary on Isa. lxiv. 4: "From of old men have not heard, nor perceived by the ear, neither hath the eye seen a God beside Thee, which worketh for him that waiteth for Him."[1] After comparing the analogous passage in 1 Cor. ii. 9, he adds: "Ascensio enim Isaiæ et Apocalypsis Heliæ[2] hoc habent testimonium." We search in vain for this reference in the existing Ethiopic text, but it occurs as an interpolation in the Latin fragment printed at Venice, where we read (xi. 34): "The angel said unto me: This is sufficient for thee, Isaiah; for thou hast seen what no other mortal man in the flesh hath ever beheld, what neither eye hath seen, nor ear hath heard, nor hath it risen into the heart of man what great things God hath prepared for all who love Him." There is no record of our work after this in the Fathers, though it is mentioned under the names Anabaticon, Ascensus, 'Ησαίου ὅρασις, in two or three catalogues of Scripture and apocryphal writings.[3] In the *Apostolical Constitutions* (vi. 16) a list of apocryphal works is given which are deemed pernicious and repugnant to the

[1] The passages above are quoted by Fabricius, *Codex Pseudepigr. Vet. Test.*, by Laurence, and by other writers.
[2] The Apocalypse of Elijah is mentioned in the *Apostolical Constitutions* (vi. 16), and by some of the Fathers, consisting, according to the *Stichometria* of Nicephorus, of 316 verses; but the text has entirely perished.
[3] See the catalogue in Anastasius, *Quæstiones et Responsiones*, Lat. Bibl. Max. Patr. ix.; and Sixtus Senensis, *Bibl. Sancta*, i. The Ascensio occurs in the catalogue of *The Sixty Books* among ἀπόκρυφα.

truth; among these appears ἀπόκρυφον 'Ησαίου, which probably represents the Ascension. For some five or six centuries the book remained in obscurity; then, for an instant, it crops up in the *Quæstiones et Responsiones* of Anastasius in the eleventh century, where, in the catalogue of canonical and apocryphal books, we find 'Ησαίου ὅρασις, the Vision of Isaiah, which describes the second section of our work. Under the same name Euthymius Zigabenus denounces it as the origin of the heresy of the Messalians with regard to the Holy Trinity. Many of the Gnostic sects found support in the statements or wording of the Ascension, and it is said to have been employed in the same way by the Cathari of Western Europe, the Albigenses, and similar sects. On the other hand, Archbishop Laurence adduces passages from the work in defence of orthodoxy against the Unitarians and depravers of the Gospel history, endeavouring, and with partial success, to show that the doctrine of the Holy Trinity and the miraculous conception and birth of our Lord were known to the author, as well as other events narrated in the Christian story. We shall meet with these statements when we investigate the contents of the book.

A critical examination of the work confirms Dillmann's opinion that it consists of three or four sections composed by different authors and at different periods, and very clumsily arranged as a whole, the writer introducing the prophet as relating to Hezekiah his vision, after he has been recounting the deaths of Isaiah and the king. This inversion is accounted for by the mode in which the present work was put together. There is markedly a Jewish portion containing an account of the martyrdom of Isaiah, and a purely Christian portion embracing the ascension or vision of the prophet. Combining together these two divisions come a preface and conclusion of Christian origin, though the introduction displays a not very evident connection with what follows; and interspersed occur many Jewish and Christian additions, interpolations, and supplements. The first part, which (according to Laurence's arrangement of the work into chapters and verses, is comprised in chaps. ii. 1–iii. 12, and v. 2–14) contains the details of the murder of Isaiah, and may be reasonably supposed to have some historical basis. Thus the account runs: "It came to pass after the death of Hezekiah that Manasseh reigned, who forgat his father's precepts, Sammael [= Satan] dwelling in him and adhering to him. He likewise ceased to worship the great and good God of his father, serving Satan, and his angels, and his hosts. And he changed in his father's house the words of wisdom which had been in the presence of Hezekiah and the worship of Almighty God (Eth.[1]). And he turned his heart to serve Berial (Belial).[2]

[1] "Eth." refers to the Ethiopic text of Laurence translated by him and by Dillmann, "Gr." to the Greek text edited by Gebhardt. The latter here has, "he turned aside all the power of his father from the service and worship of Almighty God, and they served the devil and his angels." . . . This is in agreement with 1 Cor. x. 20: "the things which the Gentiles sacrifice they sacrifice unto devils." Rabbinical writers continually refer to Sammael as using the serpent to tempt Eve (see the Targum on Gen. iii. 1, 6); and he plays a great part in the death of Moses.

[2] Berial, and elsewhere by transposition Beliar, which occurs continually in the Testimony of the Twelve Patriarchs and the Book of Jubilees, is the same as Belial, and is used as an appellative of Satan. In the New Testament, where it occurs, 2 Cor. vi. 15, all the best MSS. give Βελίαρ.

(Now Berial is the angel of iniquity, holding the dominion of this world,[1] whose name is Matanbukus,[2] and he rejoiced over Jerusalem on account of Manasseh, and held him firmly in his perversion and in the impiety which he disseminated in the city.[3]) Magic likewise was multiplied there; incantation, augury, divination, fornication, adultery, and the persecution of the righteous, by Manasseh, by Balkira, by Tobias the Canaanite, by John of Anathoth, and by Zalik Nevaj.[4] Now when Isaiah, the son of Amos, saw the manifold iniquity which was committed in Jerusalem, the worship of Satan, and the wanton conversation, he fled from the city, and dwelt in Bethlehem of Judæa. But finding that much impiety existed there also, he took up his abode upon a mountain in the wilderness. Then Micah the prophet, and Ananias the aged, and Joel, and Habbakuk, and Josab, his son, and many others who believed in the ascension into heaven, withdrew themselves, and dwelt upon the same mountain. All these were clothed in sackcloth; all were prophets, having nothing with them, naked and destitute;[5] and all lamented with great lamentation the defection of Israel. And they had no food to eat except the wild herbs which they plucked upon the mountain and cooked as they could; and they and Isaiah remained among the hills

---

[1] Comp. John xii. 31, xvi. 11; 2 Cor. iv. 4; Eph. ii. 2, vi. 12.
[2] Elsewhere written Mekembekus. Its origin and its meaning are alike unknown.
[3] This paragraph is probably a later Jewish addition.
[4] The last name is inexplicable, and the history of the persons mentioned is unknown. Balkira is sometimes confused with Malkira; but the latter seems to be identified with Sammael.
[5] One is again reminded of the passage in Heb. xi. 37, 38.

two whole years. Afterwards, while they continued in the wilderness, there was a certain man in Samaria, named Balkira, of the kindred of Zedekiah, son of Canaan, a false prophet, who dwelt at Bethlehem. Zedekiah, the brother of his father, was he who, in the days of Ahab, king of Israel, was the master of four hundred prophets of Baal, and who smote upon the cheek and reproved Michaiah, the son of Amida. . . . Now Balkira perceived and marked the place where were Isaiah and the prophets with him; for he dwelt at Bethlehem, and was attached to Manasseh. He also prophesied falsehood in Jerusalem, where many consorted with him, though he was a Samaritan. . . . Now Balkira accused Isaiah and the other prophets, saying: Isaiah and his companions prophesy against Jerusalem and against the cities of Judah, saying that they shall be laid waste, and that Benjamin also shall go into captivity, and against thee, O king, that in a cage[1] and in iron chains thou shalt be carried off. They also prophesy falsely against Israel and Judah. Isaiah says: I see more than Moses the prophet saw; Moses asserted, No man can see God and live; but Isaiah says, I have seen God, and, behold, I live. Know, therefore, O king, that these are false prophets. Jerusalem also Isaiah has called Sodom, and the princes of Judah and Jerusalem has he declared to be people of Gomorrah. Thus he constantly accused Isaiah and the prophets before Manasseh. Now Berial dwelt in the heart of Manasseh, as well as in the hearts of the princes of Judah and Benjamin, and of the eunuchs and counsellors of the

[1] "In cavea," Dillm.; γαλεάγραις, Gr.; "Galeagra," Frag. Vat. Comp. 2 Chron. xxxiii. 11; Ezek. xix. 9, Sept.

king. And the accusation of Balkira pleased him exceedingly; and Manasseh sent and apprehended Isaiah. For Berial was very wroth with Isaiah on account of the vision, concerning the advent of Messiah,[1] and sawed him asunder with a wooden saw.[2] Now while they were sawing him, Balkira stood by accusing him, and all the false prophets stood there deriding and triumphing over him. Yea, Balkira and Mekembekus stood before him uttering derision and reproaches. Then Beliar said to Isaiah: 'Say, I have lied in everything which I have spoken, and the ways of Manasseh are good and right, and good are the ways of Balkira and those who are with him.' This he said to him when they began to saw him. But Isaiah was in a vision of the Lord, with his eyes open, and he beheld them.[3] Then Malkira (*i.e.* Beliar) thus addressed him: 'Say that which I tell thee, and I will turn their hearts, and will compel Manasseh, and the princes of Judah, and the people, and all Jerusalem, to reverence thee.' But Isaiah answered and said: 'If the matter rests with me, cursed art thou in every word that thou speakest, thou, and all thy hosts, and all thy followers; for thou canst not deprive me of

---

[1] We pass on here to chap. v., the intervening portion being an interpolation giving an account of the vision, which is afterwards expanded and augmented by new particulars, containing the history of Jesus and His Church.

[2] So Eth. In the Greek legend the king orders him to be sawed asunder with an iron saw; but the instrument, though plied for some hours, is unable to enter his flesh. Then Isaiah reminds Manasseh that it is ordained that he shall be sawed in pieces with a wooden saw; the tool accordingly is changed, and the execution is accomplished.

[3] In the account of the vision given later, chap. vi. 10, the prophet is rapt in ecstasy, and does not see the men who stand before him.

more than the skin of my body.' Then they seized Isaiah, the son of Amos, and sawed him asunder with a wooden saw. And Manasseh and Balkira and the false prophets, the princes and the people, all stood looking on. But Isaiah said to the prophets who were with him, before he was cut asunder: 'Go ye into the country of Tyre and Sidon, for the Lord Almighty hath mixed the cup for me alone.' And neither, while they were sawing him, did he cry out nor weep, but he continued in converse with the Holy Spirit till he was sawn asunder."

Such, with a few omissions which merely add some particulars concerning persons named, is the original Jewish account of the martyrdom of Isaiah. This, as we have seen, was known to the early Fathers. Round it have gathered various legends and accretions, which the critical acumen of scholars has now separated from the body of the work and assigned to different authorship and later periods. But the simple record itself is founded on Jewish tradition which still exists in Talmudic writings, though there is some variety in details, one story being that the prophet, flying from his enemies, was miraculously hidden by a carob-tree which swallowed him up; and that workmen came and sawed down the tree, when the blood of Isaiah flowed.[1] In this portion of the work there is no trace of a Christian hand; all is unmistakably Jewish, and is filled with Jewish names, Berial, Sammael, Matambukus, Balkira, Malkira, etc.; so that we may regard the section as an independent pamphlet, embodying a very ancient tradition, widely disseminated and largely credited.

[1] See Laurence, pp. 151 ff.

The second division of the present book is an account of the Ascension or Vision of Isaiah composed by a Christian Jew, and probably in its original form quite distinct from the treatises with which it was afterwards associated. In the Venetian edition it appears as a complete work, with the title, *Visio mirabilis Ysaiæ Prophetæ*, etc., and concluding with the words, "Explicit visio Ysaiæ Prophetæ." It is found in chaps. vi. 1–xi. 1, 23–40 (Eth.), the gap in chap. xi. between vers. 1 and 23, which in the existing Ethiopic is occupied by a Christian interpolation, being supplied by a few words in the Venetian edition, where the interpolation is not inserted. It is separated from the rest of the work in the Abyssinian book by a distinct heading: "The vision which Isaiah, the son of Amos, saw in the twentieth year of the reign of Hezekiah, king of Judah." Herein Isaiah recounts to the king, his own son Josab, and the assembled prophets how that he was rapt in spirit and conducted by an angel through the firmament to the highest heaven, and shown first all the mysteries of the six lower spheres, and at last those of the seventh heaven, as well as Christ's future advent on the earth; His descent into hell; His return and glorious Ascension through each of the seven heavens in reward of the redemption which He won. Of this narrative the following particulars will give some idea. While Isaiah was conversing with Hezekiah on the subject of righteousness and faith, all those who were gathered there heard the door of the chamber opened and the voice of the Spirit, and they all fell down and worshipped the glorious God. And Isaiah held converse with the Holy Spirit: his soul was rapt in ecstasy; he no longer saw the men who were before him; his eyes were open, his mouth silent, yet he continued to breathe; and he beheld a vision which was shown to him by an angel sent from the highest heaven, whose glory and office were inexpressibly great, but his name was concealed. First, he was taken to the firmament where Sammael and his powers reigned, and were at continual strife with one another, even as the battle is always raging on earth, and will continue till He that is coming shall appear and put an end to it. Thence he mounts to the first heaven, where he sees a throne in the midst, and angels on the right hand and on the left glorifying One whom he saw not; but those on the right were more splendid and more perfect than the others. In the second heaven the same scene, only more magnificent, is beheld; and the prophet falls down to worship, but is checked by the angel, who bids him reserve his adoration till he reaches the seventh heaven. (Comp. Rev. xxii. 8, 9.) "For," he says, "above all the heavens and their angels thy throne is set, and thy clothing and thy crown which thou thyself shalt behold." The third heaven, whither Isaiah was next conducted, was notable for there being no mention there of what goes on in this world, though all is perfectly known. The fourth heaven was reached, and the glory of the angels and of Him that sat on the throne was still greater than before, the distinction between those on the right and left hands being still maintained. The same effects still more intensified were found in the fifth heaven. But the sixth heaven was more glorious than any which he had seen, so that he deemed the brilliancy of the five lower spheres mere darkness in comparison with this. Here was no throne, and all the attendant angels were equal in splendour, the difference between the sides existing no longer; and all invoked with one voice the First, the Father, and His Beloved, and the Holy Spirit. At this stage of his ascension, Isaiah received a dim intimation of the fate that awaited him—viz. that he should participate in the lot of the Lord, a tree being concerned in the future of both (*i.e.* the wooden saw and the cross). It was further said to him: "When from an alien body by the angel of the Spirit thou hast ascended hither, then thou shalt receive the clothing which thou shalt behold, and other numbered, laid-up clothings shalt thou see; and then thou shalt be equal to the angels in the seventh heaven." Hearing this, the prophet entreats that he may never again return to earth, but is told that his time is not yet accomplished, Then, lastly, he is raised to the æther of the seventh heaven. And the angel who dwells above the splendour of the sixth heaven would fain have prohibited his ascent; but the Lord, whose name he cannot know while in the body, bade him come up, for his clothing was there. Arrived there, he saw a marvellous light and angels innumerable; he saw also all the saints from Adam, Abel, and Enoch, not clothed upon with flesh, but vested in their heavenly clothing, yet not seated on thrones or decorated with crowns, for these latter glories they should not attain to until the Beloved has descended into the world in the form of man.[1]

---

[1] The expression in the original Ethiopic is this: "He is made like unto your form, and they shall deem Him flesh and man." This looks like Docetism, but it may mean merely that man shall

But the prince of this world will lay his hand on the Son of God, and hang Him on a tree, and slay Him, not knowing who He is; and His descent to the earth shall be concealed also from the heavens. Then he shall descend into hell and make havoc there, and, having escaped from the angel of death, on the third day He shall rise, and shall continue in the world five hundred and forty-five days;[1] and He shall ascend into the seventh heaven, and many of the saints shall ascend with Him, and then at length they shall receive their clothing, and thrones, and crowns. Then Isaiah is shown books in which were contained all the history of Israel: and everything that is done upon earth is known in this region. He is bidden worship One standing, whose glory was great and wonderful, and whom all the saints adored, but who was transformed into the likeness of an angel before Isaiah worshipped Him; and also another glorious being on the left of the other, who, he was told, was the angel of the Holy Spirit who speaks in the saints and prophets. The great glory that was next revealed blinded him, and neither he nor the angels could look thereon; only the saints were enabled to behold it. "Then," it is added, "I saw that my Lord worshipped, and the angel of the Holy Spirit, and both

---

fail to recognise His divinity. The Venetian document has simply: "He shall be in your form." The rest of the clause, as well as the introduction of the name Christ here and elsewhere in the vision, is doubtless an interpolation.

[1] *I.e.* 365+180 days. This was an opinion held by the Valentinians and Ophites, according to Irenæus, *Adv. Hæres.* i. 1. 5 and i. 34. This statement of time is absent from the old Latin version, and seems to be a heretical gloss which has crept into the text.

together glorified God Almighty."[1] He to whom all the worship in heaven and earth is addressed, is the Highest, "the Father of my Lord;" and He sends forth the Lord Christ into the earth, even unto the infernal regions, and no one, not even the angels of the lower heavens, know who or what He is, as He assimilates His form to that of the inhabitants of the various regions through which He passes, till the time come when judgment shall be executed on the evil principalities and powers, and He shall ascend with great glory and sit at the right hand of God.[2] Then He is recognised, and all the saints and angels adore Him, while He sits at the right hand of the great Glory, and the angel of the Holy Spirit is seated on the left hand. Having seen and heard these things, Isaiah is dismissed, and his spirit returns to earth to wait till the time of his martyrdom is fulfilled. It is far from improbable that the author of this section was acquainted with the Revelation of St. John, if we may judge from the language and images which he employs, though unhappily his loose and unqualified expressions bore a very different meaning to Arians and other heretics.

Such is the second portion of our book, which, together with the first part containing the martyrdom, is combined into one volume by additions in the form of prelude and epilogue, which may be called the third part, and which is comprised in chap. i. (excepting vers. 3 and 4*a*) and the

[1] The error which endeared the treatise to heretics leaks out here.
[2] The passage which here follows in Eth. (chap. xi. 2-22) contains a garbled account of the birth of Christ, and of His life and death. It does not occur in the old Latin, nor in the Greek version edited by Gebhardt, and seems to be out of place in the vision.

two final verses of chap. xi. This part merely repeats the information, that Hezekiah in the twenty-sixth year of his reign delivered to Manasseh, in the presence of Isaiah and Josab, the visions which had been imparted to himself and the prophet, and impressed upon him certain warnings and instructions; all of which Manasseh soon forgot and disobeyed; and Isaiah predicted his own death at the command of Manasseh. These brief details are amplified by some rabbinical and Christian fictions. The tractate thus arranged has been at various times increased and decorated by many additions and supplements, the work of Christian hands, so that what Dillmann terms Part IV. contains a large amount of the present text—viz. chaps. iii. 13–v. 1, xi. 2–22, 41, i. 3, 4*a*, v. 15, 16. Of the first part of this section, viz. chaps. iii. 13–v. 1, there is, as we have said, no trace in the Greek legend lately published, which certainly contains extracts from the other three divisions of the work, and hence we may conclude that it was a separate tractate not at first connected with our book. In this fourth section we have not only an account of Manasseh's crime, but also an apocalypse of Christ's life upon earth, and the fate of the Christian Church between the Lord's ascension into heaven and His return to judgment. We may note a few points worthy of observation in this section. The rancour of Berial against Isaiah is here stated to be caused by the prophet's vision and denunciation of Sammael, and revelation respecting the coming of the Beloved, and the doings of His twelve followers. Christ's sepulchre is opened on the third day by the angel of the Christian Church which is in heaven, and the angel of the Holy Spirit, and the archangel Michael. The term "angel of the Spirit" occurs, as we have seen, elsewhere in our book (cf. xi. 4), and is supposed by Dillmann to be used, because in the later writings of the Old Testament an angel is represented as discharging the prophetical office of the Spirit, *e.g.* in Zechariah, where the visions are unfolded by the angel that talked with him. Thus in the *Pastor of Hermas* we read of "the angel of the prophetical spirit," and in the Apocalypse of Baruch there is mention of "Ramiel who presides over the visions of truth." And by a loose kind of terminology all the inhabitants of heaven, save God the Father, are called angels; even as Origen speaks of "the two seraphim with six wings, the only-begotten Son of God, and the Holy Ghost."[1] In this portion of the book Isaiah foretells the existence of great disputes respecting the second coming of Christ, many on this subject forsaking the doctrine of the apostles, a fact which we know also from St. Peter's own words and from expressions of others, *e.g.* Clemens Romanus.[2] There shall be multitudes of iniquitous "elders and pastors, oppressors of their flocks," and but few prophets or teachers of assured truths, on account of the worldliness and vice which shall prevail. Before the end Antichrist will come, Berial, the prince of this world. Here we have an enunciation of the curious myth concerning Nero which is found in the Sibylline Oracles.[3] According to this opinion, Berial

---

[1] Herm. *Past. Mand.* xi. 9; Apoc. Bar. lv. 3; Orig. *De Princip.* i. 3.
[2] 2 Pet. iii. 1 ff.; Clem. Rom. *Epist. ad Cor.* xxiii.
[3] Orac. Sibyll. ii. 167, iii. 63, iv. 119, where see Alexandre's note, and the account in our next section.

descends from the firmament in the form of this impious monarch, "the matricide;" in his hand are all the powers of this world and the material forces of nature, and he shall use them to draw men unto him, and create a very wide Apostasy, so that numbers believe in him and serve him, and own him as God. This evil dominion lasts for three years, seven months, and twenty-seven days, the duration here specified being a little longer than the forty-two months of canonical Scripture;[1] but the writer has arranged the 1335 days named at the end of Daniel's prophecy according to the Julian computation. It is interesting to note this quasi-solution of the "Beast" of St. John's Revelation (xiii. 17, 18). Jolowicz[2] reckons that, taking the death of Nero as happening June 9, A.D. 68, the reign of Berial would begin October 29, A.D. 64. At the close of this reign, "after 332 days"[3] the Lord shall come from the seventh heaven with all His angels and saints, and shall cast Berial and his companions into Gehenna; and the resurrection shall then take place, and the final judgment. To the holy who shall be found on earth rest ($\mathring{a}\nu\epsilon\sigma\iota\varsigma$, 2 Thess. i. 7) shall be given, and they shall be clothed with heavenly garments, and associated with the saints who descend with the Lord, and they shall leave

---

[1] Dan. vii. 25, xii. 7; Rev. xiii. 5. Comp. Dan. xii. 12. Georgius Cedrenus, quoted by Dillmann, says that "in the Testament of King Hezekiah Isaiah asserts that Antichrist shall reign for three years and seven months, being 1290 days."

[2] *Himmelfahrt und Vision des Proph. Jesaia*, p. 9.

[3] It seems probable that the numerals are here corrupt, and that "one thousand" has fallen out at the beginning, and that the "five" at the end has been changed into "two," the original number being, as above, 1335.

their bodies in the world. There is no mention here, or elsewhere, of any millennial opinions, nor is Christ expected to reign on earth. He comes to judge and to "consume all the ungodly, who shall be as if they had never been created."[1] There are two or three other points in this section worthy of attention. The last portion (xi. 2–22) is occupied with the life of Christ on earth, wherein can be recognised some of the additions contained in the spurious Gospels. To induce Joseph not to put away Mary, "the angel of the Spirit appears in the world;" Joseph does not approach her, but guards her as a holy virgin; after two more months the pair were alone in the house together, "and while Mary was gazing on the ground she suddenly perceived with astonishment an infant lying before her, and found that she had been delivered of a child." Joseph, observing what had come to pass, "glorified God because the Lord had come to His inheritance." He is warned to tell the occurrence to no one, lest the Divine nature of the child should be divulged. But reports were circulated in Bethlehem, some saying that the Virgin Mary was confined before she had been two months married; others affirming that she did not bring forth at all; for "all knew about Him, but knew not whence He was;" and He "was concealed from all the heavens, and the principalities, and the gods of this world." This last assertion is found in many passages of the Fathers,

---

[1] This expression does not necessarily point to the absolute annihilation of the wicked; it is parallel to the words in Job x. 19: "I should have been as though I had not been; I should have been carried from the womb to the grave."

and notably in the Epistle of Ignatius to the Ephesians (xix.), where it is said that the prince of this world comprehended neither the virginity of Mary, nor her bearing of the child, nor the death of the Lord.[1] Christ's descent into hell is plainly affirmed, the expression being in one place (xi. 19), "He descended to the angel" (*i.e.* of death), and in another (iv. 21), "the descent of the Beloved to the infernal regions." The old Latin of ix. 15 adds particulars not in the Ethiopic version: "He shall descend into hell, and make it desolate and all its visions, and shall seize the prince of death, and shall make him His prey, and confound all his powers." And in an earlier passage (x. 8) a distinction is drawn between hell (*inferi*) and the abyss of perdition (*abaddon*); the latter region Christ does not enter. It is "the pit of the abyss" of St. John (Rev. ix. 1, etc.). Isaiah adds that this event in the life of the Beloved is written in the section of his prophecy where the Lord says, "Behold my servant shall understand." This can refer only to chap. lii. 13, where we read: "Behold, my servant shall do wisely," which is the introduction to the famous Messianic chapter liii. The following paragraph is remarkable: "All these things are written in Psalms: in the Parables of David the son of Jesse, and in the Proverbs of Solomon his son, and in the words of Kore, and Ethan the Israelite, and in the words of Asaph, and in the rest of the Psalms, which the angel of the Spirit has inspired; also in the words of those whose name is not inscribed, and in the words of Amos, my father,"

[1] References will be found in the commentators on the above passage of Ignatius, *e.g.* Funk, p. 187.

and of the other eleven minor prophets, "and in the words of righteous Joseph and Daniel." Here, we may note, "Psalms" is a general title, including what follows; "Parables" would be applied to the didactic poems in the Psalter, called *Maschil* in the titles. The composite authorship of the Psalter is acknowledged, the songs of the sons of Korah being distinguished from those of Ethan and Asaph. Ethan is called "Israelite" by the LXX. (Ps. lxxxviii. 1), where the Hebrew gives "Ezrahite." It is strange that neither Jeremiah nor Ezekiel are mentioned; but Nitzsch gives a parallel from the Second Book of Esdras i. 39, 40,[1] where the twelve minor prophets are enumerated, and none of the four greater ones. The confusion between Amos the prophet and Amoz the father of Isaiah is not peculiar to our author; even the great Clemens Alexandrinus fell into the same error, owing to ignorance of Hebrew. What is to be understood by "the words of Joseph" is a disputed question. Dillmann conjectures that the expression refers to a pseudepigraphal work mentioned by Fabricius,[2] and entitled *The Prayer of Joseph*,[3] though it is not clear why this spurious book should be alone named among the canonical writings specified.

Having thus briefly examined the contents of the whole work, we are in a position to consider its origin and date.

That the book was written originally in the Greek

[1] The Fourth Book in the old Latin.
[2] *Cod. Pseud. Vet. Test.* i. 761 ff.
[3] In the *Chronographia* of Nicephorus among the Old Testament Apocrypha occurs Προσευχὴ Ἰωσήφ, containing 1100 verses; it is also found in Montfaucon's Catalogue.

language might be presupposed from the ascertained source of analogous works which have been found in Abyssinia; the presumption is confirmed by internal evidence. We are often confronted with expressions which are plainly derived from, or are clumsy or erroneous renderings of, Greek terms. Thus an angel is sent expressly from the seventh heaven to make a revelation to the prophet; but in vii. 21 we read: "Worship not the throne of him who is of the sixth heaven, *from whence* I have been sent to conduct thee, . . . worship in the seventh heaven;" where the translator has been misled by the ὅθεν, which here means "wherefore." The Venetian edition gives "propter hoc." Again, what is evidently δι' αὐτοῦ in the original (iii. 13) is translated "on account of him," instead of "by means of him." "He who rests in the saints" is ὁ ἐν ἁγίοις ἀναπαυόμενος (vi. 8); in vii. 9 the translator has confused ὁμιλία with ὅμιλος, and given "speeches" instead of "assemblies;" "I preserve thee," xi. 34, is a mistaken version of ἀπαλλάσσω σε, "I dismiss thee;" iii. 26, 28: "there shall be calumnies and calumniators many," "the spirit of empty honour (κενοδοξίας) and of love of money" (φιλαργυρίας); "the pious worshippers," τοῖς εὐσεβέσι; "Him of the great glory," τὸν τῆς μεγάλης δόξης. Joseph "came unto her (Mary's) portion" (μερίδα), *i.e.* she was allotted to him as wife; where Dillmann compares the expression in *Protevang. Jacobi*, viii.: σὺ κεκλήρωσαι τὴν παρθένον Κυρίου παραλαβεῖν. There are many tokens of the use of the Greek version of the Old Testament. Thus we read, iv. 19: "the remainder of the vision is written in the vision of Babylon." The reference is to Isa. xiii. 1, where the Hebrew has "the burden of Babylon," but the Septuagint, "the vision which Isaiah saw against Babylon." Again, Isa. lii. 13 is quoted (Ascens. iv. 21) thus: "Behold, my son shall understand," which is in accordance with the Greek, while the Hebrew gives, "My servant shall deal wisely." The Latin Vulgate, the Sibylline Oracles, and the *Apostolical Constitutions* agree here with the Greek and the Ascension. In calling Ethan "the Israelite," our book, as we have seen, reproduces the error of the Septuagint. Zedekiah, son of Chenaanah (1 Kings xxii. 11) is called (Ascens. ii. 12) "son of Canaan," which is the appellation given him by the LXX. In chap. iii. 2, it is stated that Shalmaneser carried away nine of the tribes captive to Media, "and the rivers of Tazon;" the Hebrew has "Gozan," but some MSS. of the Septuagint show "Tazan," 2 Kings xvii. 6 and xviii. 11. There is evidence that the old Latin versions were rendered from the Greek; thus where the Ethiopic gives "will destroy" as the translation of a certain word (vii. 12), one Latin version gives "interficiet," another "emundabit," which variety could arise only from the original verb being καθαρεῖ or καθαιρήσει. The presumption that the Abyssinian version was made from a Greek original is thus greatly confirmed. Indeed, throughout, so closely is the Greek followed that Dillmann avows that it would be an easy task to retranslate the Abyssinian into the very wording of the original. That the present version was made in the earliest days of the Abyssinian Church is considered to be demonstrated by its agreement in diction with other similar works composed under the same circumstances, by the occasional introduction of unusual or obsolete words, and by the uncertainty of the orthography which appertains to all primitive Ethiopic literature. But how it came to be thus honoured and preserved is a question not yet satisfactorily solved. Probably, as the "vision" was considered to support certain Gnostic or quasi-Gnostic opinions, it obtained currency in Egypt where such tenets prevailed, and the other sections were usually combined with it in one volume. Certainly Origen and Tertullian were acquainted only with the "martyrdom" proper, without any of the additions and interpolations afterwards added to it.

The section containing the martyrdom is doubtless of purely Jewish origin, and of earlier date than the rest of the work. It is simply a legendary narrative, invented, or compiled from tradition, in order to glorify the prophet, and containing nothing apocalyptic. The author, or authors, of the remainder were Jewish Christians, well versed in Hebrew lore and the legends which rabbinical literature had accumulated. The opinion that the heavens are seven in number is found in the Talmud, and in such works as the Testaments of the Twelve Patriarchs; the name Sammael, for Satan, is a rabbinical term not occurring in Scripture;[1] the notion of the clothing of souls being stored up in heaven in readiness for assumption at the proper moment is one that appears in Talmudic writings.[2] From such considerations we

---

[1] For rabbinical lore concerning Sammael, or Satan, consult Dr. Edersheim, *Life and Times of Jesus*, vol. ii. App. xiii.

[2] See Jolowicz, pp. 11 ff., where quotations from Talmudic works are given.

may conclude what were the religion and nationality of the writer. The vision is founded on the fact that Isaiah is represented in Scripture as having seen the Lord. This, of course, was felt to be impossible in the ordinary sense of the words. The vision must be vouchsafed under supernatural conditions; hence the prophet is raised to an ecstatic state; his soul is separated from its earthly tenement, and is exalted to the highest heaven. Accordingly, the work which records this rapture is properly named 'Αναβατικόν, *Ascensio*, as well as ὅρασις, *visio*. We find a similar double appellation applied to the Revelation of St. John, which in the early Christian centuries was also known as 'Αναβατικόν.[1] There is no similar trance recorded in the Old Testament; for an analogous transaction we must refer to the scene where the beloved apostle "became in the spirit on the Lord's day," or where St. Paul was caught up even to the third heaven, and carried into Paradise on another occasion, whether in the body or out of the body he knew not, and heard unspeakable words.[2] Both in St. Paul's case actually, and in that of Isaiah supposedly, the vision was granted in order to strengthen the recipients for the trials that awaited them, and to teach that all things are foreknown and foreordained, and that the troubles of this life are not worthy to be compared with the glory that shall be revealed.

As regards the date of this production, we see that its various parts belong to different ages and authors. The

---

[1] Nitzsch in *Stud. und Krit.* 1830, i. 215.
[2] Rev. i. 10; 2 Cor. xii. 2-4.

first section narrates an ancient Jewish tradition; but there is nothing found therein to afford any indication of its age. If, as we have seen to be probable, it was known to Justin Martyr, it was composed at least towards the beginning of the second Christian century. It is, however, probably very much earlier, and may be regarded as pre-Christian, as it contains not the remotest allusion to any but Jewish matters. But the ascension or vision contains many suggestions which would assign it to a period immediately succeeding the apostolic period, at any rate not later than the first ten years of the second century.[1] One recognises a compilation of ideas gathered from the New Testament, and not yet reduced to a formal system or any authoritative statement. The spirit testified in old time the sufferings of Christ, which were not revealed unto the angels; the Lord comes down from heaven; ascends far above all heavens and principalities and powers, having overcome all enemies; the beatitude of the saints of the old covenant is not perfected till the Redeemer has triumphed; the glory of the righteous exceeds that of the angels. Such facts as these, based on Holy Scripture, are overladen or interspersed with notions very alien from the simplicity and purity of apostolic doctrine, and indicating the taint of Hebrew and Gnostic error; but it is Gnosticism in its early stage, as existing among the Essenes and Jewish sects, and recognised in some of the books of the New Testament. This section shows traces of having been edited and glossed

[1] These indications have been carefully noted by Dillmann, Nitzsch, and others.

by a Christian of unorthodox sentiments, who held the
malignity of matter, and many of Origen's opinions, and
likewise views concerning Christ which Arians found
agreeable to their minds. Of the doctrine of Æons and
Emanations there seems to be no trace. The opinion touching the seven heavens was current among the Jews before
Christian times, and is found in many apocryphal works
as well as in the Talmud.[1] The Homoousian controversy
is unknown to the writer of the Ascension, who introduces statements which a later age justly branded with
heresy. Thus he makes (ix. 37-40) the Son inferior to
the Father; and although he calls Him the Beloved, and
Lord of all the heavens and thrones, whose voice alone
they obey, he represents the Father as worshipped in
heaven by Him and the Holy Ghost. It is true that
They are supposed to have assumed the appearance and
attitudes of angels when They pay this worship, but no
one who held the Nicene faith would have made such a
statement, which is evidently anterior to the closer
definition of a later age. The assertion that Christ
remained on the earth between His resurrection and
ascension for one and a half years, or 545 days (ix. 16),
was a very early error, known, as I have already
mentioned, to Irenæus, and therefore extant in the
second century. Indeed, in the earliest times the
tradition of the Great Forty Days which afterwards
obtained seems not to have been universally held. St.
Luke, in his Gospel, apparently joins the Ascension

---

[1] Comp. *Test. XII. Patr.* "Levi," 2 and 3; and Wetstein's note on
2 Cor. xii. 2. Authorities are given by Dillmann on vi. 13 of our
book, and in Kitto's *Cyclopædia*, art. "Heaven," note, p. 245.

on to the resurrection, though in the Acts he speaks of Christ being seen at intervals during forty days; none of the other evangelists mentions the length of His earthly sojourn in this interval. In the Epistle of Barnabas (chap. xv.), that Father omits all mention of any space of time intervening between Easter Sunday and the ascension; Bede reckons forty-three days; so that opinion on this matter fluctuated, and had not arrived at a general conclusion in the primitive age. Another mark of high antiquity is found in the address to God (vi. 8, x. 6), "the God of righteousness, higher than the highest, that dwelleth in the saints," which recalls the expressions in the apostolical Father, Clemens Romanus (*Ep. ad Cor.* lix. 3). The occasional allusions to the *Parousia* of Christ denote a primitive time. The question, as we know from references in the New Testament,[1] was largely debated in apostolic days, but ceased to have like interest in succeeding ages. In our author's view the Second Advent was close at hand, and there is in the work no trace of the early opinion being corrected by later circumstances or events. Again, the writer knows of only one persecution which takes place before the final judgment; and this can be none other than that which was organised by Nero; for he could not have omitted that under Domitian had he lived after that tyrant; and we have seen above that he plainly adumbrated Nero, when he prophesied of the coming of Berial under the form of an impious king. And as he assigned the end of the world and the day of judgment to less than a year after this event, it is reasonable to conclude that this

---

[1] Comp. 2 Thess. ii.; 2 Pet. iii.

part of the treatise was composed at the beginning of A.D. 69. This inference, of course, proceeds on the assumption that the writer wishes his calculations to be understood literally; if his allusions and statements are to be regarded as ideal, emblematical, visionary, no definition of time can be assigned to them, but the references to events which they contain indicate the age of the author.

The apocalyptic section is of much the same antiquity. The corruptions of doctrine and practice spoken of in chap. iii., the disputes about the Second Advent, the vice and greed of the pastors who spared not their own flocks, the worldliness and immorality of professors of Christianity, the envy and hatred even among the teachers of religion—such errors and declensions are noticed both in the New Testament and in the writings of the earliest Fathers, such as Hermas. The organisation of the Church was evidently still in its infancy; the rulers are called presbyters and pastors, and the title episcopus nowhere appears; whereas in the *Didache* both episcopus and diaconus are found. Prophecy is not yet silenced, though greatly diminished, being confined to a few localities and persons. It is mentioned, we may remark, as extant in Hermas's days, and rules are given in the *Pastor* for distinguishing the real from the false pretender to inspiration; and we meet with analogous statements in the *Didache*. These and such like hints indicate a primitive origin, and could not have been afforded by an age greatly exceeding the first Christian century. It is solely from internal evidence that we gather the date of this portion of the work, as none of the Fathers or early writers make any reference to it. Offering no special support of catholic dogma, — or rather containing some very questionable statements and expressions,—it was naturally disregarded and discountenanced by orthodox believers; and, indeed, the whole work was brought into public notice only for polemical purposes, first by Gnostic controversialists, and afterwards by Arians, and it was from a collection of the writings of these latter heretics that the old Latin versions were obtained.

From what has been said we may reasonably conclude that the purely Jewish section of our book was composed just before or in the first Christian century; that the second portion, containing the "Ascension" or "Vision," is not of later date than the first ten years of the second century, after which it was known to various heretics, and used by them to confirm their erroneous opinions. The third and fourth parts are of somewhat later date, added probably towards the last half of the second century. The work continued known unto the fifth century, when it almost disappeared from notice, till rediscovered in the manner mentioned above, unless we may infer that it always formed part of the Abyssinian canon, and had never fallen out of use in the Church of that country, which, as we know, retained much of Hebrew ceremonial and sentiment.

Unlike some of the apocryphal and pseudepigraphal books, the "Ascension" was never admitted to the catholic canon of Scripture. Opinion for some ages fluctuated as to the admissibility of the Wisdom of

Solomon, Ecclesiasticus, Judith, Tobit, etc. Some Conciliar and some private catalogues allowed their claim without hesitation; others admitted them only to a secondary position; but none assigned a first or even a second place to the "Ascension:" if it ever occurs in any of the lists it is mentioned as certainly apocryphal, and entitled to no respect as inspired. If, then, it be asked wherein lies its interest for us, we reply that it is a standing witness of the care taken in the early Church to confine the books of Scripture, in the highest sense, to those whose inspiration was approved by sufficient testimony. Shall we not say rather that the Holy Spirit guided the councils and authorities of the Church in their final arrangement of the canon, and that the rejection of such works as that which we have been considering was divinely ordered? In point of antiquity, indeed, parts of it might probably compete with portions of the New Testament, but weighed in the scale with undisputed Scriptures, and tried by the standard of Catholic doctrine, it failed to stand the necessary test, and was deservedly rejected.

It is interesting also for another reason. It affords a new example of that literature which, as we have said, has been called Pseudepigraphic, from the fact that the author writes under a false name, not so much with any intention of deceiving his readers, but with the view of obtaining a hearing for his own feelings and opinions.

And, lastly, as we have seen in the sketch which we have given, the book is capable of conveying valuable hints concerning the history of the early Church, and the heresies then coming into existence; and is a noteworthy contribution to that apocalyptic literature which prevailed so greatly in the centuries immediately preceding and succeeding the advent of Christ, and which even now for many minds possesses an absorbing interest.

IV.

MIXED.

---o---

THE SIBYLLINE ORACLES.

THE work thus named is a collection of Judæo-Christian poems, of various dates, designed to propagate certain ideas among heathens, and assuming this form in order to win acceptance in such quarters. Various derivations have been suggested for the word Sibylla, and it has been attributed to the Hebrew and other Oriental languages; but many suppose that the word is really Greek, compounded of the Æolic σιός = θεός and βόλλα or βύλλα = βουλή,[1] and thus meaning, counsel of God. However, it may well be doubted whether it is not a feminine form of the old Latin word *sibus*, meaning "wise." Persibus, or Persicus, is found in this sense in Plautus and Nævius, where it is explained by old grammarians as = *peracutus*. Hence the term signifies "wise woman, witch." The name was applied to any female who affected to foretell the future, so that it may be taken to mean an inspired prophetess, or, as Varro puts it, "cujus pectus numen recipit, et quæ vaticinatur." She

[1] So Alexandre, *Excurs. ad Sibyllina*, pp. 1 f.

is not an official priestess, but one abnormally influenced by the Deity. The most ancient authors speak of *a* Sibyl; but this idea did not long continue, and we soon find them multiplied and assigned to different localities. The number of accredited Sibyls has been stated sometimes as three or four, sometimes as ten; and the writings that are current under their name have been increased by later discoveries from eight books to fourteen—though the whole of these are not extant, of many of them isolated fragments alone having been preserved. That some lines of the ancient heathen poems have been preserved by classical authors is well known; only one or two of these, however, as far as I know, are found in our present collection, though there are passages and expressions which show distinctly a pagan origin, as the account of the tower of Babel, quoted from a Sibyl by Josephus,[1] where it is said that the *gods* sent a mighty wind and overthrew the building. In Asia Minor and Greece the Sibyllines obtained only a private circulation, and were never officially collected or publicly used, though, even from the scanty notices existing, we gather that they exercised a very potent influence and were largely credited. The original Libri Sibyllini, with which the name of King Tarquin is connected, and which reached Rome from Asia by way of Cumæ, perished in the fire which consumed the temple of Jupiter Capitolinus, B.C. 82. Their place was supplied by a collection gathered from various places in Greece, Italy, and Asia Minor, and amounting to about 1000 verses. This was revised by order of Augustus, and

[1] *Antiq.* i. 4. 3.

again by Tiberius; but has been preserved only in fragments found in classical authors. The widespread belief in the authority of such productions led to the composition and circulation of a quantity of professed oracles, which demanded critical investigation, and received some such attention at the hands of the emperors Julian and Honorius. The verses, however, thus authorised as genuine have not come down to us in their integrity, and what we know of them is little and unsatisfactory. Servius, in his commentary on Virgil, mentions a hundred as the number of these *Sermones*, and Suidas names twenty-four as the production of the Chaldæan Sibyls alone. How many more were attributed to the other Sibyls cannot be known. Our present collection is of Jewish and Christian origin, and can lay no claim to any high pagan antiquity. So common, indeed, had the forging of these poems become in early Christian times, that Celsus [1] sneers at Christian writers as Σιβολλισταί, sibyl-mongers, or sibyl-believers. The exact relation of these later compositions to the early group it is impossible to determine. Their acceptance as authentic in an uncritical age is no argument in their favour; but they seem to have been considered to possess some supernatural authority, far inferior, of course, to that of Jewish prophets, but still originated by Divine influence. Doubtless the later Sibyls used some of the old material which was found ready to their hand, though it is now almost impossible to say what was borrowed from floating tradition. A line here and there, indeed, may be identified. Thus, as of heathen origin and pro-

[1] Orig. *Cont. Cels.* v. 6.

bably remnants of old oracles or Sibylline verses, we may cite the punning couplet in iv. 71 and elsewhere:—

καὶ Σάμον ἄμμος ἅπασαν ὑπ' ἠϊόνεσσι καλύψει·
Δῆλος δ' οὐκέτι δῆλος, ἄδηλα δὲ πάντα τὰ Δήλου.

The Latin versifier has attempted to reproduce the second line thus:—

Et Delus, non jam Delus, deleta latebit.

From the same source come some of the lines in Book iii., which, as we shall see, narrate the reign of Saturn and the demigods of pagan theology, beginning with the building of the Tower of Babel on the plains of Assyria, when all men were of one language, and were animated with the one desire of invading the starry heaven. This is partly scriptural; but then follows a heathen episode: Chronos and Titan fight one with the other, but are reconciled by "Rhea and Guia and Aphrodite, with her fair crown, and Demeter, and Vesta, and Dione with her beautiful locks." The birth of Zeus gives occasion for a wonderful piece of etymology. To save him from the fate of her previous children, Rhea sent (διέπεμψε) him away to Phrygia secretly, hence they call him Δία because διεπέμφθη." On a par with this derivation is that of Hades (i. 85), which takes its name from Adam, who was the first to enter it, the death of Abel being ignored for philological purposes.[1] Another etymology, not unrecognised by the Fathers,[2] is given to this name in Book iii. 26, which Alexandre

---

[1] I. 82 f.: "Αιδην δ' αὖτ' ἐκάλεσσαν, ἐπεὶ πρῶτος μόλεν Ἀδὰμ
γευσάμενος θανάτου, γαῖα δέ μιν ἀμφεκάλυψε.
[2] Alexandre, p. 350 (iii. 26).

calls "ingeniose absurdus." Here it is commended as a name of four letters which represent the four quarters of the earth, as the Latin versifier writes:—

> Qui nomine solo
> Occasus ortusque refert boreamque notumque.

In the original:—

'Ἀντολίην τε Δύσιν τε Μεσημβρίαν τε καὶ Ἄρκτον.

Another paragraph owed to heathen sources is one concerning the destruction of Troy (iii. 414 ff.), where Helen is called "the Erinnys from Sparta," which reminds one of Virgil's "Trojæ et patriæ communis Erinnys" (Æn. ii. 578); and another where Homer, "the blind old man who writes lies," is accused of plagiarising from the Sibyl whose oracles he was the first to use.[1] Diodorus mentions this accusation as made by the Erythræan Sibyl, and is not referring to our present book.

The primary cause of the composition of these productions is not far to seek. Given the existence of a body of such prophetical utterances among the heathen, which were considered of superhuman authority and universally credited, it fell naturally into the mind of Jew and Christian to endeavour to gain acceptance for the truths which they had to teach, not only by tracing these truths in the extant words of poet and prophetess, but also by themselves expressing them in the form and under the guise of Sibylline inspiration. The mystery that enveloped these oracles greatly helped the impersonation, and the authors thought themselves quite justified in their undertaking if by this means they might insinu-

[1] Alexandre, p. 356.

ate the truths of God's unity and righteousness, and disseminate the hopes which animated their breasts. That the Sibylline Oracles were held in high honour during the early Christian centuries is proved by the frequent appeals to them made by the Fathers. The list of the writers who thus used them includes the names of Athenagoras, Theophilus, Justin Martyr, Lactantius, Clemens Alexandrinus, Eusebius, and Augustine. Some of these authors apparently were acquainted only with the heathen books; others, as Clemens Alexandrinus and Lactantius, cite passages of pagan, Jewish, and Christian authorship; and while some attribute to them an authority almost conclusive, others quote them with reserve, and own that their testimony is disputed and not always of decisive importance.[1]

Every one is familiar with the verse of the "Dies Iræ," which, if an interpolation, at any rate proves the estimation in which the Sibyl was held:—

> Dies iræ, dies illa,
> Solvet sæcla in favilla,
> Teste David cum Sibylla.

The manufacture of Sibylline verses continued for some centuries. It was natural and easy to employ this means of disseminating correct opinions among piously-disposed minds. What had been done by heathen Greeks might become a power for good in Jewish and Christian hands. For two centuries before Christ writers used this form to propagate Jewish opinions; in the early days of the Christian era, Sibyllines attempted to force Christian

[1] Comp. Euseb. *Constant. Or. ad. Sanct. Cœt.* i. 19 ; August. *De Civit.* xviii. 17 ; *Cont. Faust*, xiii. 2.

views into prominence in pagan circles. Existing poems were largely used, adopted, and published. Imitations were freely made, and these additions to the already copious collection enlarged the stock to an unwieldy extent, which defied every effort at order or classification. Every writer allowed himself full liberty of inserting his lucubration wherever he chose; isolated fragments, therefore, abound, many duplicates occur, and the result is confused and chaotic. But as paganism disappeared, and Christianity grew stronger and less in need of such adventitious support, the composition of Sibylline verses gradually ceased, and no additions to the collection seem to have been made since the fourth century. The use of them dying out, their existence became forgotten, and in the Middle Ages the Greek text seems to have been unknown. Of course the passages quoted by the early Fathers and the Christian apologists, and the testimony borne to the "Prophetess," as Clemens Alexandrinus calls her, served to keep alive the knowledge of the existence of such writings; but the collection of oracles gathered into books, such as we now possess, was not current; and from their very mystery and obscurity these unknown verses were regarded with more respect and deference than their intrinsic merits deserved.

The literary history of the Sibyllines is soon told. The earliest known quotation is that mentioned above concerning the building of the Tower of Babel. This is cited by Alexander Polyhistor, who lived between B.C. 80 and 40, and is found in Eusebius, *Chron.* i. 23, and in almost identical words, though with only a vague reference to the Sibyl, in Josephus, *Antiq.* i. 4. 3. In what form the book existed from whence this citation is taken we do not know. Whether Clemens Romanus quotes any part of our work is uncertain; Hermas Pastor mentions the Sibyl, but not her verses. Quotations abound most in Clemens Alexandrinus and Lactantius, who, however, seem to have been acquainted chiefly with the Jewish portions of the work as well as with some passages now no longer extant. In the time of Lactantius there was circulated a rude and undigested mass of verses in the Greek language, which had no pretence to order or completeness. Some unknown author, who has left a preface of untrustworthy character, collected these scattered elements, arranged them into books, with many interpolations of his own, designed to express his view or to facilitate the transition from one subject to another. The collector, probably a monk, and an adept at transcribing manuscripts, lived in the sixth century under Justinian. From his work our present collection took its origin. As has been already said, we are not here to look for the mysterious Sibylline books which were offered to Tarquin; nor yet for those which replaced the perished Oracles in later times. Our collection is of later date and different origin, being merely imitations of the original utterances, and only, as it were, by chance embodying any of the ancient heathen verses. A portion of what we now possess was first published at Basel in 1545 from an Augsburg, now a Munich, MS. by Xystus Betuleius (= Sixtus Birke—*i.e.* birch-tree); this, which comprised eight books, was followed immediately by a metrical Latin version, the composition of Sebastian

Castalio (Chateillon), who also republished the Greek text with emendations some ten years later. The fourth edition appeared at Paris in 1599 (repeated in 1607), under the auspices of John Opsopœus (*i.e.* Koch = ὀψοποιός, cook), purified by the aid of some newly-discovered MSS., and enriched with some short but useful annotations. Amsterdam produced the next edition in 1687, undertaken by Servatius Gallæus (Servais Gallé); but this is of no critical value, and is full of typographical errors and irrelevant learning. A portion of the Sibyllines is printed in Gallandi's *Bibliotheca Veterum Patrum*, Venet. 1788. All these editions above - mentioned contain only the first eight books. Some additions to the received text were made by Angelo Mai, who in 1817 and 1828 found and published some of the missing books, making the complete work to consist of fourteen books, the ninth and tenth, however, not having been recovered. The first perfect edition, and one that left little to be desired, is due to C. Alexandre, who, in 1841 and some subsequent years, put forth a carefully revised text, with Castalio's Latin version improved and augmented, and with a large body of critical and exegetical notes, and a volume of excursus, which treat copiously of all matters connected with the Oracles.[1] This edition was repeated in a handier form in 1869. Another edition of the whole work is that by J. H. Friedlieb (Leipzig 1852), which is supplied with a translation into German hexameters, but disfigured by a faulty text.[2] An Englishman, Sir John Floyer, pub-

---

[1] *Oracula Sibyllina*, curante *C. Alexandre*, Paris 1841–1856.
[2] Subsidiary aids to the elucidation of the text are found in some

lished a prose translation of the first seven and part of the eighth books in 1713, in the authenticity of which he implicitly believed, taking the trouble to compare them with the prophecies of Daniel and the Revelation, and finding in them a marvellous heathen testimony to the truth of Divine prophecy. As an instance of human credulity few books are more curious than that of this simple and uncritical knight-errant.

The work as at present arranged is a mass of confusion and incongruity, no pretence at chronological order being aimed at. The production of several authors—Gentile, Jewish, and Christian—taking very different standpoints, and living in very different ages, the Oracles must be examined separately, if we wish to weigh their contents accurately and estimate their real value and importance. Each book is not in itself a whole, the production of one author, or of one age. Often it contains incongruous elements, or is simply a congeries of unconnected fragments. But thus much is evident, that two chief elements are forthcoming, viz. a Jewish with some trace of heathen colouring, and a Christian which is more uniform. But it is very difficult to decide as to the character of many portions which are only of a neutral tint. The critics are not agreed as to the arrangement of the several books, but from the considerations adduced by Alexandre and Ewald, we may divide the whole collection into eight pieces of different date and author-

---

treatises of Ewald, *e.g. Abhandlung über Entstehung ... der Sib. Bücher* (Göttingen 1858); and of Bleek in Schleiermacher's *Zeitschrift*, i. 2, 3; and in the *Edinburgh Review*, July 1877. There are numerous German treatises, many of which I have not seen.

ship. The first and oldest is undoubtedly the prologue of Book i. and parts of Book iii. (97–828). This portion was the work of an Alexandrian Jew, who wrote under Ptolemy VII. Physcon, about B.C. 140. It is by far the most important of all the poems, and worthy of the fullest investigation, as it is the longest pre-Christian production in the whole series. There is one other, and only one other, certainly pre-Christian section in the whole collection. This fragment is found in vers. 36–92 of the same third book, and from internal evidence is assigned to B.C. 40, the time of the first Triumvirate. The second piece, Book iv., is regarded as the most ancient of the Christian Sibyllines, though there is nothing in it distinctively Christian, and it may well have been the work of a Jew. Its date is considered to be about A.D. 80. The third is a conglomeration of Jewish and Christian compositions, the Jewish preponderating. Much of it belongs to the first Christian century. It consists of the whole, or nearly the whole, of Book v. The fourth piece is composed of Books vi. and vii., and, as Ewald thinks, the first part of Book v.; but this latter assertion is doubtful. This is of a Christian character, though decidedly heretical, and is referred to the early part of the third century A.D. The fifth is found in Book viii., vers. 1–360, Christian and orthodox, a little later than the last. The sixth consists of the rest of the eighth Book. The seventh is composed of Books i., ii., and the first thirty-five verses of Book iii., and was written about the middle of the third Christian century. The last piece contains Books xi., xii., xiii., xiv., and is the production of a Jew in Egypt, who had some acquaintance with Christian rites and doctrine. Thus these "Oracles" cover a space of more than four hundred years, and give an insight into the tenets and feelings of Jews and Christians at an epoch the most important in the religious history of man.

Being of this miscellaneous character, the Sibyllines must be regarded as speaking each one for itself alone. In tracing any particular view or tenet or idea, we cannot, as in the ordinary case of a book composed at a definite time and place by a single author, say generally the Sibylline Oracles express this or that opinion; but we must carefully regard the passage where the opinion occurs, and decide when it was written, and whether by Jew, Christian, or semi-pagan; for on our determination of these questions depends the value of the given statement. Unfortunately, the interpolations of later hands are so numerous, that it is impossible in all cases to assign date or locality with absolute certainty. We are not about to attempt any critical examination of the text in this paper; the design is more humble, viz. to give readers some idea of the contents of these books, keeping distinct the groups into which they seem naturally to divide themselves, and to show their bearing on the religious ideas of the two centuries preceding and subsequent to the time of our Lord.

For the benefit of those who have not seen the original, it may be premised that the poems take the same form as, and endeavour to assume the outward character of, the ancient heathen oracles. They are written in Homeric hexameter verse, but with great licence as to the quantities of words, accent often being taken to lengthen a short syllable, *e.g.* iii. 1: Οὐράνι' ὑψιβρεμέτα μάκαρ, ὃς ἔχεις τὸ Χερουβίμ, and quantities are in the most regal manner made to give way to the necessities of the verse, even without the excuse of accent, *e.g.* v. 272: αὐτοὺς δὲ κρύψουσιν ἕως κόσμος ἀλλαγῇ, the last two feet doing duty for spondees. It is supposed that the most ancient Sibylline verses were acrostics.[1] Of this kind of verse one celebrated specimen occurs in Book viii., vers. 217–250, part of which in a Latin form has been preserved by St. Augustine (*De Civit.* xviii. 23). The passage in the Greek consists of thirty-four lines, the initials of which make the words ΊΗΣΟΥΣ ΧΡΕΙΣΤΟΣ ΘΕΟΥ ΥΙΟΣ ΣΩΤΗΡ ΣΤΑΥΡΟΣ. The Latin version omits the last word, employs C and S to represent Σ, and finding a difficulty in the use of the Greek letter υ, has substituted others in its place, which may possibly represent the current pronunciation; so that, as it stands, the initials compose the words: JESVCS · CREISTOS · TEV · DNIOS · SOTER.[2]

The earliest portion of the work is found, as has been said, in Book iii., combined with some older Gentile verses and some later Christian interpolations. All critics agree in this view, and many consider the prologue placed now before Book i. to be of equal antiquity. There are fragments not found in the extant MSS. of the Sibylline Oracles, but preserved by Theophilus and

---

[1] Dionys. Hal. iv. 62; Cicero, *De Divin.* ii. 54.

[2] Alexandre gives a revised Latin version, which forms the acrostic "Jesus Christus Dei Filius Salus in Cruce."

Lactantius,[1] and ascribed by the latter to the Erythræan Sibyl. After enumerating ten Sibyls, he proceeds (*Instit.* i. 6): "The verses of these Sibyls are all in circulation except those of the Cumæan, which are reserved in secret by the Romans, and are inspected by none but the Quindecimviri. They are the work of different authors, though often ascribed to one, who passed by the generic name of Sibyl. It is impossible to discriminate the writers, except in the case of the Erythræan, who inserts her own name in her poem, and is called Erythræan, though sprung from Babylon." Some of the lines have been inserted by the original collector in the first part of the third book, and it is probably owing to this that the MSS. have ceased to contain the prologue, as it was thought unnecessary to transcribe what would be found in another place. The prologue, which probably formed the original introduction to Book iii., begins with an exhortation to the Gentiles to leave their false deities, and to worship the one true God, "who reigns alone, almighty, unbegotten, seeing all yet seen of none." "Ye shall have the reward of your evil counsel," says the Sibyl, "because, neglecting to honour the true, everlasting God, and to offer to Him sacred hecatombs, ye have made your sacrifices to the deities of Hades." The Fathers[2] have seen in these words a wonderful advance of heathenism towards right religion. But, of course, they are not the genuine utterances of a heathen; they are written by a Jew personifying the pagan Sibyl. The following argument, however, seems to be genuine. It

[1] Theoph. *Ad Autol.* ii. 36; Lact. *Div. Inst.* iv. 6.
[2] Clem. Alex. *Protreph.* pp. 23, etc.

T

is preserved by Theophilus in his second book against Autolycus (p. 348), and takes the form of a kind of syllogism: "If gods beget, and are indeed immortal, they would be far more numerous than men, nor would any place be found for mortals whereon to stand. And if all that is begotten perishes,[1] no god could ever have sprung from a human womb. But God is one, alone, supreme, who made heaven and sun," etc., "incorruptible, creator, eternal, dwelling in the air; who to the good proffers good as an exceeding great reward, and against the evil raises up wrath and anger, war and pestilence, yea, lamentable woes." The closing lines of the prologue point to a late Jewish origin, the mention of Paradise in the sense of the abode of spirits never occurring in the Old Testament save in Ecclus. xliv. 16, and then only in the old Latin version, speaking of the translation of Enoch. The prologue ends thus: "But they who honour the true, eternal God shall inherit life, dwelling for ever in the fair garden of Paradise, feasting on sweet bread from the starry heaven." The inheritance of life, the abode in Paradise, and the feeding on manna savour of New Testament terminology, and, if not of Christian derivation, are remarkable as anticipative of Christian doctrine.[2] That the author was an Alexandrian Jew, and assumed the position of the writer of the Book of Wisdom, seems tolerably certain, if we regard his allusions to beast-worship. "O ye men," he cries, "are ye not ashamed to make gods of pole-cats ($\gamma\alpha\lambda\hat{a}\varsigma$) and brutes? Has not madness and frenzy robbed you of

---

[1] Comp. Aristot. *De Cælo*, i. 9.
[2] Comp. Matt. xix. 29; Luke xxiii. 43; Rev. ii. 17.

your senses if ye think that gods plunder dishes and pots, and, instead of dwelling in the rich, golden heaven, look upon moth-eaten robes, and are begirt with spiders' webs? Fools, to adore snakes, dogs, weasels, and birds of air, and creeping things of earth, and images of stone, and statues made by hand, and cairns by the roadside: these things ye worship and many other vanities which it were a shame even to mention." Plainly the writer of these lines must have had before his eyes the abominations of Egyptian idolatry, and was expressing his hatred of a religion, the material forms of which were daily forced upon his notice. But he differs from many of his countrymen in his eschatological views. There is no trace of millennarianism, or of a reign of Messiah before the final judgment, or of a first resurrection which shall affect the righteous only— doctrines which are found continually in later books. Here there is only one judgment for all, which shall decide the fate of good and bad, who shall at once receive their appointed lot, the former entering upon an eternal life of happiness in an earthly Paradise, the latter going away into eternal fire.

We come now to the consideration of the most important and characteristic of the Oracles, viz. the most ancient portions of Book iii., vers. 97–294 and 489–828. The intervening lines, vers. 295–488, forming the second section of the book, are an interpolation of a heterogeneous character, and will be noticed further on. The writer of the genuine poem is evidently an Alexandrian Jew, living in the second century before Christ. The determination of the date of the composition depends on internal considerations. The author is acquainted with the Book of Daniel, and with the expedition, of Antiochus Epiphanes to Egypt. This affords some clue; but there is a closer limitation. After the division of the Macedonian kingdom, it is said that another empire shall be established by "a toga-clad and republican nation,"[1] which shall deal hardly with Macedonia until "the seventh king of Grecian origin shall reign in Egypt." The allusion here must be to Ptolemy Physcon, who, after his brother Philometor's death, reigned as sole king (B.C. 145 – 117), having been associated with him for a time (B.C. 170–164) before he was banished from Egypt. He was the seventh sovereign of Hellenic race. Another criterion is the allusion to the destruction of Carthage and Corinth, which, as is well known, were overthrown B.C. 146.[2]

The beginning of the poem evidently is absent. It now commences abruptly with an account of the building of the Tower of Babel, its overthrow by violent winds, and the dispersion of mankind consequent upon the confusion of tongues. Then follows a section, derived from Hesiod and other heathen sources, detailing the legends of the sons of Saturn and the Titans from the tenth generation after the Flood, wherein the gods of antiquity appear as human kings, and which are recounted in order to show how war was introduced into the world, and how other kingdoms arose. The history of the ancient empires — Persians, Medes, Assyrians, etc.—is dismissed in a few verses, the author arriving at a stride at Rome; and then merging into

---

[1] Λευκὴ καὶ πολύκρανος, iii. 176.
[2] Schürer, *Hist. of Jewish People*, iii. 280 ff.

prophecy, the Sibyl foretells the prosperity of the kingdom of Solomon, whose dominion extends over Phœnicia, Asia Minor, the neighbouring islands, and Persia—an exaggeration which could scarcely have been made by any one but a Jew of a late period. After a short episode concerning the Greeks and Macedonians, the Sibyl proceeds to inveigh against Rome, "a nation clad in white, many-headed, which, coming from the Western Sea, shall grow into a mighty empire and shake the throne of kings." Of its rapine and luxury, its gross licentiousness and profanity, its cruelty and oppression, she speaks in severest terms, and predicts a retributive punishment soon to fall. This is to happen in times when "the nation of the mighty God shall once again be strong, and become to all peoples the guide of life." An eloquent passage follows, containing the history of the Jews unto the return from exile. The opening lines are fine :—

There is a city in the land of the Chaldæans from which arose the most righteous race of men, whose care was good counsel and fair deeds. For they regard not with anxious thought the course of sun and moon, nor the wonders that are found on earth, nor the depth of ocean's blue-eyed sea, nor the omens of a sneeze and the birds of the augur, nor seers, nor sorcerers, nor charmers, nor ventriloquists' fond deceits; they study not the predictions of Chaldæan astrologers; they observe not the stars; for merest fraud are all such things, which men in their folly day by day explore, exercising their soul in no useful work, teaching error unto hapless mortals; whence many evils have befallen the inhabitants of earth, so that they have strayed from the paths of righteousness. But, on the other hand, this people make righteousness and virtue their sole care; they shun avarice, which to the race of man brings numberless evils, wars, and famine past escape. Just bounds are theirs in town and field; no thief steals by night into their houses; they harry not their neighbours' flocks of oxen, sheep, and goats, nor violate their neighbours' boundaries; the rich man vexes not his poorer brother, nor harasses the widow, but rather aids her from his stores of corn and wine and oil; ever is he a blessing to them who have nothing; ever of his harvest he gives a share to the needy. Thus they fulfil the command of the great God, which is their ordered song; for the heavenly Father has given the earth as the common possession of all men.—Vers. 218-248.

This eloquent passage, which indeed is an amplification of the warnings in Deut. xviii., is succeeded by an abstract of the history of Israel in the form of prophecy. The exodus is noticed, and the promulgation of the law at Sinai, and the happy life in the Holy Land, "when to them alone among mankind the fruitful earth returned a hundredfold—such were the measures of God." But the exile in Assyria follows and the ruin of the once favoured land, a punishment of the people's idolatry. Therefore for seventy years the country lies desolate, till a king sent from heaven,—Cyrus,—warned by a holy dream, restores Judah, the royal tribe, and all the kings of Persia give means to rebuild the temple.

The last section of the poem (vers. 489-807) is occupied with various predictions concerning the nations of the earth. In the epilogue (vers. 808-828) the Sibyl speaks of herself (though some critics regard this notice as a later interpolation), affirming that, while fame tells that she came from Erythræ, or was the daughter of Circe, she was in fact the daughter-in-law of Noah, and shut up with him in the ark. She asserts emphatically that she came from Babylon inspired ($οἰστρομανής$) to foretell the future to mortals. "The Greeks," she says, "assert that I am from Erythræ, or the daughter of Circe and Gnostos, and that I am insane and a false prophetess; but when my predictions shall be fulfilled, then shall ye remember me, and own that I am not mad, but a true prophetess of God " (808 ff.). Of the prophecy itself the following may be taken as a summary, though very often it is difficult to see to what events in history the seer refers, and sometimes there is known no fact corresponding to the fate announced:—Phœnicia shall be utterly destroyed, so that not a tribe shall be left, because of her lying lips and lawless life, and her proud exultation against the mighty God. A horrible end awaits Crete, whose smoking ruins all the world shall see. Thrace shall pass under the servile yoke, when a mixed horde of Galatians and Phrygians (Dardanidæ) shall overrun the fields of Greece. Evil shall befall Gog and Magog, the Marsi and Daci." Under these appellations the extreme northern nations are meant; the Marsi were always formidable in Roman eyes, and the Dacians are often enumerated among Scythian tribes.[1] This loose geography may be expected in a Jew living at Alexandria. Woe is next denounced on the peoples of Asia Minor—on Moors, Ethiopians, and Arabians; and then the ruin of Greece is predicted, when a barbarous nation shall invade it, and rapine and cruelty and slaughter shall reign throughout the land. This refers to the proceedings of the Romans in the Macedonian and Achaic wars. Man's share in this destruction shall be aided by Nature: plague, fire, famine shall do their part, so that scarce a third of the inhabitants shall remain. These evils are a punishment for the idolatry which profane kings introduced into Greece " fifteen

[1] Ezek. xxxix. 1, 2 ; Horat. *Carm.* ii. 20. 18, iii. 14. 18, etc.

hundred years ago." What this limitation of time may mean cannot accurately be determined. Dating it from the Sibyl's age, it would land us in an epoch long anterior to the Trojan war, about which we can form only conjectures. But the seer looks forward to better days. Greece will some day cast away its idols and turn to the true God, and with hands uplifted implore His help, offering to Him the sacrifices which once were paid to false gods. And then, led away, as it seems, by the temporary prosperity of the Jews under the Maccabæan rule, the author utters his Messianic hopes in glowing language, contrasting the peace and happiness of the favoured people with the wars and misery which were the heathen's portion.[1] "The holy race shall cleave unto the Most High God, and honour His temple with libations and incense and sacred hecatombs, and offer on the great altar fat thighs of rams. Righteously observing the holy law, they shall live happy in city and field, and, themselves becoming prophets, shall bring joy to all men; for to them alone of mortals hath God given wisdom and faith. They make no gods of gold or silver, nor pictured forms of beasts to worship; but ever they raise pure arms to heaven, in early morning rising from their bed to cleanse their hands with water;[2] they honour the eternal God and their parents; they love chastity and the bed undefiled, nor ever practise the shameful vices of the heathen, which have brought on these infinite misery."

[1] This, according to Sir J. Floyer, is a description of the Reformation in Europe, A.D. 1517.
[2] John ii. 6.

But a day shall come when idolatry shall be abolished, and the pagans shall hide their images in the holes of the rocks [1] for very shame. This blessed change shall take place " what time a new king shall rule over Egypt, the seventh in succession of the Grecian supremacy," *i.e.* as we have seen, in the reign of Ptolemy Physcon. At that time " a mighty king from Asia, like a rapacious eagle "—Antiochus Epiphanes—shall ravage Egypt, and carry off large booty across the sea. Taught by these sufferings, the nation shall bow its knee to the great God of heaven, and burn its idols; and the Lord shall make all the land rejoice; and earth shall give her increase, and there shall be abundance of flocks and herds and of everything that sustains the life of men. This passage places us at the standpoint of the writer, who, knowing nothing of subsequent events, takes occasion from the happy circumstances of the Jews at this epoch to picture the peaceful life of the righteous nation in anticipation of the glories of Messiah's kingdom. At the same time, he warns the Gentiles that first shall arise terrible tribulation from the cruel inroads of a barbarous people, meaning probably the Romans. At the close of this distress Messiah shall come. "Then from the rising sun [2] God shall send a king, who shall make all the earth to cease from cruel war, killing indeed some, making faithful treaties with others. Not by his own counsels shall he do all this, but in obedience

---

[1] Isa. ii. 19 f.

[2] Ἀπ' ἠελίοιο (v. 652), "from the east," Isa. xli. 2; or it may mean simply "from heaven," as Cyrus is said (v. 286) to come οὐρανόθεν.

to the good decrees of Almighty God.[1] And the Lord's people shall be rich with every blessing, with gold and silver and purple raiment; land and sea shall fill them with good things." Nations shall war against the holy people, eager to destroy the temple of God, and bring in their own idolatrous worship; but the hand of the Lord shall be heavy upon them, and shall rain destruction upon them from heaven. "In those days the whole earth shall be shaken, and all the inhabitants thereof, and great fear shall be on every side. He shall rend asunder the mountains, and lay open the abyss, and fill the places with dead bodies, and lay low the walls of evil men, because they knew not the law of God, and raised their weapons against the holy place." And this destruction shall fall upon them until they recognise God, the righteous Judge. Here, as the seer unfolds the mighty future, he claims for his utterances the gift of inspiration. "The great eternal God Himself bade me prophesy these things, all of which shall be fulfilled in their season; for the Spirit of God throughout the world is true."[2] Then follows another glowing description of the felicity of the chosen people, who shall dwell in peace and plenty under the immediate protection of God. "Oh, how greatly doth the Immortal love these men! shall all the islands and cities say; for all things sympathise with them and bring them

---

[1] John v. 19: "The Son can do nothing of Himself, but what He seeth the Father do." Comp. *ibid.* v. 30.

[2] Though the Jews did not accurately distinguish the Persons of the Holy Trinity, they often speak of the Holy Spirit as distinct from the Father,—*e.g.* in the Book of Wisdom,—and look to Him as the Author of inspiration.

help,[1] both heaven, and moon, and God-moved sun." At sight of this prosperity the Gentiles shall turn to God, and call on one another to come and offer sacrifice to the Almighty, and to be obedient to His law. Now the prophet calls upon Greece (*i.e.* the land of Egypt) to aid the Jews dwelling there to return to their own country, and to take part in the struggle then being carried on under the brave Maccabees.[2] If the Egyptians shall neglect to do this, and shall still cleave to their idolatry and heathen vice, they shall lose all share in the felicity of the Messianic kingdom, "when the fated end shall arrive, and the judgment of the eternal God shall fall upon mortal men." A still more glowing description of this happy time follows, very similar to the classic accounts of the golden age; and the Lord, it is said, in the starry heaven shall give one common law to all the earth, "for He is God alone, and there is none but He."[3] And when His kingdom is established over all men, then shall they bring incense and offerings to the one house of God which shall stand for ever.[4] Here the writer

[1] Wisd. xvi. 17; Rom. viii. 28.
[2] The historical allusions may be read in Alexandre's note on v. 734.
[3] This is a phrase which often occurs: Deut. iv. 35; Isa. xlv. 5, etc.
[4] In v. 774, according to the reading of the MSS., occur the words: "And mortals shall call him *the Son* of the Mighty God," υἱὸν γὰρ καλέουσι βροτοὶ μεγάλοιο θεοῖο. The last object spoken of is οἶκος, the house of God, which Lactantius and Augustine took as denoting the Logos (see Lact. *Div. Inst.* iv. 6; August. *Contr. Hær.* v. 3). But Alexandre with great probability thinks that νηόν ought to be read instead of υἱόν, as the rest of the paragraph is concerned only with the temple, and any mention of the Son of God is alien from the passage.

evidently looks forward to the permanence and unique position of the temple at Jerusalem, once polluted by Antiochus, but now purified and restored by the piety of the Maccabees. By land and sea, he says, the peoples shall flock to the Holy City to pay their vows; and this they can do because it shall be a time of universal peace, when "the prophets of God shall take away the sword from among mankind, and they themselves shall be the kings and righteous judges of mortal men; and He shall dwell with them and be their everlasting light." What signs shall precede this happy reign of Messiah? They are these: flaming swords in the sky seen by night in the east and west; storms of dust; the light of the sun failing in mid-day, and the moon's rays falling on earth at unusual times; blood flowing from rocks; warriors and huntsmen appearing in the clouds of heaven.[1]

The book closes, as we have seen above, with an epilogue containing an account of the Sibyl's origin, and asserting her claim to inspiration. In this composition we see the object of the writer very plainly. He employs the popularity enjoyed by the "Oracles" to enforce his own views, presenting the history of his own people up to Noah's time as a past record, and narrating subsequent events in the form of prophecy, the rôle of antiquity being thus well maintained, and his own age virtually asserted. He sets before the Gentiles a high ideal, showing them to what they ought to aspire, and warning them that they can hope to attain this position only by favouring and supporting the chosen people, and following their bright example. And he

[1] Comp. 2 Macc. v. 2, 3.

recalls the Hebrews, especially those dwelling in foreign countries, to the observation of the law, and to the remembrance of Messianic hopes which are now approaching fulfilment. It is just possible that Virgil, in his description of the golden age, may have reproduced some of the ideas which had emanated from the Sibyl, whose verses may have been carried to Rome by the commissioners who were sent to seek for Sibylline books in Egypt, and that he alludes to our poet when he says (*Ecl.* iv. 4): "Ultima Cumæi venit jam carminis ætas." The second section of this book is almost wholly occupied with denunciations of judgments and calamities upon nations more or less hostile to Israel. Babylon shall suffer heavily for her offences against the holy people; Egypt shall be pierced with the sword "in the seventh generation of kings," and then shall rest in peace; Gog and Magog, whose unknown country lies between the Ethiopian rivers, shall be stained with blood; for Libya and western lands a bitter time is approaching. Nor shall signs of the coming calamities be wanting; comets, plagues, famines, wars, earthquakes, shall herald the fate of these nations. Proclamations of woes on particular towns and countries follow. Rome shall have to restore to Asia the wealth which she plundered. Then we have the paronomasias:

ἔσται καὶ Σάμος ἄμμος, ἐσεῖται Δῆλος ἄδηλος,
καὶ Ῥώμη ῥύμη.

After these tribulations peace shall ensue in Asia and Europe, and a time of Messianic prosperity. Then the Sibyl turns again to gloomy vaticinations, and utters oracles concerning Antiochus Epiphanes, "a man clad in purple, barbarous, iniquitous, fiery," and his successors; she speaks of Phrygia, Troy, Lydia, Cyprus, Italy, and other countries, taking occasion to inveigh against Homer as a writer of lies (ψευδογράφος), one who plagiarised from Sibyl's oracles, and falsified what he borrowed. The section ends with announcing the destruction of Carthage and Corinth.

The book next in age to the preceding one is the fourth, the production of a Jew or a semi-Judaising Christian, composed after the fall of Jerusalem under Titus or Domitian. The date is fixed by two allusions in the poem: first, the destruction of Jerusalem (vers. 115–127); and next, the mention of the eruption of Vesuvius (A.D. 79) as a recent calamity, and the precursor of Divine vengeance on the destroyer of the Jewish nation. "When from the cloven rocks of Italy a fire returning shall blaze unto the broad heaven, and shall burn up many cities, and destroy the lives of men, filling the vast air with flaming ashes, and drops of bloody hue shall fall from heaven, then shall men know the wrath of God for that they slew the guiltless race of the pious" (vers. 130–136). Prophecies of this calamity were prevalent among the heathen. Plutarch[1] twice alleges a supposed Sibylline oracle on the subject, which speaks of the overthrow of Cumæ and Dicæarchia, *i.e.* Puteoli, by fire from the Besbian mountain. And the astonishment with which the news of it was received, and the effect upon men's minds, may be gathered from the accounts which have come down to us. Dio

---

[1] *De Ser. Num. Vind.* t. viii. p. 240; *De Pyth. Orac.* t. vii. p. 566. Alexandre.

Cassius [1] asserts that the ashes reached even Syria and Egypt. To the Jews, suffering from their late disasters, and prone to look for God's interposition in their behalf, the calamity seemed to be a well-deserved judgment on their conquerors, and a sign of the punishment which was to subdue the enemy, and re-establish their own fallen state. The supposed Christian origin of the book is inferred from certain allusions contained in it; but these are very far from being decisive. Thus the saying of grace before meals is (vers. 25 f.) noticed as a special mark of the pious, and the turning with horror from temples which flow with the blood of sacrifices. But the grace at meals was a special rabbinic practice, and the animal sacrifices referred to may be those offered by heathens. And if the author praises the people for being averse from unlawful and usurious gain, he is not necessarily alluding to Christians, but rather applauding the ideal Hebrew, however inappropriately to what we know of their actual character. We find also a seeming reference to the total immersion practised by the early Christians in the rite of baptism. "Ah! wretched mortals, lay down your swords; away with groans, and murder, and violence, and wash your whole bodies in the perennial waters, and raising your hands on high, ask pardon for past sins" (vers. 161 ff.). But this may just as well be said of the proselyte baptism practised by the Jews.[2] In another passage the reproaches heaped on the pious are just such as are complained of in the apologetic writings of the Christians, whom their traducers "attack with derision and calumny,

---

[1] L. lxvi. 23.   [2] See Schürer, ii. 323.

attributing their own evil deeds to the holy worshippers of God" (vers. 37 ff.). This, again, is too vague to determine the question either way. An epilogue about the condition of men after the judgment was thought to be sufficiently orthodox and in accordance with Christian notions to be transferred bodily to the *Apostolical Constitutions*, where it will be found in Book v. chap. 7. The episode there is indeed somewhat longer than that contained in the MSS. of the Sibyllines, and the editors of the latter have added the verses thus preserved to their editions, judging rightly that there is sufficient authority for the insertion.

There are some points of great interest in this book. Let us glance at the contents. Commencing with an address to the nations of Europe and Asia, the Sibyl claims direct inspiration from the true God, whose attributes are finely expressed; and, in opposition to the false oracles of Apollo, she professes to be able to narrate events from the first to the tenth generation, which, in Sibylline utterance, is always the last. Before doing this she digresses into the praise of those who serve the great God and bless Him before they eat or drink, and offer no bloody sacrifices, living honestly and chastely, the laughing-stock indeed of evil men, but approved of the Lord, who shall punish the mockers at the judgment, separating the righteous from the wicked. The allusion, as we have already noticed, is not necessarily to the Christians, and the passage is remarkable as, like one above mentioned, offering no support to millennial opinions, or to the notion of a first resurrection which prevailed among some of the Jews of this period.

The view here entertained is (like that enunciated in the Ascension of Isaiah, etc.) rather that of an universal judgment to be followed immediately by the felicity of the righteous. This happy reward is to be received on earth and enjoyed in the body; that a resurrection is to precede it seems to be implied. There is no mention of Christ in this account of the last days, which is inconceivable if the book is written by a Christian. But all such speculations, not based altogether on revelation, are necessarily vague, and often contradictory. After this reference to the great consummation, the Sibyl proceeds to notice six generations of Assyrian kings, commencing from the time of the Flood, followed by two of Median origin,[1] and one each of Persian and Macedonian, the last ushering in the Roman dominion. We are told of a battle between the Medes and Persians at the Euphrates, which resulted in the victory of the latter; of the Trojan war, when "boastful Greece" brought ruin on the fields of Phrygia; of a famine in Egypt of twenty years' duration, the Nile withholding its crop-nourishing waters; of Xerxes' invasion of Greece, with its disastrous termination; of eruptions of Ætna, and earthquakes in Italy, in one of which Croton was destroyed; of the war which raged in Peloponnesus; and of the destiny of many other nations, the verses concerning which seem to be remnants of old heathen oracles, and are curious if not instructive.

The allusion to the destruction of Jerusalem and the temple gives occasion for the earliest notice of the legend

[1] In this period occurs an eclipse of the sun, which may possibly be the one noticed by Thales, B.C. 585.

concerning Nero, which was at one time so widely prevalent. According to this notion, Nero did not commit suicide on hearing of the proclamation of Galba and the desertion of the army, but escaped secretly to the East, and will return some day, enacting the part of Antichrist, and making havoc of the Church. Mention of impostors who assumed to be Nero is found also among the heathen writers who have treated of this period— Suetonius, Tacitus, and others.[1] The cruel persecution of the Christians under this emperor led them to look upon him as the type of the great enemy of the gospel whose advent they expected in the last days. Many have fancied that St. Paul referred to Nero in speaking of "that Wicked one" who was to be revealed in time (2 Thess. ii.). Indeed, so intense was the hatred of Nero, entertained alike by Jews and Christians, that no evil was too monstrous to be assigned to him—the former regarding him as virtually the destroyer of their city and polity, the latter finding in him all the attributes of the great enemy of God and man, whose appearance they were led to expect. The near approach of the final consummation was supposed to be heralded by the eruption of Vesuvius, which was regarded as an instance of Divine vengeance, and was to be followed by the return of "the exile from Rome, who should come from the far Euphrates, wielding his mighty sword, attended by myriads of soldiers." Other signs of the times are the demolition of Salamis and Paphos by an earthquake, which visited Cyprus A.D. 71, and which is mentioned by other

---

[1] Tacit. *Hist.* i. 2, ii. 8 ; Sueton. *Nero.* 57 ; Lactant. *De Morte Persec.* ii. ; Zonar. xi. 18.

authors,[1] the destruction of Antioch, and the restitution to Asia of the wealth which Rome had plundered from her. This last event was the subject of a common expectation at that time, seized upon with avidity by the Jews out of their hatred for their conquerors. Lactantius (vii. 15) expresses the general feeling or hope when he says: "The Roman name, which now is supreme in all the world, shall be utterly abolished, the empire shall return to Asia, and once again the East shall bear rule." Tacitus tells (*Hist.* v. 13) how an impression had prevailed that in certain sacred writings[2] it had been foretold that at this time the East should gain the mastery, and that Judæa should send forth conquering princes. In view of these coming occurrences the Sibyl, as we have seen, urges all men to repent and be baptized, for God was about to destroy the world and its inhabitants with fire. The book ends with the following paragraph, which is worth quoting, as showing the belief of a Jew or a semi-Christian in the latter half of the first century: "But when all things shall be reduced to dust and ashes, and God shall have put to sleep the awful fire which He kindled, He will again change the bones and dust of men, and make them such as once they were. And then shall be the judgment; and God Himself shall judge the world again; and those who have done iniquity, them the earth shall cover with its heaps, and the depths of darksome Tartarus and Stygian Gehenna. But the pious

[1] Euseb. *Chron.*; Senec. *Ep.* xci.; Dio Cass. liv. 23; Cramer, *Anecd.* i. 334.
[2] Probably Dan. ii. 44 f. is meant. Comp. Sueton. *Vespas.* 4; Joseph. *Bell. Jud.* vi. 5. 4.

shall live again in the world (κόσμον), enjoying the incorruptible happiness of the immortal God, who shall give them spirit, life, and grace. And all shall see each other, looking on the sweet, joyous light of the sun. How blessed is he who shall live in that time!"

Belonging to the same period as the fourth book, or a little later, is the fifth, a few verses possibly being interpolated at the beginning. This is partly the work of an Alexandrian Jew, and seems to have been written, like other productions of the Alexandrian school, in order to introduce among the Gentiles Jewish ideas concerning monotheism and Messianic hopes. But there are some items which are clearly of Christian origin, as the one quoted further on identifying Jesus with Joshua. The writer of some passages appears to have had some acquaintance with the Revelation of St. John, and may possibly have been a renegade catechumen, and the same person who composed the interpolations in the third book, showing such implacable hatred to Rome on account of her treatment of the holy people. The frequent references to Egypt and Alexandria sufficiently prove the birthplace of this poem; and the statements concerning the Roman emperors, down to the time of the Antonines, indicate its date. The writer, who calls herself the sister of Isis, deals largely with history, beginning with Rome, and passing thence to other kingdoms and lands, and concludes with a description of a war among the signs of the Zodiac, during which stars shall fall from heaven, and shall cause the total conflagration of the world. The Roman emperors, from Julius Cæsar to Hadrian, are indicated by the value of the numbers, which in the Greek the initials of their names afford. Thus, J. Cæsar is he whose name shall begin with "twice ten" (K), Augustus he who has the first of letters (A), Tiberius he whose initial is three hundred (T), and so on. Hadrian is not designated by his number; he is called "the man of the silver head, who has the name of a sea." After him are to follow three Antonines. This concludes the oracular utterances respecting Rome. The rest of the book concerns itself with the affairs in Egypt, Judæa, and some other countries, comprising doubtless many ancient oracles once extant. Some few points in the historical allusions are worthy of mention. Thus here and elsewhere [1] mention is made of the conquest of the Persians and Medes, and the destruction of Babylon by Tiberius,—events which history has failed to record, and which belong to that affectation of universal dominion which was the product of the early Roman empire. Of course at this period the ancient Babylon was a shapeless ruin, which sheltered a few miserable Jews and natives, who contended with the wild beasts of the desert for a home in this desolate region. The connection of the Romans with this place was very slight. When L. Vitellius had the command in Syria, he took part in a civil war among the Parthians, and on one occasion led his forces to the Euphrates, and for a short time occupied the site of Babylon. This proceeding was magnified by rumour; and becoming in the course of time confused with Trajan's expeditions to the East, and the capture of Seleucia and Ctesiphon in the days of M. Aurelius

[1] iii. 384, xii. 40 f.

Antoninus and L. Verus, it was regarded as Rome's great victory over the far-famed capital of Chaldæa. The expectation of Nero's return, as the superhuman enemy of God, crops up again in this book. He is to come from Persia and overrun Egypt (vers. 92 ff.); but, daring to attack the sacred city, shall be overthrown by a mighty king sent from heaven, and then shall ensue the universal judgment. Nero appears, too, as the devastator of Greece; and some of his prominent crimes are mentioned with abhorrence. When he flees from Rome, he is said "to leave Babylon," this name being often given to Rome in the Sibylline Oracles—a fact which may help expositors of 1 Peter and the Revelation. After the destruction of the Holy Temple, and when this Adversary shall have reigned three years, a star shall fall from heaven and dry up the sea, and consume "Babylon" itself and the land of Italy. Here there is evidently some acquaintance with Christian apocalyptic literature, though the knowledge is dim and imperfect. The writer's hatred of the Roman name has led him to attribute unheard-of atrocities to the Antonines. Beliar, Antichrist, or Nero redivivus, who will have such power as was never before given unto man, will overthrow the three princes that spring from Hadrian, and compel them not only to slay one another, but even to eat one another's flesh, so that the sons make a banquet of the father's limbs (vers. 220 ff.). Most of the so-called Oracles are saved from gross error by being confined to events that had already happened, but this was really a prediction, and was not warranted by the event; but it is curiously paralleled by a state-

ment in the Fourth Book of Esdras xii. 21 ff., which
Alexandre supposes to refer to these times: "And
whereas thou sawest three heads resting, this is the
interpretation: In his last days shall the Most High
raise up three kings, and they shall renew many things
therein, and they shall have dominion of the earth
and of those that dwell therein, with much oppression, above all those that were before them; therefore
are they called the heads of the eagle. And whereas
thou sawest that the great head appeared no more, it
signifieth that one of them shall die upon his bed, and
yet with pain. For the two that remain shall be
slain with the sword. For the sword of the one shall
devour the other; but at the last shall he fall through
the sword himself." In connection with the oracle
against Rome, occur a few lines dooming Gauls and
Britons to destruction (vers. 199 ff.) for taking part in
the ruin of Jerusalem. Vespasian, it seems, summoned
a Gallic legion from Syria to act against the Jews, and
thus gave occasion for the Sibyl's invective, which
includes the destruction of Ravenna as being the port
whence the expedition sailed.[1] Such reckless assertions,
resting on no basis of fact, are very usual with this poet.
Thus, to vilify the conqueror of Jerusalem, he states that
Titus dethroned his father (ver. 39); in another place
(vers. 227 ff.) he thus inveighs against Rome: "Unstable
and of evil counsel, and by evil fate begirt, beginning of
sorrows to men and alike their end, while nature by
thee is now outraged, now preserved,[2] teeming with evil

[1] Tacit. *Hist.* iv. 39, v. 1 ; Joseph. *Bell. Jud.* iii. 1. 4 f.
[2] The meaning is obscure. The old Latin is : "Dum per te natura

and misery, who ever longed for thee? Who did not burn with wrath against thee? What fallen king ever died in thee an honourable death? Ill hast thou everything disposed; thou hast brought in a flood of wickedness; by thee the fair frame of the earth is changed." Contrasted with the iniquity and consequent destruction of Rome is the predicted prosperity of Zion. When Persia is at peace, and war shall no longer be found in her borders, the holy race of Jews shall once more arise superior to their enemies. Here follows a passage (vers. 255 ff.) which seems of Christian origin: "Now a certain excellent man shall come again from heaven, who spread forth his hands upon the very fruitful tree, the best of the Hebrews, who once made the sun stand still, speaking with beauteous words and pure lips." There is here evidently an allusion to the crucifixion of our Blessed Lord, which reminds one of the Catholic hymn, where the cross is spoken of as a tree—"flore, fronde fertilis," and the lines in the "Lustra Sex":—

> Crux fidelis, inter omnes
> Arbor una nobilis,
> Silva tamen nulla profert
> Fronde, flore, germine;
> Dulce ferrum, dulce lignum,
> Dulce pondus sustinent.

The identification of Christ with Joshua is a mixture of Jewish and Christian legend which is unique. It is perit rursusque resurgit." Friedlieb: "Da die Schöpfung beschädigt und wieder das Schicksal erettet." Floyer: "Thy creation was pernicious; but thou art preserved by fate to be the most infamous," etc. These are supposed to be translations of the Greek: Βλαπτομένης κτίσεως καὶ σωζομένης πάλι μοίρης (al. μοίραις).

no question of symbolism here, as Joshua in Christian writings is treated as a type of Christ, but rather the confusion is such as might be made by an ignorant person reading Heb. iv. 8, "if Jesus had given them rest," and concluding that Jesus Christ led the Jews into Canaan. The author, indeed, identifies himself with the Jews, as where he prays (vers. 327 ff.): "Spare Judæa, Almighty Father, that *we* may see Thy judgments;" and were it credible that the whole book was the work of one author, we should regard his religion as syncretic, and in full accord neither with law nor gospel. But the book, as we have said, is of composite character, containing heterogeneous elements. One writer may have been a Christian, another filches occasionally from Christian sources, but has no lively faith in Christ; like many of his countrymen at this time, he suspends his judgment, and instead of making a decision expends his energies in denunciations of the hated power of Rome, and in speculations concerning the future. We need not recount these various predictions, which are of similar character throughout, and have no historical value. They commonly introduce the victories and overthrow of Antichrist, or the Adversary, and contrast them with the prosperity of Israel under the Messiah. The author in the case of the latter subject is generally, but not invariably, in agreement with Revelation. He speaks of the New Jerusalem which Messiah shall build, a city brighter than sun, and moon, and stars; but, in opposition to those who gave a spiritual interpretation to such predictions, he places therein a temple, ἔνσαρκον, corporeal, material, whereas St. John says (Rev. xxi. 22) he saw no temple there. He proclaims the extinction of the two great luminaries in the heavens, but, apparently, not at the same time. When the moon's light is quenched an universal war shall ensue, which shall be specially localised in Macedonia, where the Adversary shall overthrow the Antonines, and, returning thence, shall waste Asia Minor, Syria, and Egypt, Judæa alone being left at peace. When the sun shall set, never more to rise, the whole world shall lie in darkness, except the land of Israel, which shall have light from the Lord. This awful time shall be preceded in Egypt by the freezing of the river Nile, and an irruption of barbarians into Asia and Thrace, and shall be followed by the destruction of the Egyptian idols, Isis and Serapis, and the erection in Egypt of a temple[1] to the true God, which shall last to the end of the world, when it will be destroyed by the Ethiopians, who then, with the rest of the evil-doers, will meet with their just punishment at the hands of Almighty God. The Sibyl leaves the world in flames, saying nothing of what shall be afterwards. This gap is supplied by a later oracle.

The next piece consists of Books vi. and vii., which, from internal evidence, seem to have been written by a Christian, one, however, who was very far from being orthodox, and held the doctrines of some of the sects of later apostolic times. Ewald sets the date at the end of Adrian's reign, Alexandre nearly a century later.

[1] This is not the Temple of Onias, erected near Heliopolis in the time of Ptolemy Philometor, and long before this time dismantled and disused (Joseph. *Bell. Jud.* vii. 10. 4), but a new one, which was never built, though it may possibly have been contemplated, perhaps with some support from Isa. xix. 18 ff.

The latter relies on some lines in Book vii. (vers. 41 ff.) which speak of the rise of a new Persian kingdom, infamous with vice, and an expedition of the Romans against it, which terminated unfavourably, and which he supposes to refer to the proceedings of the Emperor Alexander Severus, A.D. 232. But the allusion is very obscure, and it is certain that the emperor on this occasion returned in triumph to Rome, and that the Persian monarch was restrained for many years from hostile operations; so that we cannot fix the date of the poem from this passage, which in fact would equally well apply to the defeat of Crassus by the Parthians. The threat against Judæa for its treatment of Messiah (vi. 21 ff.) may be a prophecy after the punishment had fallen, as are so many of the "Oracles." The heresies which the author affects are such as were rife in early Christian times, and we shall probably not be wrong in setting the date of this piece in the latter half of the second century.

The sixth book, a very short one of only twenty-eight lines, is not a vaticination, but a hymn to Christ, in which are set forth His Divine nature, His appearance and ministry in the world, and His future return. These facts are produced in orthodox language, which is deemed worthy of quotation by Lactantius and Gregory Nazianzen, and was not unknown to Augustine.[1] In the mention of our Lord's baptism occurs the legend of the fire which then appeared, to which we shall refer again below. The Sibyl applies the verb "he saw" in Matt.

[1] Lactant. iv. 13 and 18; Greg. Naz. *Ad Nemes.* t. ii. p. 144; Aug. *De Civ.* xviii. 23.

iii. 16 to Christ, not to John: "He, escaping from the fire, first shall see the sweet Spirit of God coming upon Him." Thus far all is not unorthodox; but following the tenets of the Cerinthians and Ebionites, the writer holds that Jesus, a mere man, son of Joseph and Mary, received the Divine nature at His baptism by the descent of the Holy Ghost, who united Him with Christ, the eternal Word of God. He recognises two natures in Jesus Christ, and one Person, and always professes belief in His divinity. His words concerning the Cross have continually been quoted as confirming the doctrine of the Hypostatic union for which the Council of Ephesus contended. "O blessed tree," he says, "on which God was stretched," or, as the Latin versifier puts it—

O lignum felix in quo Deus ipse pependit.

Contrary to the tradition which represented Helena as the finder of the Holy Cross (and therefore supporting the earlier date assigned to this book), the Sibyl says that the earth could not keep the sacred wood, but that it was transported to a heavenly home, to appear again at the last day, "the sign of the Son of man" (Matt. xxiv. 30). The same expectation is found elsewhere, *e.g.* in the acrostic in Book viii. 244, which is rendered—

Insigne et cunctis aderit mirabile visu
Nullo sat cultu fidis venerabile lignum.

In these early times it is plain that the Cross alone, without the figure of Christ upon it, was the object of veneration. The crucifix was of later origin. Before leaving this book we may observe that in the solitary denunciation which it contains, Judæa is addressed as

"Land of Sodom," an appellation of Jerusalem common alike to the prophets and the Apocalypse (comp. Isa. i. 9, 10; Ezek. xvi.; Rev. xi. 8).

The seventh book, which from internal considerations is rightly considered to be the work of the same author as the preceding, is of conglomerate character, and returns to the usual form of Sibyllines, consisting, that is, of predictions concerning various nations, interspersed with certain mystic and theological statements. The first part is fragmentary, containing oracles concerning Rhodes, Delos, Cyprus, and Sicily. In it is comprised a paragraph from a poem on the Flood, which is also found in Book i. This contains the curious myth that Phrygia was the first country to emerge from the waters, and became the originator of idolatry. The same legend is found in other of the Oracles, *e.g.* i. 196, iii. sect. 2. 140, v. 129, and seems to have been derived without examination from the prevalent opinion that the belief in the most ancient of the pagan divinities and the most antique rites of heathenism arose in that part of the world. There is another tradition which makes the ark ground on an Ararat in Phrygia, near the city Apamea Cibotus (i. 261). This is an offshoot of the preceding myth. After some other prophecies we come to the mention of Christ, "the Begotten, the great God," appearing in judgment. Certain signs shall herald His advent, specially a mighty column of flame in the heavens, which shall drop fiery destruction on the wicked. In mentioning Christ's dominion over the angels, the writer has expressions very similar to those used by Hermas in the *Pastor* (vers. 3, 4), where he speaks of the angels as controlling all creation. Still more striking is the parallelism concerning the three towers raised in heaven wherein dwell three daughters of God—Hope, Piety, and Religion ($\sigma\epsilon\beta\alpha\sigma\mu o\sigma\acute{\upsilon}\nu\eta$), and which are prepared by Christ for the reception of the righteous. Hermas in his third vision sees a tower raised in heaven, which is to be the habitation of the just; but instead of three Virtues dwelling there, he makes seven, viz. Faith, Temperance, Simplicity, Knowledge, Innocence, Gravity, Charity. It is strange that neither Hermas nor the Sibyl availed themselves of St. Paul's enumeration of the three theological virtues, Faith, Hope, and Charity. The Sibyl, however, errs widely from Holy Scripture and the lines of orthodoxy when foretelling the adoption of certain sacred rites (vers. 76 ff.) which shall obtain in Messiah's time. "Thou shalt offer sacrifice," we read, "to the great immortal God, not melting with fire the grain of incense, nor slaying with the knife the shaggy lamb; but, in company with all who share thy blood, taking woodland birds, thou shalt pray and let them fly, turning thine eyes to heaven, and thou shalt pour water in libation into the pure fire with these words: O Father, as the Father begat Thee, the Word, I send forth this bird, the swift messenger of my words, with holy water besprinkling Thy baptism through which from the fire Thou didst appear." The Greek is obscure, but the ceremony, consisting in letting a bird fly to convey prayer to heaven, is plain enough, and is a remnant of Judaism unknown to any Christian community. The allusion also to the fire in the Jordan at Christ's baptism is evident. A paragraph concerning false prophets who feign themselves Hebrews, Alexandre calls the last gasp of expiring Judaism (vers. 132 ff.). It upbraids these men with magnifying the evil of the coming epoch, and striving to change the ancient Jewish discipline. They and all such shall perish, and a new world shall appear "in the third allotment of rolling years, within the first octave." This mysterious date has been variously interpreted, and more pains have been wasted on it than its importance demands. Alexandre, who has examined the matter with his accustomed diligence, decides that the writer refers to the year 350 of the Actiatic era, which corresponds to A.D. 380. At this time the final age commences, Antichrist is to appear, and be finally defeated; then shall follow the last great convulsion, and the terrestrial reign of the pious under the sovereignty of Messiah, God Himself being with them and teaching them.

The book ends with a curious epilogue, which is found somewhat watered down in the second book. In this the Sibyl accuses herself of various crimes, for which she deserves and shall receive punishment. She is not immortal, but will some day be slain by a shower of stones cast upon her by sailors passing near; and she concludes with the prayer: "Stone me, stone me, all ye wayfarers; thus shall I live and fix my eyes on heaven." It is impossible to determine the reason of the introduction of this self-accusation in this place. We know nothing of its grounds, and cannot conjecture the object, unless it be a hostile interpolation intended to throw discredit on the Sibyl.

The eighth book has been divided by editors into four

parts, of which the first two are of earlier date than the rest and by a different hand. The earlier portion falls into the time of the Antonines, the latter is a little later. The writer speaks of the adopted sons of Adrian, but he knows no details concerning any but M. Aurelius, in whose time he expects the return of Nero, the fall of Rome, the end of the world, and the judgment. But his acquaintance with M. Aurelius is very superficial, as he represents him as avaricious, and flying to Asia in order to save his treasures from Nero. He must have written therefore between A.D. 161 and 180, during which years Aurelius reigned. The author of this portion is a Jew, as we may conclude from his continual references to the Old Testament and the way in which he speaks of the Hebrews, but one who had some acquaintance with Christian doctrine and writings. He is thus to be placed in the same category as the writer of Book v., if he is not to be identified with him.

At the outset the Sibyl professes an intention of proclaiming the wrath of God upon the nations and the approaching end of the world; but little mention is made of any country but Rome, and the Sibyl's mind is wholly occupied with the destiny of this enemy of her people. The vice which she specially and eloquently lashes is avarice; this sin it is which shall occasion Rome's downfall. After fifteen princes have reigned in succession, "the white-headed" Adrian shall follow, who shall be greatly regretted and mourned, as if the city itself had perished. Then, as it seems, in the time of his successor, Almighty God Himself shall come and judge the souls of the quick and dead; but before the consummation a dragon shall cross the sea, with well-filled maw, and shall afflict the Roman people. This seems to be a remembrance of the dragon or the beast of Revelation xiii., which the Sibyl represents as coming from Asia with a fleet to attack and destroy guilty Rome, which is to be thrust down into hell. A description of Hades ensues, whereon rests eternal night, where all earthly distinctions are abolished, where "there is neither slave, nor lord, nor tyrant, nor king;" no corrupt judge, no libation or sacrifice, no feasting or music, no wrath or strife, but "one common life for all, which keeps them safe for the day of judgment." Another portent, which shall precede the return of Nero and the end of the world, is the appearance of the Phœnix for the fifth time.[1] The curious myth concerning the Phœnix is given in various authors. Clemens Romanus tells it thus: In Arabia or some other Eastern countries there is a bird called a Phœnix, which lives for five hundred years a solitary life. When it feels death approaching, it constructs for itself a pile of frankincense, myrrh, and other aromatic herbs, and, lying there, dies. From its decaying carcass a worm is engendered, which assumes the appearance of the deceased bird. This young Phœnix carries the remains of its parent to Heliopolis in Egypt, places them on the Altar of the Sun, and returns whence it came. The priests keep an accurate account of this event, and compute the time of its recurrence. The fourth appearance of the bird is said to have taken place in the time of Tiberius, A.D. 34, A.U.C. 787. The Sibyl's

[1] See Herod. ii. 73; Tacit. *Ann.* vi. 28; Plin. *Nat. Hist.* x. 2; Clem. Rom. 1 *Ep. ad Cor.* xxv.; Tertull. *De Resurr.* xiii.

reckoning is quite different, as she expects the fifth resuscitation, which was to coincide with the ruin of Rome, to occur A.U.C. 948. This would be equivalent to A.D. 194, or nearly, and would fall in with the reign of Septimius Severus. The date doubtless depends on the numerical value of $ῥώμη = 100 + 800 + 48$; and the prediction, however greatly falsified by the event, was the utterance of an earnest hope, expressed confidently in this form, in order to animate the drooping spirits of the subdued and disconsolate Jews. It is difficult to arrive at any clear view of the sequence of events in these last days, the writer himself having but hazy notions on the subject, and not arranging his details chronologically. There are also many gaps in the MSS., which, if supplied, would doubtless clear up some obscurities. As far as we can understand this mysterious period, the circumstances are these:[1] At the time that Anti-Messias or Nero invades the Roman empire, and before the destruction of Rome itself, Messiah descends from heaven, "the Holy King, who shall reign over Israel, and call the dead from their graves." He shall inaugurate a new Jerusalem, with a new material temple, peopled partly by Jews collected from all parts of the world, partly by the just who have been raised to life again. Against Him the Antichrist shall conspire in conjunction with certain barbarian kings; but after various portents— stars falling from heaven, and a great comet appearing— he and his allies shall be defeated by an angel, and hurled into the abyss. And another foe, a woman, shall be overthrown. She is here called "the joyous," and in

[1] Thus Alexandre arranges them.

Book iii. "the widow;" and she shall be a powerful queen, exercising a cruel tyranny, in the tenth age of man. This woman is no historical person,—certainly not Julia, the wife of Septimius Severus, as some have thought,—but the one figured in Revelation xvii., xviii., there certainly, here probably, representing Rome. In these eschatological predictions there are some differences from the details afforded by the previous books. In the fifth the empire of the Jews under Messiah was to be terminated by an irruption of Ethiopians, and the whole world was to perish owing to some sidereal catastrophe. The earlier part of the present book takes up the story after this result, and expects a renovated earth, which is inhabited by the just of all countries, raised to life after the last judgment. Further particulars concerning the last judgment are afforded by the next portion of this eighth book, which, as it has come down to us, commences with the famous acrostic on the title of Christ already mentioned. St. Augustine gives a Latin version of this, omitting the last word "stauros;" Eusebius preserves the original thirty-four lines [1] in his account of Constantine's *Oratio ad Sanctos*, where the emperor quotes the verses, as a testimony to the divinity of Christ, uttered by the Erythræan Sibyl many centuries before the Christian era. The acrostic itself contains a description of the day of judgment and the events that shall succeed, and has many points of resemblance with the Prœmium, at which we have already glanced. The author was a Christian, though he probably worked up

[1] In some MSS. the ninth line, representing the "E" of Chreistos, is absent, which shows that the spelling of the word still fluctuated.

Jewish materials in composing his poems; and in the present case, wishing to emulate the ancient Sibyl in the form of his oracle, he prefaced his prophecy with this acrostic, which has become more celebrated than its author could have ever expected. We may suppose that in his desire to give verisimilitude to his utterance he took words which were oftenest on the lips of Christians, adding Σταυρός at the end as the most venerated of memorials, and perhaps (as Alexandre suggests) with the view of making the title into a spondaic hexameter. Whether the author intended to carry the same form through the whole of the book cannot be discovered; at any rate, he soon abandoned it, finishing his labour with the words: "This is our God, written in these acrostics, the Saviour, the King immortal, who suffered for us, whom Moses prefigured when he extended holy hands, by faith overcoming Amalek," etc. The acrostic ends at "who suffered for us;" from thence the poem proceeds in the ordinary manner. It must be noted that the initials of the title compose the word ΙΧΘΥΣ, "fish," the emblem of the Christian faith so frequently sculptured on early monuments. In the account of the great consummation, we are told little that is novel. Fire shall destroy earth, sea, and sky, and the gates of hell itself, and shall convict the unrighteous of guilt; sun, moon, and stars shall fail, and the heavens shall be rolled up; hill and valley shall be levelled, rivers shall be dried, and the voice of the trumpet shall summon all to judgment. The Cross shall be seen in the sky. The closing lines of the acrostic concerning the Cross are remarkable. It is called the sign, the notable seal for all men, expressions which recall our Lord's words in Matt. xxiv. 30: "then shall appear the sign of the Son of man in heaven," and St. Paul's in 2 Cor. i. 22 and Eph. 1. 13, where he speaks of believers being "sealed," though not with the Cross, nor with the sign of the Cross (as some Roman Catholic expositors take it), but with the Holy Spirit. Further, it is named "the much-desired horn," which seems to be an interpretation of the phrase "horn of David" in Ps. cxxxi. 17 and Luke i. 69; and it is said to be "the life of the pious, but an offence to the world," in agreement with the language of St. Paul (Gal. v. 11), where he speaks of "the offence of the Cross." Then follows a curious verse, "which enlighteneth the elect with water by twelve springs." This is explained to refer to the mission of the twelve apostles, which, as it were, originated from the Cross; but the writer seems to insinuate that the office of baptizing was committed to the twelve apostles alone, and presumably to their successors,—an opinion which he repeats again below (ver. 271), and which was not common in any section of the Church. He ends by terming the Cross "the rod of iron which tends and rules the flock," expressions which may come from Ps. ii. 9 or Rev. ii. 27. It is interesting to find this adaptation of scriptural figures to the Cross at this early age; later, of course, nothing is more common.

From the remaining portions of this poem we obtain some further glimpses of primitive eschatology. First, we meet here with the use of the word "judgment" for Christ's first advent into the world. The first judgment, in this view, is the Incarnation, which is regarded as the initiation of the final judgment, perhaps with some reference to such passages as John xvi. 11 : "The prince of this world hath been judged," and xii. 31 : "Now is the judgment of this world," though plainly in conflict with the forty-seventh verse of the same chapter: "I came not to judge the world." In accordance with this theory the Sibyls here and elsewhere speak of Christ judging the world "again," when they refer to the final award. Concerning the sojourn in the unseen world, we are told that Christ went thither to carry hope to the dead saints, and to announce to them the end of the world. Where the Gospel says that, for the elect's sake, the last days shall be shortened, our present text affirms that God has given men seven ages for repentance " by the hand of the holy Virgin," *i.e.* at her intercession. These words are allowed to be an interpolation, but of how early a date it cannot be determined. Certainly any such doctrine is centuries later than this Oracle; and, as Alexandre remarks, the Sibyllines always represent the final consummation as close at hand, and any postponement of this event for seven ages is quite alien from their view. A similar interpolation (probably the work of the writer of the preface) occurs in Book ii. 312 ; and with the same view of honouring the Virgin Mary a very clumsy alteration has been made in Book i. 359, where, in the accounts of the miracle of the five loaves and the five thousand, the glosser has changed the words, which he has quoted from Book viii. 275 ff., " the fragments shall fill twelve baskets, *a hope for the peoples,*" into, "*for the holy Virgin,*" as if the remains were reserved by Christ for His mother's use.

Before quitting this portion of the book, we may observe that the writer firmly believes in baptismal regeneration. Christ, he says (vers. 314 ff.), rose from the dead that the elect, "washed in the waters of the immortal fount, and born again (ἀναγεννηθέντες ἄνωθεν), might no longer serve the lawless customs of the world." He supposes that the saints in glory will wear crowns of thorns like their Master. He sees in the rending of the temple's veil and the supernatural darkness at the Crucifixion an intimation that the old law was no longer to be observed by men hitherto blinded by the deceits of the world. He considers that in the creation of man the Father says to the Son, "Let us make man," taking Him as His counsellor (σύμβουλος) not only in the creation, but also in the redemption of the same. "I with my hands will make him, Thou hereafter shalt heal him with the word" (ver. 267). Thus in the ancient document called the "Epistle to Diognetus" (chap. viii.), it is said that the Father communicated His wise counsel concerning man to His Son alone. In Christ's hands extended on the cross the writer recognises the comprehension of the whole world in the benefits of the Passion; in the wounds in His hands and feet he finds a representation of the four quarters of the globe as being concerned in His death. He puts into the mouth of God some lines which are quoted by Herodotus (i. 47) as a Delphic oracle: "I know the number of the sands, the measure of the sea. I understand the dumb, and hear the silent speak;" and he makes Him, in commanding men to show charity to their fellows, direct that they feed the hungry with vegetable food, "a table pure and of unbloody food," whence it is argued that the author belonged to the Therapeutæ, one of whose distinguishing peculiarities was abstention from animal diet.[1]

The next portion of this book is a hymn in praise of God the Father and God the Son, and cannot be regarded as an oracle; it is probably of the same authorship as the former parts, and its date is the same, or a little later. Like the writer of the last section, this poet makes the creation of the world and man the joint work of the Father and the Son, or the *Logos*, and speaks of man being made like to the form ($\mu o \rho \phi \acute{\eta}$) of God. He then proceeds to note the message of Gabriel and the Incarnation of Christ: "Receive, O virgin, God in thy immaculate bosom." The visit of the wise men is mentioned, and there the narrative part of the poem abruptly breaks off, the rest of the section being lost. This doubtless contained an account of the life and actions of Christ, and the foundation of the Church, merging naturally into an argument concerning Christian doctrine and ethics. The fragment with which the book closes contains a portion of the latter subject, and is written in language of no mean order. The author professes himself a Christian, and, in opposition to the heathendom still prevalent, announces that he and his brethren are bound to live a holy life, to serve God, to love their neighbour as themselves. They frequent not temples, offer not prayers or libations to statues, nor deck their altars with flowers, nor adorn them with lights. They hang not the walls with costly gifts, nor offer

---

[1] Philo, *De Vit. Contempl.* 9 (vol. ii. 483).

incense, nor sacrifice animals; but in happy concord, with pure and cheerful hearts, they worship God, delighting in continual feasts of love (*agapæ*) and generous offerings, praising God with psalm and hymn. This is a beautiful picture of primitive Christian worship, confirmed by other notices, and quite in accordance with the simplicity of early times.

The next piece of the Oracles is composed of Books i. and ii., and as Ewald thinks, the first portion of Book iii. vers. 1–96, though Alexandre sets this fragment as the production of the author of the anonymous preface, and written by a monk in Justinian's time; but it is more probably of a composite character, and derived from more than one source. It may be divided into two sections, vers. 1–35, and vers. 36–96. The whole piece is of Christian origin, and for the most part of orthodox character, though containing some trace of Origen's opinions, and it is to be referred to the third century. It has been compiled and arranged in its present form by some later hand, which has also contributed some prose interpolations to connect the various fragments of which the work is composed. Indications of its date are afforded in various passages. Thus in ii. 45 ff., ii. 63 ff., there is mention of the persecutions which were being carried on, and the constancy of the martyrs, and this could refer to nothing subsequent to Diocletian (A.D. 302), and from the expressions used is considered to allude to something of earlier date. The doctrine of Universalism, which is found in Origen's works, in the middle of the third century, is brought forward in more than one passage of this piece.

The first book sketches the history of the world from the Creation to the Flood, and subsequently up to the second generation after Noah, and passes on to the advent of Christ, His life, death, and resurrection, the foundation of the Church, and the dispersion of the Jews. The second book takes up the story, and prophesies of events to the end of the world. The writer for the most part keeps close to the Mosaic account, but occasionally differs from it either in details or by additions. Thus he makes Noah send from the ark on the third occasion a bird of black plumage, which remained on the earth and returned no more; he considers Noah's sojourn in the ark to have lasted only forty-one days; and he introduces God as commanding Noah to preach repentance unto the Antediluvians, and gives the discourse of the patriarch in full. Friedlieb notes that Theophilus[1] derives the name, if not the legend, of Deucalion from the first words of Noah's warning on this occasion, which he gives in these words: δεῦτε, καλεῖ ὑμᾶς ὁ θεὸς εἰς μετάνοιαν. That Noah is called by St. Peter (2 Pet. ii. 5) "a preacher of righteousness" is an intimation of the same tradition which the Sibyl follows. Here, too, occurs the famous enigma on the name of God, which has exercised the minds of scholars for some centuries, and still awaits satisfactory solution (vers. 141 ff.). It is not worth while to waste time upon it, as the numbers given are uncertain, and differ in some manuscripts, and their interpretation is only conjectural. The *griphus* is supposed, with some appearance of probability, to mean

[1] *Ad Autol.* iii. p. 129.

θεὸς Σωτήρ. We give it here in the original, as it would be spoiled by translation :—

Ἐννέα γράμματ' ἔχω· τετρασύλλαβός εἰμι· νόει με·
αἱ τρεῖς αἱ πρῶται δύο γράμματ' ἔχουσιν ἑκάστη,
ἡ λοιπὴ δὲ τὰ λοιπά, καὶ εἰσὶν ἄφωνα δὲ πέντε·
τοῦ παντὸς δ' ἀριθμοῦ ἑκατοντάδες εἰσὶ δὶς ὀκτώ,
καὶ τρεῖς τρὶς (al. δὶς) δεκάδες, σὺν γ' ἑπτά.

The last words are intended to represent the numerical value of the enigmatical name. There is another riddle on the name Ἰησοῦς in this book (vers. 326 ff.), which is plain enough. The appellation, it is said, is composed of four vowels and one consonant twice repeated, and its numerical value in 888. The number of generations between Adam and Noah in the Sibyl's history does not correspond with the Mosaic account, the former making only five, the latter ten to intervene. But our author seems to have depended on Hesiod as well as Moses, and to have endeavoured to combine heathen mythology with Biblical history. According to him, the second generation consisted of a race called Gregori, who are named in the Book of Enoch Egregori, equivalent to the *Nephilim* of Genesis, a race between men and angels; but the Sibyl does not countenance the notion of these having any connection with the daughters of men. She figures the fifth generation as that of giants, and Noah as one of their progeny. That a Christian with the Old Testament before him should deliberately foist into the inspired record legends of no authority, and often contradictory of Holy Writ, is a strange anomaly, but one which can be paralleled by the treatment which the Bible experiences at the hands of theologians in modern times, who place floating myths in the same category with Biblical stories, and find as much truth in a heathen fable as in a scriptural narrative. The remainder of the book is not open to the same objection as the preceding portion, being founded on the New Testament, and keeping pretty accurately to the details therein narrated. The writer quotes St. Matthew v. 17 : " He shall fulfil the law of God, and not destroy it" (ver. 332, and refers to St. John iii. 3 in the words, " being born again," γεννηθέντες ἄνωθεν, though he certainly errs in ascribing this effect to the baptism of John the Baptist (ver. 340). He calls Christ (ver. 345) "the fair stone," against which the people of Israel shall stumble. This is evidently a remembrance of 1 Pet. ii. 6, 8 : " I lay in Zion a chief corner-stone, elect, precious, . . . a stone of stumbling and a rock of offence;" and the statement that Jesus goes to Hades to preach to the dead (ver. 378) is derived from the famous passage in 1 Pet. iii.

The second book takes up the story where the first left it, and foretells the events that shall happen from the time of the overthrow of the Jewish polity to the end of the world. It contains many lines attributed to the gnomic poet Phocylides, and a long fragment of the spurious ποίημα νουθετικόν which passes under his name. Alexandre has shown that Phocylides' verses had become a text-book in the Alexandrian schools, where his gnomes were committed to memory, and formed the groundwork of ethical teaching from the time of Ptolemy Philadelphus. Many of these lines found their way into the earlier Sibylline books, and were adapted to Jewish doctrine. The " carmen suasorium " here introduced by the Sibylline author may have been founded upon the words of the original poet; but it has suffered so many alterations and additions at the hands of Jewish and Christian manipulators that it is impossible to consider it as in any real sense the composition of Phocylides. The fragment is introduced to explain wherein Christian virtues consist, and what must be the lives of those who shall attain to the reward of Messiah's kingdom. The contents of the book are briefly these: After the dispersion of the Jews there shall ensue a general corruption in the world, and tumults and wars, in the course of which Rome shall be overthrown and idolatry abolished; then shall good men have opportunity of showing their virtues and triumphing over evil. Great calamities and portents presage the last times, *e.g.* the appearance of Belial or Antichrist, the return of the twelve tribes, the coming of Elijah from heaven. The last judgment follows, with the punishment of the wicked and the felicity of the righteous.

In this book, a great part of which is derived from others of the Oracles, there are some points to be remarked. Before the great consummation a star is to be seen for some days in the sky, as a signal for those who earnestly contend for the faith. The contest then begun is well called (ver. 39) a "ludus iselasticus," one, that is, where the conqueror is carried in triumph through a breach in the city walls to the temple of the guardian deity.[1] In the fragment from Phocylides there are many passages introduced from the Gospels, one also from Tobit (iv. 16): "Clothe the naked, give of thy bread to

[1] Plin. *Ep.* x. 119.

the hungry;" and from James (ii. 13): "Mercy saveth from death, when judgment comes," and from Acts (xxi. 25): "Eat not blood, and abstain from things offered to idols." Among the portents which shall precede the last day, and which are mostly the same as those named in our Lord's discourse, occurs one that is strange to Christian ears, and is derived from a heathen source, viz. the birth of children with grey hair.[1] Another prodigy, mentioned also elsewhere, is the interchange of seasons; a third is the cessation of parturition among women. This last omen is cited by Clemens Alex.[2] as contained in the apocryphal "Gospel of the Egyptians." The appearance of Beliar has been already mentioned. This name of Antichrist is derived from St. Paul's use of it (2 Cor. vi. 15) as a designation for Satan, and it is found in the Testaments of the Twelve Patriarchs. The return of the rest of the Hebrews from Assyria is expected also by the writer of the Second (iv.) Book of Esdras, who says (chap. xiii. 40 ff.) that in the latter time they shall cross the Euphrates, coming from a distant land, and settle once more in their own country. The Tishbite shall come from heaven in a chariot, not to "restore all things" (Matt. xvii. 11), but rather as a sign of the destruction of this world. Then the four archangels — Michael, Gabriel, Raphael, and Uriel — shall bring from Hades all the souls of men to the tribunal of God, who shall clothe them again with flesh and bones. And all shall pass through the probationary fire, from which the just shall emerge purified and saved, but the wicked shall perish therein. This last opinion is after-

[1] Hes. "E. καὶ 'H. 179.   [2] *Strom.* iii. 6 (p. 532).

wards modified. The "ignis probatorius" is a notion derived from 1 Cor. iii. 13 ff., and is acknowledged by Augustine, Lactantius, and other early writers.[1] The Sibylline writer seems to hold that this fire will destroy the whole world at the same time that it will try every man's work. From it the just shall be borne on angels' hands to a land where the blessings promised to Canaan shall be realised to the full, and one unending day of happiness shall reign. And in their own felicity the saints shall think of the misery of the cursed, and God shall hearken to their prayers, and save some from the pains of hell. The author does not, like Origen, believe in universal salvation. His words are these (vers. 335 ff.): "Having chosen out the stedfast" ($εὐσταθεῖς$, probably, those who have endured the fire) "from the unwearied flame, and removed them in safety, He shall send them among His own people to another and immortal life." This notion of the salvation of any of the condemned is, as we have seen, opposed to the sentiments elsewhere expressed, especially in vers. 309 ff. of this book, where, in picturing the torments of hell, the writer asserts that there is no place for repentance or mercy or hope. The statement in the text appeared so dangerous and erroneous to the editor of the Oracles in the sixth century that he introduced a refutation of the opinion, composed by himself in some execrable iambics, which Fabricius has thus translated:—

> Hæc falsa perspicue : nec unquam desinet
> Ille impiorum tortor ignis fervidus.
> Optarem et ipse equidem ista sic contingerent,

[1] Aug. *De Civit.* xx. 18. 25, xxi. 26 ; Lact. *Div. Inst.* vii. 21.

> Qui maximis maculis inustus criminum
> Deformor ipse, queis plus gratia est opus.
> Verum erubesce, nugigerule Origenes,
> Qui desituras esse pœnas dictitas.

The remainder of this portion of the Oracles, which is made up of the first section of Book iii., begins with an exhortation to the Gentiles to turn from idols to the worship of the true God, where we may note that the mention of cats and serpents as objects of adoration places the author at once in Egypt. It then proceeds to speak of the fall of Rome and the eternal kingdom of Christ, preceded by the appearance of Beliar. In former books we have seen the expectation of the return of Nero as the great enemy of God's Church; in these later writings we hear no more of this particular phenomenon, but the Antichrist is announced as the devil personified. He is to come from the people of Sebaste (which was the name given to Samaria when rebuilt by Herod the Great), owing doubtless to the prediction in Gen. xlix. 17: "Dan shall be a serpent by the way, an adder in the path, that biteth the horse heels, so that his rider shall fall backwards." Rabbinical interpretation saw in this a reference to Antichrist, and the Fathers adopted the view. Samaria, indeed, appertained to Ephraim, not Dan; but national hatred overlooked this slight discrepancy, and satisfied itself by teaching that the hated race was to give birth to this Enemy. If we can identify Dan with Sebaste, we can more easily see why this place is singled out for its bad pre-eminence. This tribe had become a by-word for idolatry, and the serpent, which was its emblem, represented the power of evil. It is thus excluded from the tribes of Israel whose elect are sealed in Rev. vii.; and St. Gregory could write:[1] "Some say that Antichrist is coming out of the tribe of Dan, because Dan is asserted to be a serpent and a biting one. Whence also in the partition of the camp, Dan most rightly pitched his camp to the north, signifying him in truth who had said in his heart, 'I will sit upon the mount of the testament, in the side of the north: I will be like the Most High'" (Isa. xiv. 13 f.). This Beliar will show forth signs and wonders, will level mountains, stop the tides, quench sun and moon, raise the dead, and by these lying wonders deceive even the elect Hebrews, as well as Gentiles who know not the law. Then all the world shall fall under the sway of a widow woman, as we have seen in Book viii., but who or what she is, is a mystery as yet unsolved. Friedlieb takes her to be Cleopatra; Ewald holds that she is Julia Domna, the widow of Septimius Severus, and mother of Caracalla and Geta. But she is evidently intended to be, not a historical character, but a mythical personage, whose existence is imagined, as has been already noticed, from some hazy remembrance of a scene in the Apocalypse of St. John. Her dominion, and that of Beliar, shall be brought to an end by God Himself, who shall rain destructive fire upon His enemies, "and then shall the judgment of the mighty God come to pass in the midst of the mighty age when all these things have fallen out."

The last piece of our Oracles consists of Books xi., xii., xiii., xiv., Books ix. and x. being either wholly lost or else once contained in some of the other books (probably

[1] *Moral.* xxxi. 24.

in Book viii.), afterwards differently arranged. This portion was that which was latest found and edited, and is last in merit as in date. Alexandre sets it as written by an Alexandrian Jew about the time of Gallienus and Odenathus, A.D. 264. Friedlieb considers Book xi. to have been composed by an Egyptian Jew in Trajan's days, the others by Christians about the middle of the third century. Ewald places some of them as late as A.D. 650, and sees in them traces of an opposition to Mohammedanism; but this opinion will not stand against a closer examination. The author is undoubtedly a Jew, who, by mixing with Christians, has learned some of their opinions, and modified some of his own. Thus he speaks (xii. 30 ff.) of the time when a luminous star appeared at mid-day above the brightness of the sun as synchronising with the coming of "the Word of the Most High, wearing flesh like (ὅμοιον) to that of mortals." And in another passage he tells how in the time of Augustus "the Word of the great immortal God came upon earth." But generally he shows himself a true Hebrew, with most of the prejudices of his nation. The date of the composition is about the middle of the third Christian century, and it seems to have been the work or composition of a single author. We need not delay long on these poems, as they consist mainly of plagiarisms from former oracles, and, where original, contain crude accounts of past and senseless conjectures concerning future events which time has completely falsified, and which are only interesting if they can be considered to represent current opinion at the period when and in the place where they were composed. They profess to

embrace the whole history of man from the Deluge to
the time of Aurelian, and contain some difficulties which
are probably impossible of solution, and are certainly not
worth the labour that commentators have bestowed upon
them, as they doubtless arise either from the writer's
ignorance, or from a vivid imagination which has played
havoc with history, chronology, and geography. Such as
they are, they present some few points worthy of notice.
We meet with that continual confusion in the names of
Eastern nations with which the Christian Fathers have
familiarised us, so that Parthians, Persians, Medes, and
Assyrians are used almost interchangeably. Solomon is
said to have secured the submission of the Assyrians,
and induced them to receive the law of God. Homer,
whom earlier Sibyls have treated with scant respect, is
here called the wisest of men, and the great instructor of
the world. But he is said to have lived after the rise of
the Parthian kingdom. The computation followed in
counting the years of Rome differs from that in ordinary
use. Instead of taking A.U.C. 725 as the date of Augustus,
the writer deliberately adopts A.U.C. 620, probably with
the view of saving the credit of some prediction concerning the fall of Rome which had not occurred at the
specified time. The account of the emperors of Rome
from Augustus onwards is full of mistakes and unhistorical details. Among the better authenticated
circumstances is found the story of the "Legio Fulmina-
trix," attested also by Christian and heathen authors.[1]
The Sibyl, however, makes the marvel due to the piety

[1] Tertull. *Apol.* v. p. 63 ; *Ad Scap.* iv. p. 87 ; Euseb. *Eccl. Hist.* v. 5 ;
Greg. Nyss. *Or. XI. in XL. Mart.;* Oros. vii. 15 ; Dio Cass. lxxv. 8.

and prayers of Aurelius himself, not to those of the
Christians in his army; and this was the view taken by
the Roman court and the Gentile world generally. A
proper appreciation of Nero's character is shown, who
is called "a double pest," in allusion to his deeds as
emperor and as Antichrist; but Domitian is highly
lauded, and the whole world is said to have loved and
honoured him—a proof, if one was needed, that no man
is so bad but some will be found to regret his loss. The
prediction concerning the final destruction of Rome is
similar to one which has been already noticed in an
earlier book. The catastrophe is to occur in the 948th
year—a number obtained by taking the numerical value
of the name in Greek. The author must have written
just before the death of Odenathus, king and priest of
Palmyra, A.D. 271, which, according to Sibylline computation, would be A.U.C. 920, and thus the fall of Rome
was to happen only twenty-eight years afterwards. But
the whole reckoning is utterly inconsistent, as in Book
xiv. a long series of princes is introduced between
Aurelian and the destruction of Rome, which would
have occupied some centuries. This calamity is not, in
these last books, always connected with the appearance
of the Anti-Messias. This personage is more vaguely
described than previously. He is no longer Nero, nor
Beliar, but "that man," "the warrior," some mysterious,
unknown person, who was to bring untold evils on the
world. Some of the circumstances formerly ascribed to
Nero are here assigned to Cyriades, the mock emperor
set up by Sapor, king of Persia; and there are certain
details about this tyrant which have been neglected by

historians, but which, coming from a contemporary, have doubtless a basis of truth. Palmyra is named "the city of the sun," and Odenathus, as its king and priest, is called "the sun-sent warrior." That it was besieged by the Persians and defended by Odenathus is a fact not otherwise supported in the history of these times, though very probable in itself. It is curious, and corroborative of the date of the composition, that as the author approaches his own times, he abandons the use of easy alphabetical and numerical riddles in naming the emperors, and in their stead employs animals to designate royal or celebrated personages. Thus Sapor is a serpent, Valerian and his son are bulls, Macrianus is a stag, Balista a goat, Odenathus a lion. This change in indication seems to show that discretion was needed in making remarks on contemporaries. In the prophecies concerning the future, which could offend no one living, the former plan of designating princes by the initials of their names is resorted to, with the result that we are presented with a number of puzzles which are incapable of solution, and which, if solved, would only show the utter absurdity of the whole series. Out of the inextricable confusion of this pretended vaticination Ewald has attempted to produce some meaning by assigning the book to the seventh century, and endeavouring to find the names of Roman and Byzantine emperors under the enigmatical designations of the poem. The attempt is decidedly a failure, as the list of princes has evidently no historical basis, and has been evolved from the fervid imagination of the writer, whose insane ambition of acting the prophet has led him into ridiculous errors. Of Ewald's ingenious theory Alexandre speaks thus : " Ita vir summus, quod in vario incepto necesse erat, nihil profecit, nisi ut novam sibi laudem, Sibyllinæ rei lucem nullam afferret."

The common opinion, that after Christ's advent the heathen oracles became silent and ceased to be consulted, is refuted by this Sibyl, who more than once refers to the answers lately given by their media. That their credit had greatly diminished, and that the ancient shrines were less frequented for fatidical purposes in the first Christian century, is true enough ; but superstition dies hard, and we may take the Sibyl's testimony as true, that up to the close of the third century oracles in Greece itself and in the islands, in Cilicia and elsewhere in Asia, were still consulted, and their responses obtained some credit. Indeed, we know from history that Titus, Adrian, and even Constantine himself were not above inquiring at the mouth of a soothsaying priestess. There was no reason in the nature of things why one author should not add his contribution to the Oracles then extant, little foreseeing how soon it would be made a criminal offence to have recourse to such means of divination. And though for a short time this enactment was abrogated by the Emperor Julian, who, on the eve of his expedition against the Persians, consulted all existing oracles, yet it was soon reimposed and enforced, and thus at length Delphic utterances were silenced.

The latter part of this final book is taken up with an account of the disputes between the Greeks and Jews dwelling at Alexandria. The latter were a very strong body, amounting to one-third of the whole population, and living in a separate quarter of the city. After many conflicts peace is established between the two rival communities, and then begins a time of happiness, which is described in glowing terms, such as are generally used in picturing the reign of Messiah. But there is no such reference in this book; and it is worthy of notice that the promised felicity should assume this novel form. After the prosperous period at Alexandria shall have endured for some long indefinite time, "the harvest of men" shall arrive, and the dead being recalled to life, a new state of things shall be introduced. "The holy nation shall reign supreme in all the earth under the eternal rule of its ancient worthies." This is a remarkable statement, as it is deliberately altered from that in Books viii. and iii., where the advent and dominion of a "holy king" is announced; and it seems in part to favour the notion of the earlier sect of Zealots, who would have no monarch except Jehovah to reign over them; but it introduces an innovation, as it foretells for the Hebrews a kind of republic, of which the presidents should be Abraham and Moses, and other celebrated leaders risen from the dead.

Such is a brief account of the Sibylline Oracles. From what has been said it will be clear that they are to be regarded as literary productions, assuming the form of predictions, and taking the place of the lost books, but possessed of no claim to inspiration, conscious or unconscious, and intended to give a fictitious support to tenets which the pagans would receive with disfavour. The historical portion, which forms two-thirds of the whole collection, contains very little that is really valuable, though there are doubtless some additional details which may be authentic, though otherwise unsupported. But the difficulty of severing the true from the mythical renders such paragraphs almost useless.

There are many allusions to the facts mentioned in the Gospels in these post-Christian "Oracles," but scarcely any additions to the matters narrated therein The most notable is the story of the fire kindled in Jordan when our Lord was baptized, a legend which is also mentioned by Justin Martyr (*Dial.* 88), and (though under a different tradition) in the Ebionite Gospel. Justin writes: "When Jesus came to the river Jordan, where John was baptizing, and descended into the water, both a fire was kindled in the Jordan, and when He came up out of the water the apostles of our Christ recorded that the Holy Spirit as a dove lighted upon Him." The Sibyl, as we saw above, thus alludes to the same event: "When, in the flesh which was given Him, He came forth, having bathed in the stream of the river Jordan, which rolls, sweeping on its waves with grey foot, He, escaping from the fire, first shall see the sweet Spirit of God coming upon Him with the white wings of a dove." Nothing else of moment as an addition to the Christian story is noticeable; and the variations in the histories derived from the Old Testament are only such as are found in the Targums and other apocryphal Jewish authorities. The "Oracles," indeed, are valuable only as showing the development and modifications of thought at the momentous period covered by their production. Jew and Christian alike availed themselves of heathen sibyllism for some four or five centuries, and the result is shown in the heterogeneous collection which has reached us under the general title of Sibylline Oracles.

INDEX.

---o---

A
Abraham, 213 ff., 218, 221.
Acrostic, 288, 323 f.
Adam, 146, 208 f.
—— life of, 195.
Age, present and future, the, 10 ff.
Alexandria, 342.
Angels, evil, 21 f., 58 f., 94, 227.
Angels, fall of, 22, 57 f., 148.
Angels, good, 20 f., 61, 93 f., 227 f.
Antichrist, 22, 313, 319, 322, 334, 336, 340.
Antiochus Epiphanes, 116 f., 297, 301.
Antonines, the, 310 f., 320.
Apocalypse, the, 85.
Apocalyptic works, 7 ff.
Apocryphal works, 5.
Archangels, 20 f., 58, 61, 94, 160.
Archontici, 246.
Aristobulus, 37 f.
Asher, 174.
Asmoneans, 112.
Assumption of Moses, the, 7, 21, 95 ff.
Atonement, day of, 226, 229.
Azazel, 21, 58.

B
Babylon, 309, 310.
Balkira, 250 f.
Baptism, 303, 325, 327, 332.
Bar-Cocheba, 116, 181.
Baruch, Apocalypse of, 7, 130 ff.
Baruch, Book of, 132 f., 137.
Beast, the, 261.
Behemoth, 155.

Beliar, 22, 168, 249, 334, 337.
Benjamin, 176.
Berial, 249, 260 f.

C
Canaanites, 231.
Cerinthians, 187, 316.
Christ, 17 f., 41, 89, 184 f., 254, 262 f., 270, 315 f., 317, 328, 332.
Christ, baptism of, 186, 188, 315, 318, 343.
Christ, descent of, 165, 188, 262.
Christology, 89, 257 f.
Chronology, 218 f., 223, 319, 322, 339.
Cross, the, 316, 324 f.

D
Dan, 172, 336 f.
Daniel, Book of, 82, 85.
Dead, prayer for the, 335.
Diocletian, 329.
Docetism, 256.
Domitian, 145, 340.

E
Ebionites, 179, 316.
Ecclesiastes, Book of, 2.
Eden, Garden of, 93, 208 f., 216.
Edom, kings of, 224.
Elijah, Apocalypse of, 247.
—— return of, 334.
Enoch, 210 f.
Enoch, Book of, 7, 49 ff., 180, 198 f., 210.

Esau, 182.
Eschatology, 22, 91, 229, 297 f., 306, 313 f., 322 ff., 333.
Esdras, Fourth Book of, 5, 7, 136 f., 200.
Essenes, the, 122, 203.
Evolution of Christianity, the work so called, 85 ff.

F

Festivals, the Jewish, 206, 215.
Fire, the proving, 334 f.
Flood, the, 63 f., 66, 146, 218, 317, 330.

G

Gad, 174.
Gentiles, 23, 154, 156, 179, 230, 300.
Gnosticism, 267, 269, 273.
Gods, heathen, 289 f., 292.
Gog and Magog, 295, 301.
Grace before meat, 303.
Greece, 295 f.

H

Hades, 60, 279, 321.
Haggadistic writings, 8 f.
Heathen, fate of, 128 f.
Heavens, the, 161, 246, 254 f., 267.
Hebrew language, the, 201, 228.
Hebrews, Epistle to the, 240 ff.
Herod the Great, 113.
Herodian Princes, 115.
Hezekiah, 259.
Hieracas, 246.
History in type, 145 f.
Homer, 302, 339.
Hyrcanus, 37, 77, 112.

I

Idolatry, 290 f.
Isaiah, Ascension of, 7, 236 ff.
Isaiah, death of, 240 f., 249 f., 267.
Israel, supremacy of, 230.
Israelites, history of, 67, 109 f., 146 f., 219 f., 293 ff.
Issachar, 171.

J

Jacob, 173, 209 f., 232.
Jannæus, Alexander, 37.
Jechoniah, 133, 141.
Jeremiah, 141.
Jerusalem, 187 f., 317.
—— destruction of, 133, 138, 141 f. 302.
—— the heavenly, 160 f., 190, 313.
Jesus, 316.
Jews, prosperity of, 312, 342.
Jonathan, 77.
Joshua, 108, 312 f.
Joseph, 169, 175, 183 f., 209, 218, 220.
Jubilees, Book of, 8, 193 ff.
Jubilee system, the, 204 f., 219, 221.
Judah, 169, 171, 175, 182, 187.
Judas Maccabæus, 77.
Judas of Galilee, 119.
Jude, quotation from Assumption of Moses, 95, 97, 99 f., 106.
—— quotation from Enoch in, 49, 57, 73, 83, 97, 99.
Judgment, the final, 24 f., 40, 45, 58, 70, 91, 159, 261, 291, 304 f., 307, 320, 334.

L

Lamb of God, the 176, 190.
Legion, the thundering, 339 f.
Levi, 169 f., 171, 175, 182, 187, 209, 218, 226.
Leviathan, 155.

M

Maccabees, 77, 296, 299.
Machpelah, 212.
Man, son of, 62, 89 f.
Manasseh, 244 f., 249.
Manasses, 147 f.
Mary, the Virgin, 262.
Mastema, 227.
Matanbukus, 250.
Mattathias, 77.
Matthias, 119.
Mediator, the, 173.
Melchisedek, 246.
Messiah, 13 ff., 17, 22, 40 ff., 44, 62, 89 f., 143, 153 f., 185 f., 297.

INDEX. 347

Messianic hopes and theology, 23, 43 f., 58, 62, 68 f., 79, 91 f., 142, 151 ff., 189, 192, 296 ff., 313, 319, 322.
Millennium, the, 157, 159.
Mosaic law, the, 178 f.
Moses, 125, 213, 220.
Moses, Apocalypse of, 196.
—— Assumption of, 7, 95 ff.
—— burial of, 95 ff.

N

Naphtali, 173, 185.
Natural phenomena, 65.
Nazarenes, 179, 187.
Nero, 22, 260, 271, 306 f., 310, 340.
New Testament referred to, 190.
Noah, 81 f., 209, 237 f., 330.

O

Odenathus, 338, 340 f.
Oracles, the heathen, 341 f.

P

Palestine, 82 f.
Papias, 132, 139.
Paradise, 60, 93, 161, 290.
Parousia, the, 129 f., 151, 187, 229, 271, 320.
Parthians, 80, 139.
Passover, Feast of, 215 f.
Patripassianism, 187.
Paul, St., writings of, 190.
Pentecost, Feast of, 215.
Pharisaism, 39.
Phocylides, 332.
Phœnix, the, 108, 321 f.
Phrygia, 317.
Pistis Sophia, 28.
Place, the holy, 211.
Pompey, 37 ff., 114.
Potiphar, 183.
Prophet, the, 121, 129.
Pseudepigraphic, meaning of, 1, 5, 6.
—— writings, character of, 2 f.
—— writings, number of, 4 f.
Ptolemy Physcon, 292, 297.

R

Ramiel, 146, 149.
Repentance, 45.
Resurrection, the, 23 f., 40, 44, 46, 62, 69, 92, 128, 143, 156 ff., 307, 334, 343.
Reuben, 168.
Revelation, how made, 149 f.
Righteous, fate of the, 57, 63, 69 f., 156 ff., 189, 261, 305, 307 f., 335.
Rome, 152, 293, 307, 308 f., 310 f., 320, 340.

S

Sabbath, 224 f., 234.
Sadducees, 116, 215.
Sammael, 267.
Sapor, 340 f.
Satan, 21, 94, 227, 249.
Sebaste, 336.
Seven, the number, 221 f.
Sheol, 92 f.
Shepherds, the seventy, 67 f., 74 ff.
Sibylla, 276 f., 289, 294.
Sibylline Oracles, 9, 276 ff.
Simeon, 169, 182.
Sin, original, 150 f.
Solomon, Psalter of, 6, 25 ff.
Solomon, Wisdom of, 1, 6.
Soul, immortality of, 228 f.
Spirit, angel of the, 257, 260, 262.
Spirit, the Holy, 189 f., 246, 298.
Stars, the disobedient, 59 f.
State, the intermediate, 93.
Symbolical representations, 66 f.

T

Tabernacles, feast of, 215, 235.
Tablets, the heavenly, 65, 69, 70.
Taxo, 118 ff.
Testaments, Apocryphal, 8.
Testaments of the XII. Patriarchs, 8, 162 ff., 199.
Theocracy, 123, 128 f.
Therapeutæ, 328.
Tiberius, 309.
Time, how divided, 10.
Torment, place of, 71.
Trajan, 145.
Tree of life, 60.

U

Universalism, 329, 335.
Ur, 212.
Uriel, 149.

V

Varus, 113 f.
Vesuvius, 302, 306.
Vine, legend of, 132.

W

Weeks, apocalyptical, 69, 91, 145.
Wicked, fate of the, 46 f., 57, 70, 158, 162, 307, 335.

Wisdom of Solomon, the, 1, 6.
Woman, the mystical, 322, 337.
World, end of the, 141, 145.

Y

Years, the seventy, 75, 111.

Z

Zabulus, 121.
Zealots, the, 105, 109, 112 f., 119, 123, 127 f., 343.
Zebulon, 172, 183.

T. and T. Clark's Publications.

Just published, in demy 8vo, price 10s. 6d.,

BOOKS WHICH INFLUENCED OUR LORD AND HIS APOSTLES:

Being a Critical Review of Jewish Apocalyptic Literature.

BY

J. E. H. THOMSON, B.D.

CONTENTS:—Introduction.—BOOK I. Background of Apocalyptic.—II. Evolution of Apocalyptic.—III. Criticism of Apocalyptic.—IV. Theological Result.

In demy 8vo, price 10s. 6d.,

THE JEWISH
AND
THE CHRISTIAN MESSIAH.

A STUDY IN THE EARLIEST HISTORY OF CHRISTIANITY.

By Professor VINCENT HENRY STANTON, M.A.,
TRINITY COLLEGE, CAMBRIDGE.

'Mr. Stanton's book answers a real want, and will be indispensable to students of the origin of Christianity. We hope that Mr. Stanton will be able to continue his labours in that most obscure and most important period, of his competency to deal with which he has given such good proof in this book.'—*Guardian.*

'We welcome this book as a valuable addition to the literature of a most important subject. . . . The book is remarkable for the clearness of its style. Mr. Stanton is never obscure from beginning to end, and we think that no reader of average attainments will be able to put the book down without having learnt much from his lucid and scholarly exposition.'—*Ecclesiastical Gazette.*

T. and T. Clark's Publications.

GRIMM'S LEXICON.

'The best New Testament Greek Lexicon. . . . It is a treasury of the results of exact scholarship.'—BISHOP WESTCOTT.

In demy 4to, Third Edition, price 36s.,

A GREEK-ENGLISH LEXICON OF THE NEW TESTAMENT,

BEING

GRIMM'S 'WILKE'S CLAVIS NOVI TESTAMENTI.'

𝔗ranslated, 𝔑evised, and 𝔈nlarged

BY

JOSEPH HENRY THAYER, D.D.,

BUSSEY PROFESSOR OF NEW TESTAMENT CRITICISM AND INTERPRETATION
IN THE DIVINITY SCHOOL OF HARVARD UNIVERSITY.

EXTRACT FROM PREFACE.

'TOWARDS the close of the year 1862, the "Arnoldische Buchhandlung" in Leipzig published the First Part of a Greek-Latin Lexicon of the New Testament, prepared upon the basis of the "Clavis Novi Testamenti Philologica" of C. G. Wilke (second edition, 2 vols. 1851), by Professor C. L. WILIBALD GRIMM of Jena. In his Prospectus, Professor Grimm announced it as his purpose not only (in accordance with the improvements in classical lexicography embodied in the Paris edition of Stephen's Thesaurus and in the fifth edition of Passow's Dictionary edited by Rost and his coadjutors) to exhibit the historical growth of a word's significations, and accordingly in selecting his vouchers for New Testament usage to show at what time and in what class of writers a given word became current, but also duly to notice the usage of the Septuagint and of the Old Testament Apocrypha, and especially to produce a Lexicon which should correspond to the present condition of textual criticism, of exegesis, and of biblical theology. He devoted more than seven years to his task. The successive Parts of his work received, as they appeared, the outspoken commendation of scholars diverging as widely in their views as Hupfeld and Hengstenberg; and since its completion in 1868 it has been generally acknowledged to be by far the best Lexicon of the New Testament extant.'

'The best New Testament Greek Lexicon. . . . It is a treasury of the results of exact scholarship.'—BISHOP WESTCOTT.

'I regard it as a work of the greatest importance. . . . It seems to me a work showing the most patient diligence, and the most carefully arranged collection of useful and helpful references.'—THE BISHOP OF GLOUCESTER AND BRISTOL.

'The use of Professor Grimm's book for years has convinced me that it is not only unquestionably the best among existing New Testament Lexicons, but that, apart from all comparisons, it is a work of the highest intrinsic merit, and one which is admirably adapted to initiate a learner into an acquaintance with the language of the New Testament. It ought to be regarded as one of the first and most necessary requisites for the study of the New Testament, and consequently for the study of theology in general.'—Professor EMIL SCHÜRER.

Just published, in post 8vo, price 7s. 6d.,

MESSIANIC PROPHECY:

Its Origin, Historical Growth, and Relation to New Testament Fulfilment.

By Dr. EDWARD RIEHM.

New Edition, Translated by Rev. LEWIS A. MUIRHEAD, B.D.

With an Introduction by Professor A. B. DAVIDSON, D.D.

'No work of the same compass could be named that contains so much that is instructive on the nature of prophecy in general, and particularly on the branch of it specially treated in the book.'—Professor A. B. Davidson, D.D.

'I would venture to recommend "Riehm's Messianic Prophecy" (Clark's translation) as a summary account of prophecy both reverent and critical.'—Principal Gore in *Lux Mundi*.

Just published, in crown 8vo, price 5s.,

MESSIANIC PROPHECIES IN HISTORICAL SUCCESSION.

By FRANZ DELITZSCH.

Translated by SAMUEL IVES CURTISS,
PROFESSOR IN CHICAGO THEOLOGICAL SEMINARY.

'The proofs of this volume were corrected by the author on his deathbed, and the Preface was dictated by him five days before his death. There is something sacred about such a book. It embodies the results of the most recent scholarly investigation, and at the same time breathes the spirit of deep and fervent Christian faith. In times when it needs the greatest care to handle wisely the subject of Messianic Prophecy, the student could not well have a better guide than this short but comprehensive volume. It is as full of instruction as it is a help to discriminating faith. We heartily wish it a wide circulation.'— *Methodist Recorder.*

WORKS BY PROFESSOR A. B. BRUCE, D.D.

Just published, in post 8vo, New Edition, Revised, price 7s. 6d.,

THE KINGDOM OF GOD;
OR, CHRIST'S TEACHING ACCORDING TO THE SYNOPTICAL GOSPELS.

By A. B. BRUCE, D.D.,
PROFESSOR OF NEW TESTAMENT EXEGESIS IN THE FREE CHURCH COLLEGE, GLASGOW.

'To Dr. Bruce belongs the honour of giving to English-speaking Christians the first really scientific treatment of this transcendent theme . . . his book is the best monograph on the subject in existence. . . . He is evidently in love with his subject, and every page exhibits the intense enthusiasm of a strong nature for the Divine Teacher.'—Rev. JAMES STALKER, D.D., in *The British Weekly.*

BY THE SAME AUTHOR.

In demy 8vo, Fourth Edition, price 10s. 6d.,

THE TRAINING OF THE TWELVE;
OR,
EXPOSITION OF PASSAGES IN THE GOSPELS EXHIBITING THE TWELVE DISCIPLES OF JESUS UNDER DISCIPLINE FOR THE APOSTLESHIP.

'Here we have a really great book on an important, large, and attractive subject—a book full of loving, wholesome, profound thoughts about the fundamentals of Christian faith and practice.'—*British and Foreign Evangelical Review.*

BY THE SAME AUTHOR.

In demy 8vo, Third Edition, price 10s. 6d.,

THE HUMILIATION OF CHRIST,
IN ITS PHYSICAL, ETHICAL, AND OFFICIAL ASPECTS.

'We have not for a long time met with a work so fresh and suggestive as this of Professor Bruce. . . . We do not know where to look at our English Universities for a treatise so calm, logical, and scholarly.'—*English Independent.*

'The title of the book gives but a faint conception of the value and wealth of its contents. . . . Dr. Bruce's work is really one of exceptional value; and no one can read it without perceptible gain in theological knowledge.'—*English Churchman.*

T. and T. Clark's Publications.

Now complete, in Five Volumes, 8vo, price 10s. 6d. each,

HISTORY OF THE JEWISH PEOPLE IN THE TIME OF OUR LORD.

By Dr. EMIL SCHÜRER,
PROFESSOR OF THEOLOGY IN THE UNIVERSITY OF KIEL.

TRANSLATED FROM THE SECOND EDITION (REVISED THROUGH-OUT, AND GREATLY ENLARGED) OF '*HISTORY OF THE NEW TESTAMENT TIMES.*'

*** Professor Schürer has prepared an exhaustive INDEX to this work, to which he attaches great value. The Translation is now ready, and is issued in a separate Volume (100 pp. 8vo). Price 2s. 6d. *nett*.

'Under Professor Schürer's guidance we are enabled to a large extent to construct a social and political framework for the Gospel History, and to set it in such a light as to see new evidences of the truthfulness of that history and of its contemporaneousness. . . . The length of our notice shows our estimate of the value of his work.'—*English Churchman.*

'Messrs. Clark have afresh earned the thanks of all students of the New Testament in England, by undertaking to present Schürer's masterly work in a form easily accessible to the English reader. . . . In every case the amount of research displayed is very great, truly German in its proportions, while the style of Professor Schürer is by no means cumbrous, after the manner of some of his countrymen. We have inadequately described a most valuable work, but we hope we have said enough to induce our readers who do not know this book to seek it out forthwith.'—*Methodist Recorder.*

In post 8vo, price 9s.,

THE TEXT OF JEREMIAH;

OR,

A Critical Investigation of the Greek and Hebrew, with the Variations in the LXX. retranslated into the Original and Explained.

By PROFESSOR G. C. WORKMAN, M.A.,
VICTORIA UNIVERSITY, COBURG, CANADA.

WITH AN INTRODUCTION BY PROFESSOR F. DELITZSCH, D.D.

Besides discussing the relation between the texts, this book solves the difficult problem of the variations, and reveals important matter for the history, the interpretation, the correction, and the reconstruction of the present Massoretic text.

'A work of valuable and lasting service.'—Professor DELITZSCH.

'The most painstaking and elaborate illustration of the application of his principles to this end that has yet been given to the world. . . . Scholars will hail it with gratitude, and peruse it with interest.'—*Guardian.*

WORKS BY PROFESSOR DELITZSCH.

In One Volume, 8vo, price 12s.,

A SYSTEM OF BIBLICAL PSYCHOLOGY.

'This admirable volume ought to be carefully read by every thinking clergyman.'—*Literary Churchman.*

In Two Volumes, 8vo, price 21s.,

COMMENTARY ON THE EPISTLE TO THE HEBREWS.

KEIL AND DELITZSCH'S
COMMENTARIES ON, AND INTRODUCTION TO, THE OLD TESTAMENT.

'This series is one of great importance to the biblical scholar, and as regards its general execution it leaves little or nothing to be desired.'—*Edinburgh Review.*

INTRODUCTION, 2 Vols.	(*Keil*).	PSALMS, 3 Vols.	(*Delitzsch*).
PENTATEUCH, 3 Vols.	(*Keil*).	PROVERBS, 2 Vols.	(*Delitzsch*).
JOSHUA, JUDGES, AND RUTH, 1 Vol.	(*Keil*).	ECCLESIASTES AND SONG OF SOLOMON	(*Delitzsch*).
SAMUEL, 1 Vol.	(*Keil*).	ISAIAH, 2 Vols.	(*Delitzsch*).
KINGS, 1 Vol., AND CHRONICLES, 1 Vol.	(*Keil*).	JEREMIAH AND LAMENTATIONS, 2 Vols.	(*Keil*).
EZRA, NEHEMIAH, AND ESTHER, 1 Vol.	(*Keil*).	EZEKIEL, 2 Vols.	(*Keil*).
		DANIEL, 1 Vol.	(*Keil*).
JOB, 2 Vols.	(*Delitzsch*).	MINOR PROPHETS, 2 Vols.	(*Keil*).

THE above Series (published in CLARK's Foreign Theological Library) is now completed in 27 Volumes, and Messrs. CLARK will supply any EIGHT VOLUMES for TWO GUINEAS (Complete Set, £7, 2s.).

Separate Volumes may be had at the non-subscription price of 10s. 6d. each.

So complete a Critical and Exegetical Apparatus on the Old Testament is not elsewhere to be found in the English language; and at the present time, when the study of the Old Testament is more widely extended than perhaps ever before, it is believed this offer will be duly appreciated.

'Very high merit for thorough Hebrew scholarship, and for keen critical sagacity, belongs to these Old Testament Commentaries. No scholar will willingly dispense with them.'—*British Quarterly Review.*

T. and T. Clark's Publications.

WORKS BY PROFESSOR DELITZSCH.

Now complete, in Two Vols. 8vo, price 21s.,

A NEW COMMENTARY ON GENESIS.

NOTE.—While preparing the translation, the translator was favoured by Professor Delitzsch with such numerous improvements and additions, that it may be regarded as made from a revised version of the New Commentary on Genesis.

'Thirty-five years have elapsed since Professor Delitzsch's Commentary on Genesis first appeared; fifteen years since the fourth edition was published in 1872. Ever in the van of historical and philological research, the venerable author now comes forward with another fresh edition, in which he incorporates what fifteen years have achieved for illustration and criticism of the text of Genesis. . . . We congratulate Prof. Delitzsch on this new edition, and trust that it may appear before long in an English dress. By it, not less than by his other Commentaries, he has earned the gratitude of every lover of biblical science, and we shall be surprised if, in the future, many do not acknowledge that they have found in it a welcome help and guide.'—Professor S. R. DRIVER in *The Academy.*

'We wish it were in our power to follow in detail the contents of Dr. Delitzsch's most interesting introduction, and to give specimens of the admirable, concise, and lucid notes in his exposition; but we have said enough to show our readers our high estimate of the value of the work.'—*Church Bells.*

'The work of a reverent mind and a sincere believer; and not seldom there are touches of great beauty and of spiritual insight in it.'—*Guardian.*

Just published, in Two Vols. 8vo, price 21s.,

BIBLICAL COMMENTARY ON THE PROPHECIES OF ISAIAH.

With an Introduction by Professor S. R. DRIVER, D.D., Oxford.

NOTE.—By special arrangement with the author, Messrs. CLARK secured the sole right of translation of this Fourth (*and last*) Edition of his 'Isaiah.' It is dedicated to Professors Cheyne and Driver of Oxford. In his preface the author states that this Fourth Edition contains the fruit of his continued labour, and that a thorough revisal of the whole work has been made.

Canon CHEYNE says:—' Students of Isaiah will greet so early a translation of Delitzsch's "Isaiah." . . . Prefixed to it is an interesting critical sketch by Professor Driver, which will be a useful guide to students, not only of this, but of the other works of the accomplished author.'

'Delitzsch's last gift to the Christian Church. . . . In our opinion, those who would enter into the meaning of that Spirit as He spake long ago by Isaiah, words of comfort and hope which have not lost their significance to-day, cannot find a better guide; one more marked by learning, reverence, and insight, than Franz Delitzsch.'—Professor W. T. DAVISON in *The Expository Times.*

'Commentaries in Europe are not often republished after their author's death, whatever is of permanent value in them being appropriated by their successors. But it may be long before one undertakes the task of expounding the Prophets possessing so many gifts and employing them so well.'—*Guardian.*

T. and T. Clark's Publications.

LOTZE'S MICROCOSMUS.

In Two Vols. 8vo, FOURTH EDITION, price 36s.,

MICROCOSMUS:
CONCERNING MAN AND HIS RELATION TO THE WORLD.

By HERMANN LOTZE.

CONTENTS:—Book I. The Body. II. The Soul. III. Life. IV. Man. V. Mind. VI. The Microcosmic Order; or, The Course of Human Life. VII. History. VIII. Progress. IX. The Unity of Things.

'These are indeed two masterly volumes, vigorous in intellectual power, and translated with rare ability.... This work will doubtless find a place on the shelves of all the foremost thinkers and students of modern times.'—*Evangelical Magazine.*

'The English public have now before them the greatest philosophic work produced in Germany by the generation just past. The translation comes at an opportune time, for the circumstances of English thought, just at the present moment, are peculiarly those with which Lotze attempted to deal when he wrote his "Microcosmus," a quarter of a century ago.... Few philosophic books of the century are so attractive both in style and matter.'—*Athenæum.*

'Lotze is the ablest, the most brilliant, and most renowned of the German philosophers of to-day.... He has rendered invaluable and splendid service to Christian thinkers, and has given them a work which cannot fail to equip them for the sturdiest intellectual conflicts and to ensure their victory.'—*Baptist Magazine.*

In Two Vols. 8vo, price 21s.,

NATURE AND THE BIBLE:
LECTURES ON THE MOSAIC HISTORY OF CREATION IN ITS RELATION TO NATURAL SCIENCE.

By DR. FR. H. REUSCH.

REVISED AND CORRECTED BY THE AUTHOR.

Translated from the Fourth Edition
By KATHLEEN LYTTELTON.

'Other champions much more competent and learned than myself might have been placed in the field; I will only name one of the most recent, Dr. Reusch, author of "Nature and the Bible."'—The Right Hon. W. E. GLADSTONE.

'The work, we need hardly say, is of profound and perennial interest, and it can scarcely be too highly commended as, in many respects, a very successful attempt to settle one of the most perplexing questions of the day. It is impossible to read it without obtaining larger views of theology, and more accurate opinions respecting its relations to science, and no one will rise from its perusal without feeling a deep sense of gratitude to its author.'—*Scottish Review.*

T. and T. Clark's Publications.

Just published, in post 8vo, price 7s. 6d.,

THE LIFE AND WRITINGS OF ALEXANDER VINET.

By LAURA M. LANE.

WITH AN INTRODUCTION BY THE VEN. ARCHDEACON FARRAR.

'I may say, without hesitation, that readers will here find a deeply interesting account of a sincere and brilliant thinker. . . . The publication of this book will be a pure gain if it calls the attention of fresh students to the writings of a theologian so independent as Vinet was, yet so supreme in his allegiance to the majesty of truth.'—Ven. Archdeacon FARRAR.

'Miss Lane deserves the grateful thanks of all students of theology for her praiseworthy attempt to revive interest in a man whose views have a special message for these times, and whose lofty and beautiful spirit cannot fail likewise to attract all students of human nature.'—*Glasgow Herald.*

Just published, in demy 8vo, price 7s. 6d.,

ELEMENTS OF LOGIC AS A SCIENCE OF PROPOSITIONS.

By E. E. CONSTANCE JONES,

LECTURER IN MORAL SCIENCES, GIRTON COLLEGE, CAMBRIDGE;
JOINT-TRANSLATOR AND EDITOR OF LOTZE'S '*Microcosmus.*'

'What strikes us at once about the work is the refreshing boldness and independence of the writer, which, however, is not mere waywardness or idiosyncrasy. In spite of the long-drawn previous history of the science and of its voluminous records, Miss Jones finds plenty to say that is freshly worked out by independent thought. There is a spring of vitality and vigour pervading and vitalising the aridity of even these abstract discussions.'—*Cambridge Review.*

Just published, in demy 8vo, price 9s.,

KANT, LOTZE, AND RITSCHL:
A Critical Examination.

By LEONHARD STÄHLIN, BAYREUTH.

TRANSLATED BY PRINCIPAL SIMON, EDINBURGH.

'In a few lines it is impossible to give an adequate idea of this learned work, which goes to the very root of the philosophical and metaphysical speculations of recent years.'—*Ecclesiastical Gazette.*

'We are grateful to the publishers for this volume, which deserves to be carefully read and studied.'—*London Quarterly Review.*

'The book is worthy of careful study.'—*Church Bells.*

WORKS BEARING ON THE

LIFE AND PERSON OF CHRIST,

PUBLISHED BY

T. & T. CLARK, 38 GEORGE STREET, EDINBURGH.

Nicoll (W. R., LL.D.)—The Incarnate Saviour: A Life of Jesus
Christ. Crown 8vo, 6s.
'It commands my warm sympathy and admiration. I rejoice in the circulation of such a book, which I trust will be the widest possible.'—*Canon Liddon.*

Lange (J. P., D.D.)—The Life of Our Lord Jesus Christ. Edited,
with additional Notes, by Prof. MARCUS DODS, D.D. Second Edition, in Four vols. 8vo, Subscription price 28s.

Stalker (Jas., D.D.)—A Life of Christ. Bible Class Handbooks.
Crown 8vo, 1s. 6d.; large type Edition, handsomely bound, 3s. 6d.
'As a succinct, suggestive, beautifully written exhibition of the life of our Lord, we are acquainted with nothing that can compare with it.'—*Christian World.*

Naville (Ernest)—The Christ. Seven Lectures. Translated by Rev.
T. J. DESPRÉS. Crown 8vo, 4s. 6d.
'Ministers who wish for suggestions and guidance as to the manner in which they can treat of the pressingly important subject which is considered by M. Naville, should take pains to acquaint themselves with this volume.'—*Christian World.*

Caspari (C. E.)—A Chronological and Geographical Introduction to
THE LIFE OF CHRIST. 8vo, 7s. 6d.
'No Bible student should fail to make this treatise his constant friend and companion.'—*Bell's Weekly Messenger.*

Bruce (A. B., D.D.)—The Kingdom of God; or, Christ's Teaching
according to the Synoptical Gospels. Fourth Edition, post 8vo, 7s. 6d.

Bruce (A. B., D.D.)—The Training of the Twelve; or, Exposition
of Passages in the Gospels exhibiting the Twelve Disciples of Jesus under Discipline for the Apostleship. Fourth Edition, 8vo, 10s. 6d.
'A really great book on an important, large, and attractive subject; a book full of loving, wholesome, profound thoughts about the fundamentals of Christian faith and practice.'—*British and Foreign Evangelical Review.*

Bruce (A. B., D.D.)—The Humiliation of Christ, in its Physical,
ETHICAL, AND OFFICIAL ASPECTS. Third Edition, 8vo, 10s. 6d.
'This noble theological treatise.'—*Evangelical Magazine.*

Scrymgeour (Wm.)—Lessons on the Life of Christ. Bible Class
Handbooks, 2s. 6d.
'A thoroughly satisfactory help both to teacher and scholar.'—*British Messenger.*

Lehmann (Pastor E.)—Scenes from the Life of Jesus. Crown 8vo,
3s. 6d.
'There is in these lectures a tender sympathy, and a spiritual devoutness and simplicity, which gives to them a real charm.'—*Literary World.*

[*Continued.*

T. and T. Clark's Publications.

Smeaton (Professor)—*The Doctrine of the Atonement as Taught by* CHRIST HIMSELF. Second Edition, 8vo, 10s. 6d.
'We attach very great value to this seasonable and scholarly production.'— *British and Foreign Evangelical Review.*

Stier (Dr. Rudolph)—*On the Words of the Lord Jesus. Eight* vols. 8vo (or the 8 vols. bound in FOUR), £2, 2s. *nett.* Separate volumes may be had, price 10s. 6d.
'The whole work is a treasury of thoughtful exposition.'—*Guardian.*

Ullmann (Dr. Carl)—*The Sinlessness of Jesus: An Evidence for* Christianity. Third Edition, crown 8vo, 6s.
'Ullmann has studied the sinlessness of Christ more profoundly, and written on it more beautifully, than any other theologian.'—Canon FARRAR in his *Life of Christ.*

Ebrard (Dr. J. H. A.)—*The Gospel History: A Compendium of* Critical Investigations in support of the Four Gospels. 8vo, 10s. 6d.
'Nothing could have been more opportune than the republication in English of this admirable work.'—*British and Foreign Evangelical Review.*

Steinmeyer (Dr. F. L.)—*The Miracles of Our Lord: Examined in* their relation to Modern Criticism. 8vo, 7s. 6d.
'Will take its place among the best recent volumes of Christian evidence.'—*Standard.*

Steinmeyer (Dr. F. L.)—*The History of the Passion and Resurrection* OF OUR LORD, considered in the Light of Modern Criticism. 8vo, 10s. 6d.
'Will well repay earnest study.'—*Weekly Review.*

Krummacher (Dr. F. W.)—*The Suffering Saviour; or, Meditations* on the Last Days of the Sufferings of Christ. 8th Ed., cr. 8vo, 7s. 6d.
'To the devout and earnest Christian the volume will be a treasure indeed.'—*Wesleyan Times.*

Dorner (Professor)—*History of the Development of the Doctrine of* THE PERSON OF CHRIST. Five vols. 8vo, £2, 12s. 6d.
'So great a mass of learning and thought so ably set forth has never before been presented to English readers, at least on this subject.'—*Journal of Sacred Literature.*

Weiss (Dr. Bernhard)—*The Life of Christ.* 3 vols. 8vo, 31s. 6d.
'From the thoroughness of the discussion and clearness of the writer, we anticipate a very valuable addition to the Great Biography.'—*Freeman.*

The Voice from the Cross: *A Series of Sermons on our Lord's* Passion by eminent Living Preachers of Germany. Edited and translated by WM. MACINTOSH, M.A., F.S.S. Crown 8vo, 5s.
'Is certain to be welcomed with devout gratitude by every evangelical Christian in Britain.'—*Christian Leader.*

Salmond (Professor)—*The Life of Christ. Bible Class Primers.* Paper covers, 6d.; cloth, 8d.
'A scholarly and beautiful presentation of the story of the Four Gospels.'—*Sunday School Chronicle.*

Hall (Rev. Newman, LL.B.)—*The Lord's Prayer: A Practical* Meditation. Second Edition, crown 8vo, 6s.
'The author's thoughts are sharply cut, and are like crystals in their clearness and power.'—*British Quarterly Review.*

T. and T. Clark's Publications.

PROFESSOR GODET'S WORKS.
(Copyright, by arrangement with the Author.)

In Two Volumes, demy 8vo, price 21s.,

COMMENTARY ON ST. PAUL'S FIRST EPISTLE TO THE CORINTHIANS.
By F. GODET, D.D.,
PROFESSOR OF THEOLOGY, NEUCHATEL.

'A perfect masterpiece of theological toil and thought. . . . Scholarly, evangelical, exhaustive, and able.'—*Evangelical Review.*

'To say a word in praise of any of Professor Godet's productions is almost like "gilding refined gold." All who are familiar with his commentaries know how full they are of rich suggestion. . . . This volume fully sustains the high reputation Godet has made for himself as a biblical scholar, and devout expositor of the will of God. Every page is radiant with light, and gives forth heat as well.'—*Methodist New Connexion Magazine.*

In Three Volumes, 8vo, price 31s. 6d.,

A COMMENTARY ON THE GOSPEL OF ST. JOHN.
A New Edition, Revised throughout by the Author.

'This work forms one of the battle-fields of modern inquiry, and is itself so rich in spiritual truth, that it is impossible to examine it too closely; and we welcome this treatise from the pen of Dr. Godet. We have no more competent exegete; and this new volume shows all the learning and vivacity for which the author is distinguished.'—*Freeman.*

In Two Volumes, 8vo, price 21s.,

A COMMENTARY ON THE GOSPEL OF ST. LUKE.

'Marked by clearness and good sense, it will be found to possess value and interest as one of the most recent and copious works specially designed to illustrate this Gospel.'—*Guardian.*

In Two Volumes, 8vo, price 21s.,

A COMMENTARY ON ST. PAUL'S EPISTLE TO THE ROMANS.

'We prefer this commentary to any other we have seen on the subject. . . . We have great pleasure in recommending it as not only rendering invaluable aid in the critical study of the text, but affording practical and deeply suggestive assistance in the exposition of the doctrine.'—*British and Foreign Evangelical Review.*

In crown 8vo, Second Edition, price 6s.,

DEFENCE OF THE CHRISTIAN FAITH.
TRANSLATED BY THE HON. AND REV. CANON LYTTELTON, M.A.,
RECTOR OF HAGLEY.

'There is trenchant argument and resistless logic in these lectures; but withal, there is cultured imagination and felicitous eloquence, which carry home the appeals to the heart as well as the head.'—*Sword and Trowel.*

www.ingramcontent.com/pod-product-compliance
Lightning Source LLC
Chambersburg PA
CBHW020317240426
43673CB00039B/834